Stories
from the
Farm on the Hill

Copyright © 2012 by Gerry Preece

All rights reserved.
Published in the United States by Buckdale Publishing,
3158 Hawkslanding Drive, Cincinnati, Ohio, 45244.

March, 2012

ISBN: 978-0-9854427-0-5

Illustrations by Brian Preece
Cover design by Joan Preece

Stories
from the
Farm on the Hill

*Reflections and Short Stories
about Life on the Family Farm*

GERRY PREECE

The farmhouse and barns in 1955

I grew up on a small, family operated dairy farm on a dirt road in Upstate New York. My family bought the place in 1955, and I was born in 1956. I lived there until I left when I was eighteen, and my folks sold the farm four years later.

From end to end that road is about five miles long. There were ten working farms along that road when I was a kid.

Today, there are none.

"Farming at any level is a labor of love, but now the future is so uncertain. Looking forward, I don't see much opportunity for small farms to thrive. It's a tough grind. It's not going anywhere. It will always stay beautiful, open land, and will always be a piece of land with my sweat on every square inch of it."

Will Tuttle
Owner of America's oldest running family farm,
on putting it up for sale after 378 years, 11 generations
from article by Peter Schworm
The Boston Globe, July 27, 2010

Contents

	Preface - Glue and Mooring Lines	1
1	My Past Place.	5
2	Working the Soil from the Other Side	11
3	From Horses to Horsepower	21
4	A Time Between	31
5	Thomases	35
6	Ben English	55
7	Animal Farm	75
8	Hard Work	106
9	Visitors	125
10	Uncle Dean	163
11	"Vly Summit Winter Olympics" of 1968	201
12	Impetigo Park	221
13	A Day at the Washington County Fair	231
14	Farewell from the Top of the Hill	249
	Endnotes	261
	Acknowledgements	271

Preface

Glue and Mooring Lines

I felt both like I was there and like I was floating above the scene, a disembodied observer. At fifty three, I was giddy about being with all three of my brothers, it being only us now as others had retired for the night. It was late, and we were gently bourbon-plied in my brother's kitchen, tired but too delighted with our own rare company to sleep. Mom was going to make it; that much was finally clear to us now, and that realization produced a sense of relief in us. She was eighty four, and had just fallen, broken a hip, and was recovering well from surgery. We had raced to Atlanta from our four corners, united in our fear of possible loss.

Our conversation gradually turned to Uncle Dean, my dad's brother, who had died the previous month in Maine. He was a colossal character in our lives, and we relished sharing our memories of him, tasting and re-tasting his outrageous and hilarious antics which had become famous not only in our family but in other circles as well. We told of his shenanigans at football stadiums and yacht clubs, of his "discovering uranium," of his being a ship's crusty captain, and more. We guffawed at how he and Dad, when they were prank-happy teenagers, would "borrow" dinghies from the Milford Yacht Club, take them for joy rides and then abandon them, leaving them adrift in the harbor while they swam to shore. I realized in the telling that these stories are so much glorious glue, the stuff that unites us as family and the medium of memory that lifts our common heart. I could feel the bonds between us strengthen, could feel that glue of storytelling connect us, could feel our collective loneliness limp away.

Like we always do in our family, we focused on funniness, and held private the more human memories of Dean. He was indeed funny, but he was a lot more than that. My brother Casey finally verbalized what we were all thinking in some part of our minds, that we wanted to make those characters of our past one-dimensional, to categorize them more easily, and to look past their complex humanity.

The stories just kept coming and we ached from laughter, but we never mentioned Dean's softness, his heartfelt blubbering at farewells, and his sentimental stumbling for authentic words of love that escaped his otherwise gifted gab. We didn't mention the tragedies he faced and endured or his fizzled failures. He was a wonderful, soft, perfectly imperfect guy, and we loved him dearly. But that softness touched something inside us that made us uncomfortable, and we didn't want the softhearted, sweet man. Instead we wanted the brazen entertainer, the comedic actor who broke up strangers and had them whispering to each other about "that insane man" for weeks. At least that's what we told ourselves.

I hadn't seen Dean in years; he had gone his way and I had drifted in mine, thinking there would always be time. As the narrative about Dean and our shared childhood unfolded, each story proved only partially complete, with some of the important details already turning wispy and cloudlike, evaporating right in our midst, daring us to catch them, taunting us. And then, I realized with sudden clarity, there were precious few chances left to recall those story pieces, those fragments of family, which might be lost to us forever. That truth hurt me deeply. I shared that sadness with Dean in a private moment, stolen secretly there in front of my brothers. I silently shared with the softhearted Dean, the broken, loving one, and I felt his tears well up, felt my own too. It saddened me, made me wet-faced and sentimental. I was angry with myself for letting those pieces of memory drift off in the foggy night current, like little dinghies with decayed mooring lines, finally frayed to nothing from years of indifference. Lost forever.

I determined then and there to capture what I could of those people and that place, the "who" and "where" of how I grew up. And so I write this for selfish reasons, and I do it for family, for both those who will appreciate it now, and for those in the future who might wish to know. I do it because I want to and because I must. To me, this is more than just family stories and reminiscence. It is those things, to be sure. Yet it's also about what I think is a very special time, the last hurrah of the family farm and a way of life, wedged between yesteryear's horse farming and big-business farming of today. It seems to me that it was a very short, but very glorious time, a time aching to tell its story, to spill its glue on us and stick to us, lest it too drift away, mooring lines frayed from neglect.

****

What follows are reflections and short stories. There is no continuous tale as one would find in a novel. There is no story line that starts at the beginning and ends at the last page. Rather, these are discreet episodes, vignettes and snapshots of life. Because some of the details and references in a given section build on stories presented earlier, I recommend reading the stories in order, though readers may of course feel free to roam these pages in whatever fashion suits them. I will tell you a bit about the geography and history of the place, tell you how my family came to farming, and introduce you to neighboring farmers and friends and a few of our visitors. Along the way I'll acquaint you with some of the farm's animals and will share with you the work and play that was our way of life.

Because these stories are about people and place, I have abandoned a strict chronology. I believe this approach yields richness to the stories and the characters, and I hope it will provide the reader with a more satisfying experience, though it is imperfect. To ease the reader through my back-and-forth of years and dates, I state my age at the beginning of sections where that information may help.

Some of what is written here is simply small fragments of memory that as a whole are incomplete. They don't seem to exist for any particular reason; they don't seem to tell any particular story. Their existence in my modest memory vault is therefore strange and puzzling to me. I set them down here to give them time, to let them breathe, in hopes that such time and air will birth a new insight, or perhaps it will nurture other memories, emancipating them from the murky depths of recall and into daylight – and just maybe such new perspective will someday complete these fragments of story.

Nearly all of these stories are true, though I have changed some names to protect the privacy of those who prefer it. I have also bent a few details in order to make the stories flow more easily. The few tales that are fictional are stories I believed to be true until, after some five decades and having already set them to paper, I only then discovered to be family folklore. I present those fictional episodes alongside the factual ones, because to the childhood me, they were all my reality. As best as I can, I set the record straight in endnotes.

Lastly, with deference to the truth and owing to the only measure of memory the good Lord has given me, I am absolutely certain I have butchered several "facts" in these stories. I just don't know which ones.

> *"When I was younger, I could remember anything, whether it had happened or not."*
> *Mark Twain*

Chapter 1

My Past Place

Our past places get inside us and walk with us forever. They are soulless zombies that entrap us on the rusted barbed wire of former failures, and at the same time they are angelic spirits, paracletes who lift us as hang-gliders, soaring forward from the hilltops of our lives. Our past places both haunt and enliven us. They are with us always.

We say we are *from* a place, that we were born in this place or raised in that place. Our words make it sound like we were physically contained within a space, like we actually got inside the thing. But it's really the other way around: We don't get in places. Places get in us.

So too for the people who have touched us. They range from the obvious and predictable, like parents, to the most obscure and unlikely acquaintances that somehow seem to reach into us and shout to our souls in ways that mystify us. Some seemingly small encounters shape us like bulldozers, and some enduring ones nudge us along with soft spoons. Regardless, those heroes of history and circumstance, those ghosts of geography get in us and talk to us unceasingly. They live and breathe and consort with us for our whole lives, and we can no more leave them than we can leave ourselves. We move away. We pursue our lives. Most of us get jobs and some marry, and we all gradually grow different in so many ways, but our places still journey beside us. Our places are with us always.

My past place is unheralded, small and remote and quiet, nestled between the Adirondacks and Vermont, tucked softly beneath Lake George, along the eastern Hudson River Valley. The town of Cambridge, New York, neighboring Greenwich, and the surrounding hamlets with names like Vly Summit, Stump Church, Shushan, Eagle Bridge and Buskirk were and still are tiny communities with a huge sense of place. My sacred ground was not only the local area and communities, it was the place of our simple family farm, and even more specifically, it was the top of our farm's high hill. As Cambridge and these hamlets were my Jerusalem, the top of our hill was my holy of holies, my special place with a mystical power. That hill was my crow's nest as I sailed in my formative years, the height from which I could see beyond the immediate, where I could observe the forces around me, shaping me even as I watched. It was the place that suggested more, the place that gave me perspective.

View from the top of our hill, c.1958

I was born there. I grew up there. I am from there, and that place walks with me, shapes me even today. This – the Cambridge area and the farm and that hill - is my past place, and it is *in* me.

Here, for me, place and time converge into a single thing. Here history sits just so on a hillside, and a cornfield recites to me an ancient tribal tale. The Mohicans lived here for centuries and I can feel their presence as I cross through woodlands or drink pure water from a spring, when I walk the dirt roads that trace ancient trails. Towns with Mohican names like Schaghticoke, Hoosick and Walloomsac are all around, standing in testimony to time-place oneness.

Here, the county is named after George Washington, and many local families trace their histories back to the earliest European settlers. From my family's hilly farm, I could spy hallowed ground from our country's Revolutionary War beginnings. To the southeast, across a fifteen mile vista, I could make out the three hundred feet tall obelisk monument that marks the Bennington Battlefield, where the Green Mountain Boys defeated General Burgoyne's British Army Regulars. To the west, through the hazy Hudson Valley, I could spot Saratoga's sacred site, marked by its own obelisk, where American farmers-turned-soldiers dealt a stunning blow to the British - the turning point of the Revolution. As a young boy peering through my five dollar telescope, my dreaming eyes imagined the billows of smoke, colorful banners and flags flying just above the blanket of grey puffs. I could smell the gunpowder and hear the drummers urging ranks onward amid the rumble of distant cannons. Fifteen years later, as a shaken and overwhelmed cadet at West Point, full of surrender and surrounded by men in granite, I would look across this same Hudson through wet eyes, imagining what those heroes endured, doubting that I had what it took to be in their footsteps.

Looking north from the top of our hill, I could make out the distant Adirondack Mountains, gauzy lumps of grey that floated on the horizon like a spirit-sent armada, layer upon distant layer. That far corner of Washington County forms part of the Adirondacks, a vast and ruggedly beautiful area, a strangely inhabited wilderness. In this section of Upstate New York, people live and shop and work in an area protected as "forever wild" by the state's constitution. Earth and rock and water have a special living permanence, an irrevocable heritage, and people are an equally deliberate part of that formula, an elemental part of the chemistry. Here, the land and its people are indistinguishable, a fact that presses on that place with tectonic force.

Also visible through that spyglass which, for me, magically transcended time and distance, is a tall hill named Colfax, some five miles to the northeast. At the foot of Colfax, on the far side, sits the riverside crossroads of Battenville, where I used to swim. There Susan B. Anthony, temperance leader and fighter for women's rights, grew up, went to school and taught. Perhaps it's not just coincidence I later married a woman who broke gender barriers, who was in the first class of women at West Point.

With that same telescope I could make out Shaftsbury, Vermont, the little town that Robert Frost called home and where he penned some of his greatest works. Whenever I roamed those woods, or walked in the crunching moonlit snow, or placed rocks on a field's stone wall, his cadenced verse sang in my soul. Still today I hear him, feel a part of him within me when I do these things or even ponder doing them.

Stump Church

The idyllic little Stump Church with its perfect white spire stood less than a half mile from our farm, and to me it was the crown jewel and standard of the bucolic beauty of the place. The Stump Church was built in 1832 and it still welcomes local families every

Sunday. The *Washington County Post*, then the nation's oldest weekly newspaper, arrived in our mailbox each week and we perused it religiously for all the local latest.

It was and is a grand, slate roofed scene, a storybook place. Grandma Moses lived her whole life here and painted her plain country scenes with the kids and sleds and simple farm life that surrounded her. You can almost taste the maple syrup being boiled down in every gentle hollow. It looks like a place that Norman Rockwell should be from. He is. He lived in Arlington, Vermont, the next town over, a few short miles away. Orvis, the world's foremost fly fishing company named its elegant, hand crafted, bamboo fly fishing rod after the Battenkill, the pretty little river that winds its way through the place. Both rod and river are strikingly beautiful works of art, God-made. As a kid I swam in the Battenkill and canoed her, and plopped my fishing line in without any awareness whatsoever that I was in one of the most premier and picturesque trout streams in the entire world. Covered bridges seemed to be everywhere, and each bend in the Battenkill brought yet another gift of serene beauty. I thought all rivers looked like this one. How could a kid know? It was a postcard place.

Yet it was also a very real place with very real people, with love and joys and tragedies and heartache and triumph. There I met characters of all sorts, teachers, farmers, friends, schoolmates, and relatives. I picked out slices of them that I fancied, copied them, made part of them part of me. It was the place where I stumbled through my early beginnings, grew in the awkward, lurching ways of boyhood, where I first laughed and cried and stole my first kiss, where I was first hurt, and where I first hurt others in ways that still haunt me, where I first learned selfishness, and where I learned to love, to forgive, to be kind and to be humble. It is where I first became the partly perfect and partly broken person I am today. Entwined with my God, this place-time is my private and permanent North Star. It is that core part of me that knows what's "right," and it calls me ever forward. Most of all, it is the place that is in me, always. It is history and heroes, poets and painters, neighbors and farmers and friends. And it is that profound sense deep within, telling me that people, place and time are strangely inseparable.

These are more stories of place and time than stories of me. I am not nearly so fascinating. But that place, in that time is indeed the stuff of fascination to me, the stuff of goose bumps on my forearms, and the place of heroes who walk always beside me.

Covered bridge in nearby Buskirk

Chapter 2

Working the Soil from the Other Side
How the Preeces Came to Farming

(My age: three years before I am born)

"*Roberts appears to be ready on the mound…looks to deliver the first pitch of the top of the ninth. Gilliam is dug in and ready, anxiously chopping at the air with his bat…*"

"Hello?"

"Don?"

"Speaking."

"Hi Don, it's Brad Sorrels. Sorry for calling at this hour. How are you?" Brad owned the funeral home where Don worked in Norwalk, Connecticut.

"Good, just listening to the Dodgers game. What's up, Brad?"

"*Gilliam swings and cracks a sharp grounder, but right at the shortstop for an easy put out. That's one down as Pee Wee is making his way to the batter's box. Duke is on deck.*"

"Oh, hope they're playing well. Preacher's pitching, right?" Preacher Roe was the Dodger's pitcher that night and he was a favorite among Dodger loyalists.

11

"Yah, and he's keeping them off the bases. You calling to offer me more Ebbets Field tickets, Brad?" Don prodded with the lighthearted banter that marked their friendship for years, each acting like it was the duty of the other to secure gifts and give them away freely.

"No, wish I was. Hey, Don, before I forget to tell you, the Coulters mentioned that they might want you to paint their house this summer – you're still painting when you can, right? I told them I thought you were."

"Oh, great, Brad. Yes, I'm still painting and was hoping to line up some jobs soon, so I'll call them Monday. Preece Painting – where pigments have a 'brush' with destiny!" he joked, making fun of his own modest, one-man enterprise. He painted a few houses each year to supplement his mortician's income and more importantly, to thrust himself into the open air of summer. I'd later come to know my father as the loveable though annoying type of claustrophobic that drove the car with the heat on and the windows down. He loved the open air.

"And Pee Wee swings hard! Oh, it's only a lazy pop up, looks like it's gonna be foul behind first. But the second baseman Tommy Glaviano is really hustling and he's gonna put this one away for the second out."

"Good, I'm glad I told them right, Don. Say, the real reason I'm calling," Brad's tone turned business-like, "is that we've got a wreck on the Post Road near Milford. Eddie Billowski called." Eddie was a Milford policeman and knew Brad and Don well. Eddie always recommended Sorrels' when the family asked for suggestions regarding mortuary or funeral services. The fact that Eddie called Brad tonight meant that the ambulance had already been to the scene and medical workers declared the three deaths.

"I'm on it, Brad. Game's almost over anyway. Where is it?"

"Just the other side of the Housatonic, westbound. Near Flannery's drug store, along that patch of woods."

"Yep, I know right where you mean."

"Thanks, Don. You know I appreciate it. Eddie will be there until the scene is cleared. And Don?"

"Yah?"

"No need to rush. Bring some coffee. Eddie said it's a bad one. Three teenagers. You're going to be a while."

"Called strike three! Duke got fooled by that one, just froze him at the plate and that'll do it for the Dodgers in the top of the ninth."

Don's stomach sank when he heard Brad say "three teenagers." He thought he'd left that behind him, the stuff of teenagers dying. At least in the war it meant something. Teenagers dying in car crashes seemed so senseless and was hard for him to take. Each time it seemed more gut wrenching than the time before.

Don told his wife Clare about the call. She made a thermos of coffee for him and kissed him goodbye. He headed toward the door and the funeral home and the roadside role of a mortician with night duty. Twenty minutes later he arrived at the scene of the accident and quickly found Officer Billowski.

"Hey, Eddie."

"Don, good to see you. I figured Brad would ask you cover this one. Three of them in there." Eddie nodded toward the lights and the wrecker truck and ambulance that surrounded the mangled automobile. A gas powered generator droned on from behind the wrecker, providing an unending, irritating rumble of necessary noise that had to be overcome in any exchange of words. The generator powered the two floodlights that stood as somber sentinels and illuminated the devastation.

"Bad one, Eddie? Brad said it was."

Eddie just looked at Don and then looked down while the question hung heavy in the air between them. Eddie just shook his head. "They were just kids," was all he could gulp out. "I need to get back to the family for a minute, Don." Eddie took a deep breath and walked to the stoic, lost-eyed couple who stood facing him with defeated shoulders, shoulders that had just been sentenced to carry ponderous and permanent wounds that would never heal.

Don made his way to the activity to get a look for himself, nodded a greeting to Skip Morris who drove Milford General's ambulance. Skip nodded back to Don. "Thought I'd hang around until you got here," Skip said. "Nothing I can do here, Don. But thought I'd stay and give you hand getting them out."

"Thanks, Skip. What have we got here?"

As Don walked closer he smelled the mongrel mixture of gasoline, motor oil and scorched rubber that came with car wrecks and became forever connected in his mind with mutilated bodies. He braced himself for what he'd see. The four-door automobile was badly twisted against the trunk of a large, old oak tree. The car was bent and crushed in ways that hardly seemed possible to him and indicated that the driver had to be guilty of reckless speed. He saw the two bottles first, as they were impossible to miss, oddly colorful, nameless, brandless bottles of booze that his mind had no capacity to take in, no ability or interest to note further, the particulars being irrelevant. They had been drinking, that was enough.

He did, however, fully take in the three teenage faces, despite his sincere efforts at detachment and self protection. The young faces stunned and rattled him. Those brutally bloodied faces, still so close to life, still full of invincibility, still expressing surprised disbelief at the surrounding destruction and mutilation shook him. The three destroyed bodies were contorted in ghastly ways that only war veterans and death workers ever see. Don Preece was both, but he had to turn away for a moment, had to avert his eyes while his voice softly croaked out "Aw, God!" for nobody to hear.

In those ruined faces, he saw himself as a younger man, as a teenager. He grew angry with them for their foolishness and their pointless self destruction, for their refusal to heed advice and for their deadly arrogance. But because he understood each of those shortcomings, because he was still so close to all those things in his earlier self, he connected with those three souls in kinship. Don was only twenty seven, closer in age to these three teenagers than he was to Eddie or Skip, and to a degree he still understood the aimless, uncontrollable ferocity that drove teenage boys.

The three faces drew him in through their lifeless eyes and shouted to him, pleaded with him, asked him for one more chance. "Oh God, we didn't mean for this to happen!" they seemed to be saying to him with blank eyes that somehow wouldn't look at anything but him. "One more chance!" the haunting, still youthful, forsaken faces said, "*Please* give us another chance!"

Don Preece knew about second chances because of his own life-defining moment of eight years earlier. He knew about second chances from his having been hit with red hot shrapnel from a kamikaze attack on the U.S.S. Achernar as they prepared to invade Okinawa. Early on April 2, 1945, just after midnight, the bomb-laden Japanese plane hit Achernar's starboard side and exploded. Five pieces of burning metal shredded Don's belly and buttocks and the nineteen year old sailor fell into the Pacific, unconscious. Dan McPeek, his best friend and future farm-visitor and shaper of my life, told me later how Manuel Zerr, a sailor from New Orleans, dove in after Dad and fished him out, carried his limp, bloody body across the gun tub below, leaving wet footprints as evidence. Don Preece would eventually make it. Luckily, he got his second chance. He wished he could give the same to these boys, wished he could issue second chances to every young person on the planet. Wished he could issue a second chance to his brother Buddy, who died of diphtheria when Don was four. Wished he could give another chance to his brother Dicky, who suffered every day with Down's syndrome. He could not give it to any of them, not to his brothers, who did nothing to earn their misfortune, nor to these three teens, who tragically and pointlessly let their lives slip away. He could give no second chances. They were not his to give. And it sickened him.

With some effort, Don shook it off, collected his wits and his composure and looked over his shoulder, still disturbed deep inside. "C'mon, Skip," he said, mustering his own courage. "Eddie!" Don hollered to the policeman over the drone of the generator. "Can you give us a hand?"

The three men set about the business of trying to remove the bodies. They pulled on unmovable steel and tugged on dead arms and broken limbs, wrenched with all their might against brutally bent metal and pinched body parts that had been wedged into unsightly contortions. They struggled fiercely to free the bloodied bodies of the dead teenagers. They positioned themselves and repositioned themselves, tried pry bars from the wrecker truck, worked as individuals and as a single team. They did everything humanly possible to remove the metal carnage that entrapped those teenage bodies. But they could not do it. The evil and angry wreckage was too stubborn and too clutching and too furious in its insatiable appetite for its prize.

After a while, when it became obvious that they would need an altogether different approach, Skip Morris made his apologies and bid them good-night, withdrew with his empty ambulance to where he could do some good. Eddie's surrender made Don go at it even harder, but he just grew more frustrated. Something inside Don slipped and he began to become outwardly emotional, using the excuse of physical effort to manifest his growing rage. Eddie Billowski did his best to draw Don Preece back into detachment, to distract him from the frazzled nerve those teenagers struck in him. "Enough, Don," he said, breathing hard. "I'll call for the welder, Don. Get yourself a cup of coffee." His words had no effect. "Hey, c'mon, let's go. Come sit with me in the squad car and share some of that coffee – I could sure use it. And maybe we can see how the Dodgers game ended up."

Officer Billowski made the call to the welder, who agreed to come and use his torch to cut the metal wreckage, to cut loose the iron pieces and to free those dead boys from that mangled car. While Eddie called the welder, Don Preece pulled alone and in utter frustration on soulless metal for a few more moments, pleading to those faces through his tears to set themselves free and wriggle loose of their horrific bondage. He so wanted to tell them to wise up and stop wasting the precious, tragic gift of life that was already gone.

Perhaps only war veterans can feel what he felt that night. Perhaps only those brought near death in battle could know the depth of frustration he felt when faced with three lost lives, squandered and cut short for mere thrills. Battle-wounded men, who indeed risked their very existence for others, add sacred meaning to our lives, while some of us unthinkingly fritter the gift away in senseless self-absurdity. Nonsensical and unaware, the fritterer rejects the veteran's sacrifice, and in so doing, offends and injures him further. Yet the veteran, the wounded giver, forever unable to harden his purpled heart, still desperately wants to give, for only he knows the amazing, staggering, untellable value of the gift. They broke him that night. Three teenage boys whom he'd never before met, who unintentionally threw their promise of life away, they broke him. Nauseated, Don Preece shook and choked and wept in his private rage.

He finally met Eddie in the squad car and they shared the coffee. They waited for the welder to come and cut the bodies free. Eddie paid him the dignity of talking only Dodger baseball, and not mentioning Don's own wreckage, evident in his tear-streaked face and broken voice. Don finally regained his detachment. Regained his control. Regained his professionalism. And that night, while the generator buzzed and the three bodies remained trapped, while he waited in the stark floodlit night for the welder and drank coffee with Eddie Billowski and chatted about the Brooklyn Dodgers, Don Preece swore to himself that he'd find another line of work.

The following year, his father would float the idea and Don would say yes to farming.

* * * * * * *

My grandfather Ralph eventually grew tired of it all, too. Though he prided himself on being the unemotional and professional funeral director, the stuff of death eventually wore him down. It started early in his career, when he backed his car out of the Connecticut driveway and accidentally ran into six year old Dub Touhey, who despite all warnings and parental threats, was snow sledding in the street and zoomed unseen into the car's path. Poor Dub died instantly. My grandfather knelt over him and cried out involuntarily. It horrified him, made his head spin and made him turn away and retch. It was pure accident; there was absolutely nothing he could have done. But this haunted my grandfather and started the process of slow exhaustion for him.

As time went on, Ralph found that he couldn't suppress his cynicism toward the all-too-common phonies he encountered as a funeral director. He became fed up with the two-faced relatives of the deceased who worked him mercilessly in private, angled and drove and harangued him to give them dead old Aunt Betty's jewelry or poor old Uncle Charlie's watch, not to bury them in the valuable things. "They'll never know," they all insisted, referring to both the deceased and the other living relatives who would otherwise be aghast if they would ever learn the jewelry had a new owner. These same heartless thieves would then show up at Betty's or Charlie's burial ceremony, wailing in counterfeit grief. "Oh Charlie! My dear, dear Charlie! Oh, how can I possibly go on without you? I cannot bear it! I must come with you, my beloved, I must! I *must!*" My grandfather stopped one such burial ceremony mid-sentence and asked all the attendees to step back. He made a big show of it, made it clearly disruptive. "Stand back, everybody," he announced, always the orchestrating funeral director, sweeping his arms as a means of instruction. "Make room, make room. The lady is going to throw herself in…so let's give her room to do it." After a few moments of stunned silence, the lady quietly took her seat.

And because others had perceived the same phoniness my grandfather did, there were more than a few snickers from the crowd, all aimed at the pseudo-mourner, all delighted that the funeral director did what they wished they'd had the courage to do.

Ralph knew that though he was right about the lady's insincerity, he had crossed a line. And that crossing told him that it was time to move on.

Ralph Preece also loved the thrill of investing in something that would become an adventure. Shortly before World War II, he partnered with some in-laws and started manufacturing tools to make bullet casings. The war came and they made a small fortune. But they spent it as fast as they made it. For example, in 1943 they needed to meet with an ammunition company in Chicago, so the boys rented a private Pullman railcar, had it fitted out with everything they "needed," such as caviar and champagne, had a limousine pick them up from the train station and made reservations for dinner at Chicago's finest. Within a few months after the war the money was completely gone. But Ralph's appetite for business adventure and investing with a little risk had been piqued, and the farm opportunity came along at just the right time.

Ralph's machine-shop buddy and business friend, Gus Stelfplug, told him about the farm for sale up in Cambridge, New York. Gus's daughter was married to a farmer on the other side of the hill up there and of course Gus had been there many times. Ralph had made some of these trips with Gus, and he loved the people up there. He also knew Don would love the clean, open air. The father-son mortician duo talked it over and it was agreed. My family's farming adventure had begun. It was as if they reversed their profession, completely inverted it, literally turned it upside down. Instead of morticians, burying the dead in the ground, they would become farmers, raising life from it. They would still work the soil, but "from the other side."

The initial entourage, the first wave of Preece-invaders to Vly Summit Road included Don and Clare (my parents), Ralph and Gertie (my paternal grandparents), Dickie (their Down's Syndrome son, Don's brother), and Rick (my older brother). Ralph's mother, who was nearly bedridden, would soon follow. They must have looked something like the Beverly Hillbillies when they piled into that brown Dodge Coronet and made the long, four hour trek to the farm they bought from Henry Thomas' family in 1955.

I doubt they had any idea what lay ahead.

Chapter 3

From Horses to Horsepower
How the Farm Came to be Available

The real story about how the farm came to be for sale is rather straightforward. Henry and Permelia Thomas owned the place and worked the horse-powered farm with the help of Henry's son and daughter, Alfred and Zilpha. (Both were born to Mary, Henry's first wife, who died giving birth. Henry later married Permelia.) Henry passed away in 1954. He was seventy-one, had a heart attack, and died in the hospital shortly thereafter. The farm was then put up for sale. I learned all this in 2011 and 2012 from Henry's family, and the records clearly back them up.

But that is not the story I grew up believing.

For five decades I believed what I have written below, and which I now present here as pure fiction and family folklore. I am not sure where the story comes from or why my family dyed the history of the place with this tale. Perhaps they wanted us boys to respect the deadly dangers inherent in farming or to fear certain tools and machinery with which boys had no legitimate business. Or perhaps I merely imagined it all by myself and made it my personal historical chronicle, never questioning its veracity. I am quite capable of such things. So is my family.

I had written all of what follows before I learned the factual history of the place. I wrote what I believed, and in that sense, for some fifty years, it was indeed my "truth." And so I hope the Thomas family will indulge this fictional fantasy and can accept that I have written honestly from family legend and without any intent to deceive. Most of all, I hope I have captured some of the work of farming with horses in a way that honors Henry and his family for their remarkable craft.

* * * * * * *

(My age: two years before I am born)

In 1955 my family moved to what had been a horse farm. When the Preeces arrived, the horses were gone, but the remnants of horse farming lingered all around, in every barn and every field. Years later, you could still smell those horses. You could still feel them in the horse-hide-oiled, horse-rubbed-and-polished wood of their stables. You could still hear them in the jangle of brass and leather harnesses and in the horse-drawn farm implements that were everywhere in our barns, our museums to an ended era.

I know some of how this change came about, how horse farming ended here. I imagine the rest. I sit alone in the abandoned horse drawn sleigh, dust filled and moth eaten, parked where it has been for years, inside this narrow barn, kept in tight quarters with every necessary element of the trade. Only the horses themselves are gone. I listen to what remains of them in this silent and darkened place, sunlight streaming in through the spaces between barnboards, shining on dust particles that dance like golden slices of silent, floating foam. I hold the leather straps and collars, draw them in through my nose, fairly tasting their tales. I wake them gently from their long slumber. In hushed and patient tones I ask them about how it all happened, and they begin to whisper to me...

"Haw!" Henry Thomas issued the command to turn left with a business-like confidence, a matter-of-fact tone that registered efficiency and expected obedience. Betty and Ned, his two black Percheron draft horses, followed the command with the elegant, practiced precision of a seasoned team, moving in unison as Henry pitched the nose of the plow out of the ground so the horses could slide it along with ease. They made a full turn and started the next furrow, going back down the length of the field. After a four minute pull, it was "Gee!" and the parade of muscle and equipment turned fully to the right and furrowed back again with a subtle accuracy that even Henry marveled at.

Henry drank in the smell of springtime, the clean, earthiness of mud and new sprouts and damp air. He could look across the still blooming woods and make out the Stump Church on that May morning in 1954. He had been there yesterday and had taken note of the small, gated cemetery, making him consciously aware of his own mortality. He was seventy-one. Nothing better mirrored the cycle of life and death, the cycle of seasons better than farming did, and Henry Thomas was keenly aware of these cycles as he plowed. It had started anew yet again. Spring, the beginning of another season. Robins puffy with unlaid eggs landed close behind him, feasting on the fat worms that the plow exposed.

In the adjacent field, just on the other side of the stone wall that marked the edge of Henry's property, Joe Scully had also started plowing. Unlike Henry, Joe Scully plowed with his new Farmall 300 tractor. It made a terrible racket, but it did in a couple of hours what took Henry and his Percherons all day. Too loud, Henry thought. Far too loud and far too expensive.

By mid morning there were only the sounds of horse hooves punching into soft earth, steel slicing through it, and the occasional jingling of leather straps and brass connectors. That patient dance of plowing went on all morning. After each turn, the horses slid into a natural gait that produced an easy, rocking chair rhythm for Henry as he walked behind. Of course he had to guide the plow to keep it on track, but the work was peaceful. His subtle adjustments seemed mere suggestions on the plow, as he had learned over the years how to let the horses do the work. The plow played a soft music of csshhhhhh… with an occasional muffled scrape as a buried stone was dislodged from its underground hibernation. Henry and the team would return tomorrow to pluck the newly turned rocks and add them to the stone walls that marked the field's border, each rock piled on the next in testimony to earlier generations who had worked this field.

Henry had become so engrossed in the work of plowing that he overlooked the hour. He forgot about lunch and about resting his team. Betty reminded him. She was the undisputed horse-leader at Henry's place, as mares often are. Ned was a younger gelding and loved to work, but he lacked her stamina and seemed happy to follow her lead. Like all farm animals, Henry's horses had personalities. They had temperaments and characters that made them as familiar and distinctive as the neighborhood gang at a Saturday night poker party.

Part of Betty's character was an abiding sense of meals and knowing when it was time for a break, even if Henry didn't. She simply stopped right there in mid furrow, as if to say "Henry, you forgot to give us a break. So we're taking one." Ned followed suit, though he probably didn't know why the sudden work stoppage had been called; he'd heard no commands from Henry. But Ned followed Betty's lead in everything, even stopping, unbidden, mid-furrow.

It took Henry a moment to crawl out of his daydream, out of his absorption with the current furrow, to realize what had happened and why the sudden stop. When it dawned on him, he chuckled at the old gal, at how she knew what was right and fair, and how she'd give you her best, but she also expected consideration from her handlers. Even draft horses expect a certain dignity. He admired her awareness and her complete control over Ned. She's a labor union boss, he thought to himself, and she's a darned good one. After the break, and after some sugar cube bribery, they went back to their deliberate and methodical work, gently carving the field all afternoon.

As that day ended, Henry and his parade made their final pass along the stone wall, plowing slowly and softly, trudging westward toward the setting sun. As they did, he recalled watching Joe Scully plow his first furrow that morning, just a few yards on the other side of that stone wall, as the Farmall had raced eastward, opposite the direction Henry was now going. He had caught a glimpse Joe's face then, full of the morning sun, full of determination, full of the new zeal that comes with a farm's first tractor, charging toward the future.

Henry knew his own farming days were numbered. Tractors had long been making their way to every farm in the area, but Henry was a horse farming man and that was that. He was one of the last. He would have no tractors, and he understood that meant he couldn't keep farming much longer. Regardless, he was simply getting too old for the hard work of farming, and he knew it was almost time. His wife, Permelia, had been suggesting the same to him for a couple of years now, but Henry feared he wouldn't know what to do with himself if they sold the place.

To Henry Thomas, horse farmer, farming was an intimate, communing-with-the-earth vocation, with the farmer walking each square foot of his land and handling each stalk of corn, hefting each forkful of hay. It was a spiritual thing, a sort of calling. A farmer, with his God, patiently coaxed life from the ground with his hands. Farming wasn't some calamitous race against time. It didn't call for the frantic intrusion of clanging engines and tractor noise. To Henry Thomas, farming was meant to be hard work, but it was also meant to be peaceful.

Henry's back and shoulder pained him when he had finished the field, when he led the black Percherons into the horse barn. So he had Floyd Hill fork some hay down the chute for each horse, dropping the feed down to the main floor where Betty was first to extract the reward through the feed slot. Floyd then brushed down and cooled the horses, watered them, and put the equipment away. Floyd was Henry's hired hand on the Thomas farm. At forty-seven with a full head of hair, he lived down the road and walked to Henry's every day; he had been walking to this place of work each day for eight years. In the red barn by the road, Floyd wiped down and hung the draft horse collars and leads, the bits and driving bridles. He disconnected the hames from the horse collars and hung them on the wooden wall pegs, aligned them like soldiers above the heavy oak milk sleds that were now stored for the warmer months. Floyd then went to the horse barn to check on Betty and Ned one last time. He loved these beasts, knew them intimately, and smiled knowingly when Henry told him about Betty's mid-furrow labor strike.

It was Floyd's dream to have Betty and Ned compete at the Washington County Fair in Cambridge each August, but Henry had never gone along with the idea. It was too much of an inconvenience, Henry had told him. Too much of a commitment and too far to go at a time when there was so much to get done on the farm – mowing and haying and filling the mows for winter, weather permitting, of course.

Regardless, Floyd loved the idea of taking the horses to the fair, and he nurtured this private dream, delighted in the fantasy of it. Each year he and Henry made their way to the horse pull at the fair, just as hundreds of others did. They joined the throngs to watch local farmers prance their teams to the flat-bottomed sled, laden with ponderous blocks of concrete. Those horses would strain and pull with a will and determination that made one marvel at their bred-in appetite for work. One driver would finally walk away with the prize, would lead his team off the pitch with a bursting pride. Hamilton this year, then Herrington. Thomas. Brownell. Skellie. English. Their team would have out-pulled all others and would be champions for the year, admired and envied by neighbors and townsfolk and serious farmers from across the county.

Floyd wanted a chance, just a chance. But Henry, being somber and steadfast about the responsibilities of farming, would have none of it. He needed Floyd to focus on the work. There was so much of it to do. So in August they made their annual, one-day visit to the fair. Floyd watched the horse pull and dreamed, and Henry made the most of the social opportunity. It was the one time in the year he got a chance to talk with some farmers too distant to visit with more often. Henry talked business: prices and seeds and cows for sale, farms being sold. Meanwhile, Floyd fancied his team, Betty and Ned prancing, with Floyd in charge, the orchestra leader in his symphony of imagination.

Fall soon came and the season turned. In October, the two men and two horses brought wagon loads of oats and ears of corn to the barns. Betty and Ned stood firm while Floyd laid the sheaves of oats on the fanning mill, where Henry drove the piston-like arm that made it shake and sift so that only the oat kernels fell into the bucket. Floyd dumped the bucket into the oat bins in the back of the corn crib, and they repeated the process for what seemed like a few hundred times.

Corn came in the wagons a few days later. The men took turns at the various tasks, one shucking the ears and the other turning the crank on the sheller, which stripped the hardened kernels that would be used to feed the chickens and would be crushed into grain for the cows. The work was consuming, though not exhausting.

Neither of them spoke about the magnificent fall colors of the place, yet both regarded it in their own reserved and appreciative way. It was breathtaking. Amber, ochre, gold, crimson, and pine green mixed and popped and sang to the eye, dazzled the heart. It seemed to Henry and Floyd to be too much of heaven to comment on; any words they might use would be so incomplete. So they appreciated it in private, and reflected on cycles, on the rhythms of farming. It had been a good year. The air had become markedly crisper and colder and the cycle of seasons was making itself known again. Winter was on its way. Endings would be coming soon.

On the morning of November 4th, Henry awoke to bitter cold. Winter had come abruptly, had not crept in on cat's feet as spring did. Pasturing was abruptly over. It was now too cold for the cows to be out, and Henry decided to make the seasonal switch that day, to keep them inside the barn for the winter. He discussed it with Floyd over a cup of coffee in the kitchen that morning and the men set about the day's work. After milking, the first order of business was to feed the cows, in a sense to bring the pasture to them, since it couldn't work the other way for another five months.

In the main barn, in the hay mow, Floyd pulled the rope attached to the hay carriage and fork, a fifty-pound iron contraption suspended from the rail that ran inside the barn, along the entire length of the roof peak. The twin forks were three feet long and designed to plunge into a thick stack of hay, hold it in place by spreading its tongs, so the pile could be moved from place to place. But something far up there seemed knotted and bound; the carriage and fork moved uneasily, grudgingly. Henry went for the two pitchforks they would need and Floyd snapped the rope a few times to dislodge whatever was causing the problem.

What Floyd couldn't see through the darkness inside the barn was that the heavy carriage had partially come off the rail, slipping through a space created by Mother Nature's heating and cooling, stretching the iron rail fittings and then shrinking them. His final yank on the rope was one of frustration and determination, and it was just enough to silently dislodge the whole thing, to set the heavy carriage and forks free falling through thirty feet of nothing, toward the man who had yanked it loose.

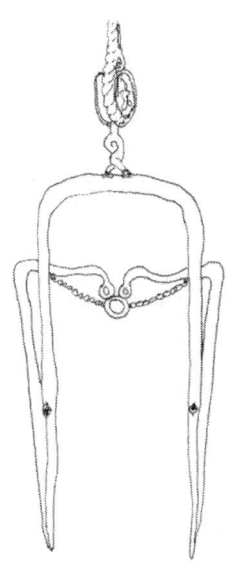

There was no poetry in Floyd's death, no dramatic elegance. It came this day unannounced, a shattering intruder. The forks didn't pierce Floyd, didn't tear through him. Instead they struck him awkwardly, glancing off his bent back. The bulk of the thing followed the forks, crushed the side of his head and slammed it over so far that the tender spinal bones in Floyd's neck gave way. He died instantly, passing from this life before his crumpled body collapsed to the floor.

Henry heard it, but he didn't see it. He was so immediately sickened that it was almost as if he himself had been hit. He knew intuitively what had happened and registered the whole event in his mind even before he could wheel around, before his eyes could take in the scene. He knew instinctively that Floyd was gone and his life, Henry's life, would never be the same. He knew his best friend and trusted helper was gone forever. He knew instantly that this horse farming way of life, which he could live only with the help of another skilled man, had ended.

Neighbors rallied, as they always do in small farming communities when tragedies strike. The Henry and Permelia Thomas house on Vly Summit Road, and the house down the road where Floyd boarded, were filled with respectful, subdued visitors over the next few days. They brought meals and food staples and flowers and offered every kind of assistance. Henry's son, Alfred and a neighboring nephew milked the cows for the next two days. Friends and neighbors and relatives - Henry didn't even know who - cleaned the barns and fed the horses. The O'Donnell brothers, the bachelor twins who farmed with horses on the other side of Henry's big hill checked in on him for several days.

This onset of winter brought a change in seasons, and also brought a change in the cycle of life for both Floyd Hill and Henry Thomas. Floyd's had ended. Henry's was changing dramatically; he would be looking for a buyer for his farm. Other changed lives, the lives of my family members who were yet unknown to Henry, would soon intersect with his in ways that would shape me forever. The Preeces would be leaving Connecticut, looking for a farmer who wanted to sell. They would find Henry Thomas. And Henry would find the Preeces.

Chapter 4

A Time Between

(My age: 55)

We farmed the old Henry Thomas place in a way that marked the change from one great era to the next. Our era, the era of my farming life, was not a great one, but rather the line that divided two others which were. Our time was a short one, sandwiched between a century of horse farmers and the lives of today's rural commuters and mega-farm businesses. It was neither night nor day, but that fleeting glimpse of bleak gray dawn before the sun announces day. It was that short string of pre-dawn moments when the sky is blue and the trees are black, caught in transition, a snapshot not belonging to either grand era that sits before or after it. Ours was a time between.

We were neither horse farmers nor commuters, but we bought the place from one and sold it to the other. Their ways, the ways of those grand eras are long and enduring, unrushed. Ours appeared suddenly, charged through the front door with loud hello's, and then, marching double-time straight through, disappeared just as quickly and quietly slipped out the back way without saying goodbye. It was a unique and brief boundary time in history, as gone now as the horse drawn plow. We farmed with tractors; our tractors were the first powered wheels that plot of land ever felt. And they were the last.

Farmers of today have air conditioned tractor cabs, GPS systems, computer driven irrigation monitors that respond to a labyrinth of weather forecasts and ground sensors, and automated everything, from feeding to milking to mixing the right batch of fertilizer. Farmers of today are hard working, sophisticated business people with enormous capital investments and complex organizations.

Our farming methods resembled more those of Civil War times than those of the 20th century. We were more subsistence farmers and manual labor practitioners than we were participants in the post World War II economy. The emergence of suburbia and industrialized technology happened around us, but not to us. We raised much of what we ate, bartered for more, wore hand-me-downs, and found ways to eke out a living that today might evoke a certain pity. But we had great company, a like-living community of eker-outers that made us feel boringly average and even fortunate at times. Hunger may have crossed our minds, and a desire for more, an ambition of hopefulness, but never pity.

On our small farm we drank milk from our cows, canned vegetables from our own garden, grew and stored potatoes to last the year, and stocked our freezer with beef and pork and mutton from our barns. We bartered for eggs and sat in second hand furniture, baked bread from scratch and made pies from our own apple tree, ate pears from another, and walnuts from one more. A barefooted man came twice a week and collected our one hundred pound milk cans and brought them to market for us. We cleaned manure from barns with forks and shovels and wheelbarrows, mixed concrete by hand, cut green corn with sickles and husked dried ears of corn by hand. We cut trees with handsaws and took our own garbage to the dump. The place had no running water when my parents bought it, but they put it in soon afterward. A working outhouse stood in our back yard for nearly all of my years there, provisioned with a new Montgomery Ward catalogue each season. We got decent reception of one TV station and barely enough for another, black and white of course. The turn of the century house wasn't insulated, had one oil-burning heater, and open windows were our only air conditioning. Doctor visits were rare events, and when they occurred, a dark suited man carrying a black leather bag would knock at our door. Our house had no key; it was always unlocked. Party phone lines and one-car households and hitchhiking and sewing machines were unquestioned, everyday things.

What amazes me most is that we made it. My undertaker grandfather and dad, a father-son mortician team from city life in Milford, Connecticut, set sail for a dirt road dairy farm in Upstate New York, landed on her rocky shore and made it work. Somehow they figured out how to care for cows and raise crops, how to plow and plant and harvest and store corn, oats, alfalfa, timothy, and clover, how to operate milking machines and balers, how to sell milk and buy calves. I think our modest success was due more to determination than anything else. The miracle within a miracle is that we did it without tragedy. Tragedies were all around us. Ten year old Johnny Schmitt, who lived on the farm next to ours, was accidentally killed when he ran into the path of a passing truck. He could not hear it over the sound of farm equipment. Other neighboring farmers broke bones, had tractors roll on them, lost limbs in machines, broke their backs from falls, and more. Farming was a rough business. We were spared.

I both hated it and loved it. I hated the isolation and unyielding, relentless demands. I hated the loneliness and the inability to socialize in ways I declared to be "normal," hated feeling different. I hated not having access to the exciting world I knew was teeming with life beyond that place, just beyond my reach.

But I loved the people and flavor of the place. They were such colorful people, straightforward and self-content. Some might say they were simple, but they would be wrong. Unrehearsed is what they were. I admired how they didn't pretend in the ways I did, or seem to even want to, and I ached to find my own portion of that same self-clarity. I loved the open air and New England prettiness of the place, the stunning blackness of new moons and the shocking brilliance of frightful, powerful lightening storms in summer skies, the likes of which I have never seen anywhere else. It was and still is a gorgeous place filled with people who were anything but boring.

I couldn't wait to leave.

I miss it so very much.

I am grateful for the lessons and the learning. I am grateful to have breathed the air of a beautiful countryside and to have had the company of such wonderful people. I am grateful to have lived in that time between.

My Aunts Lorraine (l) and Janet (r) helping build the silo, 1955. Uncle Dean is on the silo ladder. Uncle Jim Duffy is partially visible in the barn doorway.

Chapter 5

Thomases
About Neighbors

Our family was well accepted in Cambridge, but we were newly arrived, and I instinctively knew that made us quite different. I felt that, unlike other families, we were giving the place a sort of test drive, trying it out, hoping to make a go of it in this new place. Other families had been there for generations and couldn't imagine being anyplace else. Those deeply rooted families formed a fascinating tapestry of lineage, a sort of homespun weave that connected families by quilting bloodlines that were planted there many generations prior.

Their ancestral lines rippled through small streams and tributaries, fed the Battenkill and Hoosick and Hudson Rivers. Their family histories bubbled up like springs from beneath the soil, from some place deep under those ancient hills, from that very chunk of earth itself. In the same way, those same people poured their life-source into the ground, into the soil and streams and rivers of the place, a living gift to and from families who have anchored there for centuries, who long ago made an unwavering commitment to place. They stayed put, and their families grew.

The Thomases were not unusual in the Cambridge area. Other families had similar histories and, like the Thomases, were here in numbers and were here to stay. Herrington. English. Brownell. Hamilton. Buckley. Law. Willard. Pratt. Welling. Shiland. Kenyon. And more. These families took permanence from the place and gave permanence to it. We bought our farm from a Thomas, lived down the road from one and across the way from yet more Thomases, and so they were the old Cambridge family most immediately in front of us. To understand a bit about the Thomas clan is to understand a bit about Cambridge.

My First Friend

Daniel J. Thomas, Jr. was born in 1778; he came to the Cambridge, New York, area around 1800. The records don't indicate why he came, but I can offer one possibility. Daniel's father (Daniel, Sr.) was twenty five years old when war broke out at Lexington and Concord, just fifty miles from his Rhode Island home. It's hard to imagine this didn't stir him in some compelling way, as it did for so many Americans. Perhaps this twenty-five year old, third generation colonist might have joined the patriot effort, might have fought at Saratoga, might have seen this charming, promise-filled countryside. Perhaps he returned home to tell his whole family about the place. Perhaps he came soon after, around 1800, with his wife Anne and their eight children, including twenty two year old Daniel Jr., to make it their home. It's merely my guess. Colonist-soldier or not, the Thomases came to Cambridge, and Daniel Thomas, Jr. was among the first.

Daniel Thomas Jr. arrived in the Cambridge area around 1800.
Daniel, Jr.'s son, Henry Thomas, was born near Cambridge in 1827.
Henry's son, Horton Thomas, was born in Cambridge in 1853.
Horton's son, Charles Thomas, was born in Cambridge in 1884.
Charles' son, Ralph Thomas, was born in Cambridge in 1922.
Ralph's son, Daniel Thomas, was born in Cambridge in 1954.

This Daniel Thomas lived on the farm next door. Though I have not spoken to Dan in over thirty years, I will never forget him. He was my first friend.

One of the last of the local farmers, Dan Thomas still farms in Cambridge. He married Olive Herrington, whose family has roots there just as deep. An 1866 map of the local area shows eighteen different Herrington farms within a five mile radius from the house where Dan Thomas where grew up. Dan's not leaving Cambridge anytime soon. Florida's golden beaches don't have the same pull on people like Dan Thomas as they do on me. I want to go to Hilton Head and Hyannis, to the Sierras and the Sahara. I want to stroll among the moai carvings on Easter Island. I love getting away. It helps me relax, helps me clarify what I'm called to do and who I'm called to be, to better understand how I fit into the grand scheme of things on this planet. It helps me figure out where I belong. Dan Thomas already has his answers; he already knows these things. He always knew. He's a farmer, and Cambridge is home. It is where he belongs. And while I felt welcome in Cambridge, while I always felt at home, Dan Thomas, my first friend, belongs there in a way I never can or will.

Danny Thomas and His Glorious Chariot

(My age: 7)

Farms can be isolated and lonely places, quiet and mundane. Adventure approaches these rural farms slowly, when it approaches at all. It meanders down vacant dirt roads like a tottering, weathered old man, clutching his cane and ponderously, painfully placing one foot in front of the next; at every remote intersection, unsure whether to turn left or right, or to inch along directly ahead. He chooses only gradually, and at random. Years can go by without excitement, without experiencing the adrenaline-drunk thrill of something truly astounding, something that energizes or enflames, something that intensifies farm living. And so, when fortune finally sweeps down on her wings and one day whisks adventure to the farmer-boy, it is a thing even more prized because of its rarity.

Up there, with the distances between houses and with the farming way of life, you didn't see friends every day, or even close to it. And that meant that on those days when Danny Thomas did come to our place, I was all the more delighted. He was two years older than me, strong and wiry and good natured. Dan-Dee I used to call him, and he nicknamed me Joll-Doll, which I think was a take-off on the name of the Jolly family, relatives of his. Everyone there seemed to be a relative of his. To me, relatives were wonderful people who lived in faraway places with sidewalks and ice rinks and a dizzying array of restaurant choices. To Dan, relatives and neighbors were all one big ball of nearby wax.

One July day, I found myself in the middle of the lonely dirt road that ran in front of our house, bouncing a rubber ball off the side of our red barn, manufacturing my own synthetic version of adventure, imagining that I was on a real baseball team with real uniforms playing on a real ball field. I threw at an angle to the right and ran that way, anticipating the rebound, imagining a batter smacking the ball into the gap. I sprinted, caught, spun and threw from the air, as I leaped back to the left, above the base runner who was sliding into second, spikes high. I imagined the first baseman's eyes widen as my throw approached him, saw his amazement at my skill and determination.

I was seven. I did this for hours. For years.

Dirt road and barn wall, the site of my imaginary baseball diamond

I was both player and announcer in my private fantasy, lost within myself. I called the play-by-play under my breath, even more astounded as an announcer at my own skill than the first baseman was. "There's a hard crack toward the third base side, but it looks like he might get it! Holy cow – look at that throw... heeee GOT HIM!!" I patted my glove and toed the ground in my "aw shucks" humility while I secretly basked in the cheers of the crowd, listening while their applause grew ever louder. Drinking in the noise. That adoring crowd was so loud in my mind's ear that I failed to recognize that the cheering had given way to the muffled growl of a small engine now just one hundred yards away on that same dirt road, and headed swiftly my way. It was Danny Thomas on his go-cart – I nearly swallowed my announcer-tongue in my burst of sudden exhilaration!

Dan was smiling broadly as he slowed to a stop on his cobbled-together, homemade go-cart, a patchwork of two by fours and plywood, a Briggs & Stratton engine and mismatched wheels. To me, it was a spectacular, regal chariot, swifter and more glorious than Ben-Hur's, a dazzling and resplendent craft that would carry adventurers to undiscovered lands at stupefying speed. It was, to me, an utterly fantastic roadster! I can still remember every square inch of the jumbled jalopy, from how the driver would turn the thing by pivoting the front axle with his feet, to the ingenious clutch system that slid the entire engine forward and back in order to engage the belt and pulley, to the simple brown-padded seatback, to the aluminum plated thumb-throttle mounted beside the seat. It was the most wonderful piece of machinery ever assembled, and I ached to ride it whenever Danny had it out.

On this most blessed of occasions, he put me in his lap and launched us for paradise, for the Xanadu that was just beyond the next bend in the road. Dirt and gravel were soon tearing by just inches beneath us. Danny let me slide the clutch handle forward and I felt the pulley engage. I was delirious with power, intoxicated with the idea that you could control and direct such a thing as a kid, without adults. We toured a quarter of a mile to our field barn and turned, Dan skidding his sneaker soles along the dirt road to slow us. Then we were off again in the opposite direction, past our farm and all the way to Danny's, wind in our faces. He slowed us when we arrived, turned the wheels with his long legs and pressed the accelerator lever while I engaged the clutch again, hearing the engine surge, feeling the thing lurch forward, feeling wheels gripping gravel, thrusting us toward tomorrow.

It seemed to me that Danny Thomas approached perfection when he was one with his go-cart, and this day was no different. Danny seemed to love the raw power of the thing, the speed of it, the sense of taming an otherwise dominant and fantastic force. He was at his best, was more naturally at home, and I could feel it. He was being the best version of himself, and it seems that whenever somebody is completely and truly themselves, heaven smiles, and the great compass needle of the world settles itself, stops its uneasy wiggling, and locks rock-steady on true north. We know when we're in the presence of that kind of perfection, and even as a youngster I was aware that by riding on that go-cart with Danny, I was witnessing the wonder of something special, something that was exactly what its Maker had intended for it to be. Danny Thomas, driver and pilot of power.

I know now that our speed on that day must have been only ten or fifteen miles per hour. But to me, the isolated farm-boy who pined for adventure, we rode across the Bonneville Salt Flats on yet-untested technology, two Chuck Yeager test pilots with adventure in our hearts, and warm wind in our faces. Danny Thomas's go-cart was an incomparable, splendid machine, and I loved it. I still catch myself sometimes, impulsively looking down the road when I hear a distant engine, hoping to see Danny Thomas piloting it, rounding the corner and coming my way.

"Danny Thomas of Cambridge, Washington County, backed his four-turbo-charger John Deere[1] up to the sled. When it was attached, the tractor started up, a huge plume of black smoke filled the air, and the small front wheels also went up in the air as the tractor surged forward."

"He's a many-time winner," said the announcer. "Two-seventy-nine-point-oh-two is what he's hunting for. He's looking for back-to-back wins here on the circuit."

Thomas was able to make it 282.10 feet before the sled brought him to a stop, eclipsing Burt Stannard's 279.02.

"Two-eighty-two-point-ten, fans! Let's have a nice round of applause for the new leader!" he said.

from The Register Star
article by John Mason
Hudson, New York
September 5, 2010

Dan Thomas
State Champion 1995, 1996, 1997, 1998, 2005, 2007
New York Tractor Pullers Association

---

[1] see Endnotes, page 264.
Dan Thomas' tractor on that day was actually an International, not a John Deere.

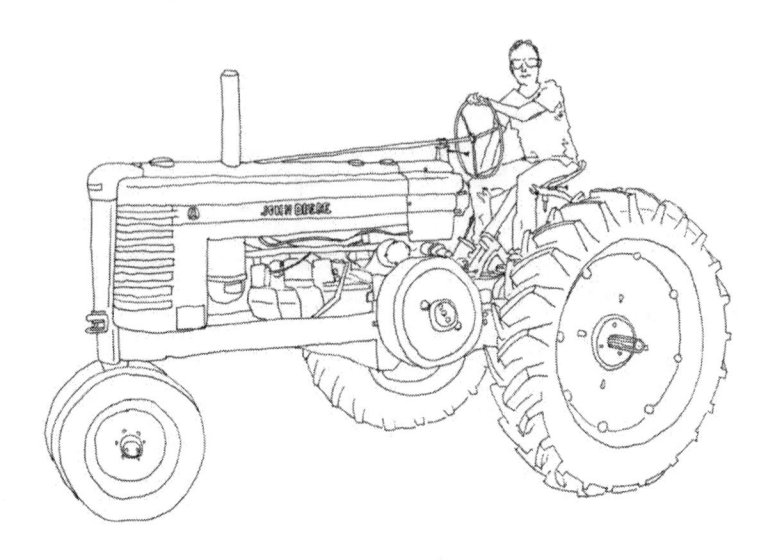

Boomer

(My age: 10)

June 28th, 1966. First field, first cutting, first hay of the year. It was rare for a farm boy to get excited about new work, but on this day, I was as nervous as a brand new batter facing his very first pitcher, his first time in uniform and his first game on a real ballfield. My job in the lower field that day was to pack the just-baled hay on the wagon, following a set pattern, tier upon tier, that interlaced the bales for stability, a process which I can still recite in my sleep today. As a fourth grader, I was already quite proficient at the method, even if my strength was still suspect.

"Is he really ready for that?" my grandfather had asked as the tasks were being planned earlier that afternoon, as if I wasn't standing right there in front of them The group of men and teenagers who formed our crew ignored my presence, and made me feel invisible. I was small and the bales each weighed more than I did. The men engaged in some debate as to my readiness, but it was decided they'd give me a "try out." It was all discussed openly, as if in a courtroom with me standing humbly by the witness box, me being on trial of sorts, never being asked for my view of the facts. Regardless, the gavel came down it was declared I was the probationary packer for that day. I desperately wanted to prove myself.

But there was another, bigger reason for my anxiety. I wanted to do a particularly good job on this hot summer day, as Doug, nicknamed Boomer, Dan Thomas's older brother, was running the baler, and being eight years older than me, was somebody I very much wanted to impress. Unbeknownst to him, I had conscripted him, pressed him into service as my newfound hero, for no other reason than he cut a handsome figure, confident and calm aboard his matching green and yellow tractor and baler. He had just graduated from Cambridge High and that put in him a higher place in my mind, a new man I saw as my future. My hope and aspiration that day was that on his occasional glances our way, he'd notice my immaculate stacking of bales, and take note of the artful packer, marking me somewhere on his mental list of names as "Gerry Preece, Good Worker."

Tractor engines finally began to rumble, the baler began its steady pounding, hay dust wafted off the equipment, and the haying season was underway. I started my packing duties strongly, placing each bale neatly in place and following the prescribed pattern without asking any questions. I kept an eye on Boomer to see if he were watching, but it was hard to tell. One tier was finished, and then the second, and the third. I had the hang of it and found that quick confidence that comes before the first real test, before you realize the true nature of the game you're in. And, being preoccupied with whether Boomer noticed my work, I failed to pack the bales tightly enough to hold well. I was moving an upper bale when the back corner of the load collapsed, and both bales and my pride tumbled. I was humiliated.

Before I could gather myself, the bales were already coming back to the wagon for me to re-pack. Boomer had seen my tragedy, stopped his tractor and baler, and had arrived as my rescuer, offering bales and words of encouragement. That one simple act lionized him for me, exalted him to the highest shelf in my mind, where he still sits today. By not criticizing or critiquing, by quietly coaching and giving me the chance to do it right, Boomer gave me a sort of peer-worker respect, a gift I could never have asked for. It is a gift that inspires me almost fifty years later, that beckons me to kindness when my first instinct is harshness. I do not always accept the gift, but it whispers to me in ways I cannot deny.

I remember him coming to our house after the work was done that day, chatting easily in our kitchen while the number of bales and prices were calculated and my parents wrote the check for the agreed amount. My failure was never mentioned. As he turned to go out, Boomer shot me a wink and a nod, Kris Kringle on a John Deere.

"Sunny 81°
165 bales from back field.
Doug Thomas baled. $21.45"
from Ralph Preece's diary
entry for June 28, 1966

A Quiet Hero

(My age: 52)

It was my father who gave me the habit of walking in cemeteries. I never knew any other family that considered visiting random cemeteries a normal pastime, but to our family it was like going for a Sunday drive. Indeed, Sunday drives with my family often included a stroll through some unfrequented cemetery, reading headstones and imagining what those names did for a living, what kind of people they were, how they may have lived and died. We looked for clues in the dates and what names were adjacent to what other ones. We imagined family connections with others of the same last name, people among the living whom we knew.

Me walking the Stump Church Cemetery

Perhaps it was Dad's brief years as an undertaker that gave him this strange habit of walking cemeteries, where he seemed as comfortable as if he had just entered a bakery on a Saturday morning. Perhaps it was the fact that his father was also an undertaker for even more years. Or maybe, it was because my father had come so close to losing his own life in World War II that made him seem impervious to what others found unnerving and morbid. He was curious and outgoing, and it seemed he wanted to know everything about everybody, even those who had died.

It was my inherited habit of cemetery walking that had us behind the Stump Church in the spring of 2009, paying a casual visit to my family buried there. Ralph and Gertie – my grandfather and grandmother, my Down's Syndrome Uncle Dickie and my Aunt Janet were there. I spent a few prayerful moments with each before I began the ritual strolling, taking note of names, a reverent roll call of familiar families. It was late afternoon. I was tired from having travelled all day and was ready to wind things down, to find a fast meal and crawl into myself for the evening and find sleep early. So I looked at the names halfheartedly that day, taking name after name, life after life, for granted. I muddled thoughtlessly through the rows of weathered headstones, through the names that whispered to me from those meek monuments of marble and granite.

When I saw Judy's name it took me a long moment to register what I was reading. It had been over thirty years. She died at nineteen, after living her entire life with a crippling disease. Though she lived less than a mile away, a small distance in farm country, I didn't know her well. I knew her only as the red haired, bright little girl too often suffering, but always with a smile that defied her pain and misfortune, and always with eyes that met mine joyfully. I knew her only as an incredibly brave girl who chose to give life her best, despite the unfairness of it.

In a special way, she was and is a hero of mine. She is an icon of that place – humble, joyful, determined and timeless. Each time I saw Judy, she was a living example of toughness and great attitude, a person with an admirable spirit. She and her wrecked body were often more full of life than I was with my healthy one, and I treasured that uncomfortable tension that naturally arrived with her presence, the tension that demanded of me to be something more. But over the decades my memory of her faded into a gossamer grey place in my mind where I seldom went and where I increasingly lost my way. She had gone to that place in memory where if somebody asked if I remembered Judy, I would answer yes, but I didn't otherwise call her to my conscience. So seeing her name on that headstone jolted my recall and enlivened my very soul, my deepest self.

Unexpectedly overwhelmed, I turned away from the others I was with, from my wife, Sue, from my brother Casey and his wife, Claire. As I strolled on, the tears came silently streaming down, and I choked hard. It was as if through sheer will, Judy had dragged her broken body from the grave, limped and struggled and made her way to me, and met my eyes yet again, sharing with me her courage, her passion for life, her selflessness. It was as if she were welcoming me back, welcoming me home, reminding me of my gifts, and quietly convicting my complacency.

In that moment, because of Judy Thomas, I chose to live larger. I cherished life with more awareness and vigor than I had in quite some time. A part of me was ashamed that I had taken so much for granted. Yet a bigger part of me, a better part wanted to reach out to Judy, to thank her for the gift of awareness and appreciation and deliberate living, and I determined to grasp all of life that I could in what was left of that day. And in making that decision, making that simple commitment, in making those changes and living better on that day, I like to think that I bestowed yet more meaning and honor on the life of Judy Thomas. Perhaps in my better living, inspired by Judy, her life became an even bigger thing.

Though I do this only in my own small way and with great imperfection, I nevertheless find myself thinking of her often, and am inspired to live better moments, larger moments in the "right nows" of my life. I thank her for helping me to live life more fully, and I hope that my doing so in some way elevates her, my long ago Stump Church neighbor, who walks with me today.

> "Every action of our lives touches on some chord that will vibrate in eternity."
>
> *Edwin Hubbel Chapin, Preacher and Author*
> *born 1814 in Union Township*
> *(later named Greenwich)*
> *Washington County, NY*

Soft Slippers and Big Hearts

(My age: 14)

Lightning startles everyone. But for a farmer with bales of hay still in the field, those first drops of rain and the accompanying bolt of lightning create an unnerving and momentous urgency. It is more than startling. It imposes panic and a loud distress onto farmers otherwise known for their calm. The hay must be gotten in dry, or it is lost – and with it, the year's efforts on that field.

Clouds had been gathering for an hour, so we knew it was coming. But we were fortunate to have the work almost all behind us, the bale buncher and final five bales were already on the wagon, and we were headed home. It had been a long day. Dad, my brother Casey, and I crossed the gravel drive that brought us up the hill to Kenyon Road, Robin Thomas's farm immediately in front of us. But to our right, in Robin's valley field, lay un-baled windrows and scattered bales of hay. Robin was baling and his daughter Sandra was driving the tractor and wagon, throwing bales and packing as she went. His younger daughter Judy was helping by gathering bales into piles for more efficient pickup, but she was small and frail and I knew her health wasn't good. I guessed they still had to bale and load seventy-five bales, about a wagon's worth. I knew what Dad was thinking, I could sense it. But, selfishly, secretly, I just wanted to be done, to get home, to get clean. We had just left the gravel drive, just arrived on Kenyon Road.

That's when the first bolt of lightning cracked. Dad stopped our rig like he had pitted at the Indy 500 and issued commands fast and crisp. We responded without question, swarming toward them like firemen rushing toward flames. Robin sent Sandra to the baler and Judy to the barn, and he leaped atop the tractor pulling the wagon. Casey went aboard their wagon and rapid-packed while Dad and I poured the bales on furiously, somehow keeping pace with Robin's desperate driving. I think we set the land speed record for collecting those last bales, the specifics of how it happened and who did what as much a blur to me then as now. But the hay was dry and now it was in; we had beaten the weather.

Robin looked right at me, gave a big smile and wave as we remounted our own parade of machinery and launched for home through the rain, unconcerned as our cargo was so insignificant. His wife Dorothy waved just as big from their front porch as we sped by; she must have observed the neighbor-team effort. I laid back against a bale on the wagon as we went, and re-ran the whole scene in the slow motion theater of my mind. I saw things now I had missed in the rush of activity a few minutes earlier.

I saw Sandra's determined face and her all-business focus on the job at hand. She was my age and cute and I wanted to befriend her, to make an eye-contact smile or have a light-hearted word. That didn't happen. Instead, I grew impressed with her work ethic and character, her passionate sense of responsibility. I saw Judy struggling without complaint, outmatched by each bale. I saw her resolute courage. I saw a gentle man operating a farm the same size as ours – almost identical in number of acres and cows, four kids of identical age to the Preece kids – but not with four healthy boys. The Robin Thomas family got it done with two healthy daughters, another who fought a lifelong illness, and a youngest son. I saw a kind hearted farmer with his belt slung very low beneath his waist, holding together the muscle tear and hernia that hampered him for as long as I knew him. I saw a farmer dashing across that field in his slippers.

His slippers... I noticed them on his feet many other times in the midst of his work, planting or plowing or haying or chopping corn. I suppose they were a way for him to steal some rare comfort, to gain some control over the unceasing pain that haunted his midsection, over the relentless work of farming. I saw them again, anew that day. Those slippers were metaphor for me. They were weathered and worn and farm-field rugged, and at the same time they were soft and comfortable and inviting. I love that he wore those slippers.

I'd later learn that Robin's wife Dorothy held a master's degree from Columbia. Ivy League. She met a farmer boy named Robin and fell in love, lived the rest of her life on a little dirt road farm less than a mile from my house. She taught school and ran a farm household and raised four children. She buried her long-suffering daughter and her husband in a tiny cemetery behind the Stump Church. I am proud, humbled to have deceased relatives in their company.

The Robin Thomases are a family I regret not knowing better, as they were people of such character and lived so close by. But our school buses pointed in different directions and that made all the difference, as the poet from beyond the other side of our hill might say.

Theirs was a farm with daughters, women, with a young son and brother. A family with more than its share of character and more than its share of misfortune. Always positive, never complaining. They were at once tough and hardworking, soft and joyful, feminine and manly. They were and still are a wonderful and big-hearted, soft-slippered farm family.

Son of a Biscuit

(My age: 6)

We went to Alfred's to get a bushel of apples. I was six. Dad pulled our "Little Green Wagon" behind the small, grey Ford 8N tractor. I sat in the wagon, which was a re-fashioned back half of an old pickup truck, welded to a frame and capped at the front and back with oak planks. It was just the thing for a thousand small jobs around the farm.

Alfred Thomas lived a hundred yards up the road from Dan Thomas's place. Dan's father was Ralph, and Ralph's father was Alfred's cousin. Alfred's father was Henry Thomas, the patriarch of the family from whom my family bought the farm on Vly Summit Road. Trying to decipher and decode these tangles of names and relations was part of living amongst a clan, and it was befuddling.

Alfred was an outgoing man, and always had a prolific garden. He was quick to give away the fruits of his labor, part from pride but even more from kindness. He worked on the county's road crew, and each year would grade our road in the spring, mow the roadside in summers, and plow the winter snows. He always made an effort to look around and spot us as he went by, quick to shoot a friendly wave our way. He was as reliable and regular as a Swiss watch.

I remember the October colors as we pulled into his manicured gravel driveway. The maples in his yard were New England perfect, and I could smell the apples he had in a basket beside the shed. He and Dad immediately dove into conversation that I didn't follow, my being too intent on the apple aroma and the woven wooden bushel basket. It was set against the rich, charcoal-brown backdrop of deeply weathered, wooden barn siding and spectacular, new-fallen maple leaves, a scene Rockwell himself would have appreciated. Noticing my interest, Alfred gave me an apple and chuckled, then promptly went back to talking with Dad. Alfred was wound up, energized about something or somebody, and clearly a bit agitated. But he was a man who refused to utter vulgarities, and so had adopted a phrase I had never heard before. I'd hear him mutter along then spit out "Son of biscuit!" which even at my young age, tickled me.

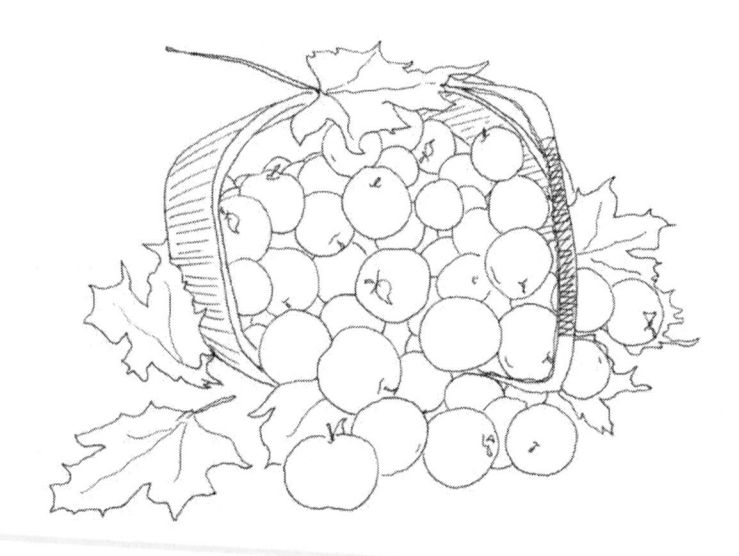

I drifted toward his pipe-in-the-ground arrangement, a thing I'd never seen before and gave it a curious eyeing. Spotting me, Alfred came over and began to operate his hand-pumped well, drawing a sloshing bucket full in just a few strokes and chortling out a cry of success. I was amazed and impressed, drank some fresh water and studied the thing further. It seemed to make water taste better, made it somehow more real, more natural and authentic. The adults talked on and I faded in and out of listening. He'd say it occasionally and always with good cheer. "Son of a biscuit!" I drank that phrase in as if he had drawn it from his well, hand-pumped and genuine, clean and refreshing and sweet.

Later, as a teen, I'd see Alfred and Ethel often, and they would always go out of their way to say hello, to show interest, to be kind. We worked the field directly across from their house, and I'd plow their driveway in winter months. Their house was compact and well kept, tidy and welcoming. I always enjoyed hearing Alfred talk, not only for what that day's conversation held, but also because I knew I'd eventually be treated, gifted with his trademark phrase. It always pleased me and I will always associate it with Alfred Thomas, a kind and generous man who was too polite to cuss. "Son of a biscuit!"

****

There were many more Thomases there, but I never really got to know them. I had met them, and knew they were in the local area. Carl, Lee, Cort and Horton, their families and others, all related. They belonged, always. The Thomas clan, and others like them made up a special part of that place. Today, there is yet another, brand new generation of Thomases there about whom I know even less. But I am sure of two things. First, they are hard workers, as that is in their ancestral blood. And second, I know where they can be found, even one hundred years from now. They wouldn't be the same without the place. And the place wouldn't be the same without them, without these long-rooted families, clans of permanence that give shape and color and flavor to place.

Gerry Preece

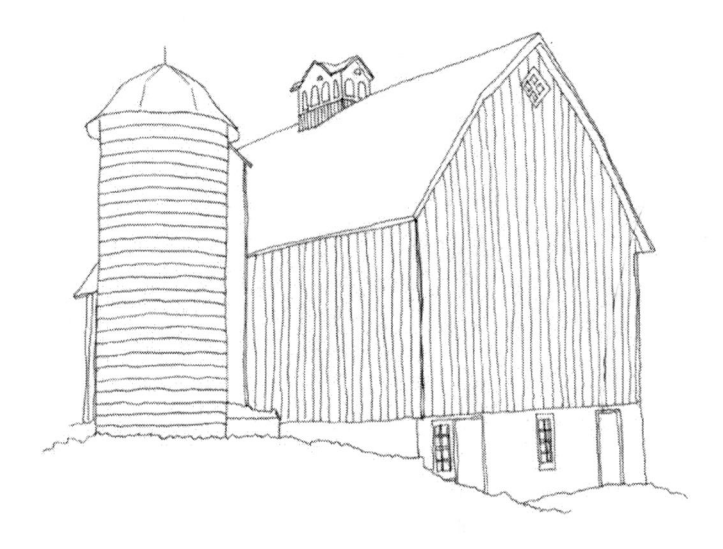

Chapter 6

Ben English

"I am a part of all that I have met."
Alfred Lord Tennyson

One of those towering figures in my childhood memories is Ben English, neighboring farmer and family friend. I hope like heck that there is a nugget of "Ben" in me somewhere. He seemed to me to find joy in everything; he laughed loudly and often. He was gravel-tough. And he was a kind and gentle giant of my youth.

#130 English Road, Cambridge, NY

"The land was ours before we were the land's"
Robert Frost

It's impossible to forget how a dairy farm smells, because it paints an olfactory mosaic on your nose unlike anything else. If you try, you can practically taste these places. Taken altogether, the symphony of smells is rich and pungent, and once you get used to it, downright beautiful, a robust palette-full of life. Yet taken one at a time, the smells range wildly, from alfalfa's newly-mown sweetness, to the salty, heavy decay of manure... it can gag the newcomer, the uninitiated visitor. In between is a cacophony of newly turned earth and timothy and fresh-chopped corn and chalky, wet cement. New-cut lumber and gasoline and musty oats, apple pies and fireplace ashes. Mounds of October maple leaves and empty fertilizer bags. Great smells. Big, robust smells, these places have.

To the farm kid, the kid that grew up here, the kid that lived every single day in these places, locations could be distinguished by smell alone. Our noses served us like magical, glorious divining rods of scent. One barn smelled different than the other, though they might be only ten feet apart. As a kid, you could tell the difference blindfolded, like you had a sort of infallible nasal night radar.

The English's farm, just like every other one, put its own, unique fingerprint on the nose. Airier on top of that big hill. Windier. But the secret ingredient was sheep. Sheep brought a sort of spoiled, ancient spice to the recipe of smells there, and the farm kid's nose could register sheep at the first whiff.

And like the nose, the eyes told you right away: this place is different. Ben English's farm was a living organism, a place where nothing stood still for long, a place where everything and every sight pointed to energy and the brute, physical force of motion. At every glance, you got the sense that equipment was only half un-hitched when it was abruptly deposited, that everything was planned for hurried use later that afternoon, and so there was no point in storing it neatly. It was a frantic and fluid place that suggested a certain urgency, and boundless, living energy.

At the same time, the place somehow held a sense of deep contentment, an underlying "all is right with the world" providence that defied the visual jumble of motion around you. I think this came from Ben himself (and certainly from Arlene), not just from the place.

In this part of the world, it was hard to separate places from people, from the men and women and growing children that lived on, *in* those places. The land, the property itself became part of the people, part of who they were and who they still are. I don't mean that just metaphorically. I think it goes deeper. It seems to me that something inside those people, something actually, *physically* inside those people, was changed or shaped by place, by the stubborn permanence of woods and water, earth and rock, which was so powerful there. And those people, those souls that every day stuck their hands in that dirt, who left so much of their sweat and their very lives in that soil, they changed the place. For those humble giants, those generations of farmer-souls, were even more unyielding than the very earth itself. And so it was at the English's place.

Ben English's farm

There were two dominions that, though distinctly different, flowed together effortlessly. The crazy, loud, hubbub of action that was Ben's kingdom of barns on the one side, and across the driveway was one of the most picturesque white farmhouses I have ever seen. Not a storybook place, not a place for show, a real home on a real farm with real people. This was Arlene's place, and it bounced her reflection off every clean window, off its fresh white paint, off its welcoming kitchen table. Charming is not too trite a word. Ben and Arlene English's place sang an easy sort of harmony to all who visited there.

To me, as a young boy, Ben and Arlene seemed to perfectly complement each other. He was bigger than life, boisterous, mischievous, and wonderfully carefree. And Arlene was gentle and modest, talented and tasteful, and she seemed to be the only force on earth capable of moderating Ben in any way. They were both also as kind and full of life as anyone I knew.

Ice Cube Terror

"People love to be scared. I guess it's a primal deal."
                                              Timothy Olyphant

(My age: 8)

Nobody got more joy out of playfully traumatizing kids than Ben English did, and we Preece kids were flattered to be his favorite targets. I think we served as a certain sort of vacation for him, a way to escape the mundane seriousness of farming for a few minutes, for him to be as simple and giddy as a child on a playground swing. He chased us hard and tickled us; he relished our fear and flight. But his specialty was pressing an ice cube against our backs, holding it there while we bellowed in laughter and it melted into our squirming spines. We loved hating it; we loved being scared. Like throngs of expectant August roller coaster riders, we anxiously awaited the joy of fear that was Ben English.

"Fear makes the wolf bigger than he is."
                                              German Proverb

You cannot sneak up on a country farmhouse. It's impossible. This truth is as certain as gravity. Farmhouse inhabitants are so attuned to the everyday sounds and smells and daily rhythms of the farm that nothing out of place, no matter how small, ever goes unnoticed. Even the simple, gentle sound of a bicycle easing along the road will set off a thousand silent alarms, making themselves known only to the inhabitants, the everyday regulars of the place. Cats scurry. Birds flutter. Dogs go on high alert, racing to their battle stations. If they are near, the cows will even stop and stare. Any one of these signals instantly catches the attention of the farmhouse resident, and two or more quicken the heartbeat.

It was this subconscious siren that brought the eight year old me to the window that day, peering over the back of the couch, using it as a sort of shield, allowing me to stay protected yet observe the outside world. I had heard the vehicle pull up and heard the clank of truck doors being shut.

And now, spying out the window, I saw the unmistakable, red and white International truck that was the brand and trademark of Ben English. He stood there, massive in his work-worn clothes, beside the truck. I tensed immediately and lasered my focus toward his shoes, my eyesight sharpened by the rush of adrenaline and my peripheral vision narrowed. I was over-wound, spring-tight. Every molecule in me waited for his first footsteps. If toward the barn, I was safe. Toward the house, toward me, meant sheer terror. A long, anxious moment passed. But his shoes didn't move. They simply stood, as if planted, like granite rocks that poked through the ground. I could feel the tension expand in me and even beyond me, filling the space in the living room. Those feet of his remained planted, and that fact allowed my eyes to take in more, to slide up the line of his leg to his worn, brown coat, and eventually to his eyes. To those eyes that stared back out from under his sweat-lined, Bear Bryant style hat, those eyes with their wild, electric intensity. Those eyes were looking, glaring... right at me!

I shrieked. Before I could gain awareness, I was halfway up the stairs, flying in terror and my heart was pounding in my chest so hard it hurt. In spite of my frantic flight, I heard his bellowing war whoop, his larger than life roar that was part laughter and part mock anger, and I knew in that moment that he was already to the front porch – and moving much faster than me.

I heard the front door burst open and heard my mother say something, but her voice was drowned out, overwhelmed. He was yelling and laughing much louder now, his sounds thundering through the house, literally shaking the walls. Something crashed in the kitchen; I heard an ice tray rattling loudly, and he just got louder as he bounded up the stairs.

I dove into the closet, cowering in fear – in real terror. I knew he wouldn't stop until he found me. He had come after me and my brothers so many times before. At first these were fun adventures, but now his new, favorite thing was to put an ice cube down my back. That took things to another level. And as I grew older and bigger, he seemed to feel obliged to become rougher and more relentless, yanking me up a bit too harshly, causing real pain, and tickling a bit too long, turning delight into a sort of frightful anguish. It hurt now; it was dangerous now. I was *really* afraid now. It wasn't a game anymore… which is why I loved it more than ever.

Things went flying as he went from room to room, and he made quite a show of it. He feigned that he had little restraint regarding personal property or for the concept of privacy – he rampaged through another closet, pretending to root for me in there, as if I had hidden beneath a few bales of hay in the barn. I could sense his intensity growing, his pseudo-anger at the fact that it was taking so long to find me. He was in my room now. I could hear him breathing hard between his howls and suppressed giggles as he came toward the closet where I hid. I could smell his old coat; I was sure he could smell my fear. Before the closet door opened, I screamed, giving myself away, and plunging the two of us into a nightmarish blur of wild flailing and ear-rattling roaring and uncontrollable, involuntary tickle-laughter and the inescapable, cruel, harsh chill of ice against the backbone. I nearly blacked out as he grabbed me by the ankle and whipped me out of there like a wet towel. It hurt. A yelp shot out of my throat and that both startled me and made me laugh, which in turn made his eyes widen frightfully. And big Ben English boomed another deafening roar.

I was both laughing and almost crying now, pleading for him to stop tickling me. The ice on my back was a dribbling mess. My shirt was twisted and mopped with ice and the sweat of fear. I was both defeated and delighted, as if the monstrous roller coaster had gotten the best of me this time. Eventually, gradually, his loud, laughing howls eased, and I felt that at last I could breathe again. I slowly regained my bearings. My family and Arlene were huddled around us. The faces were giddy with delight, with a certain disbelief at the wonderful wildness they had just witnessed. But Arlene was scolding him, calling him a big bully, and telling to stop frightening the poor little boy. My brothers stood there too, standing behind the others, where it was safer. I could see it all in their eyes – the thrill of the safari, the exotic hunt – and the relief that on this day they were not his prey. Yet their eyes still held a crazy, inexplicable hope, and a fear, that he wasn't finished yet, that they would suddenly become his next target of tickling.

Later, I recovered slowly, retreating into the corner of the kitchen, nursing a hot chocolate Mom and Arlene had made for us kids. I stayed in the background, drew no attention to myself, and listened to the adults as their conversation turned from farming concerns to politics to things in the news. And I eased into a peaceful exhaustion, a sort of waking dreamland, and thought of what an incredible thrill it was to be scared like that, to be really terrified. I felt myself beginning to nod off, and I hoped Ben English would be back again soon.

Jimmy Shanley and Ben's Air-Conditioned Silo

> *"If you don't know where you're going...*
> *you might end up someplace else."*
>
> *Yogi Berra*

(My age: 11)

Ringers. City kids. These were the young people who visited the farms and tried their best to help out with farm chores. Most of them made genuine, honest efforts. But those sincere attempts were rarely enough to overcome their lack of familiarity, which blinded them from the nuances of tasks that we everyday practitioners rehearsed in our sleep. There's a right way to throw a bale of hay, for example. A way that's efficient and smooth and that saves your skin for the next hundred bales. But the newcomer approaches the first bale with too much determination and too much raw forearm and spends too much precious energy in the process. This constituted a minor crime in the mind of the farm kid, and the novice often took the brunt of our playful but relentless ridicule. Some folded under our scrutiny. A rare few endured. My cousin Jimmy Shanley did more than endure; he thrived.

Jimmy visited the farm every summer without fail. Winters too. His wonderful and well-off parents raised him in their upscale suburban home in Woodbridge, Connecticut, where Jim attended private schools, attended Scout camps, and spent weekends at the Mill River Country Club in Stratford. His home was three hours away by car, but to us it might as well have been Shangri-La in the Orient. Miles couldn't measure the distance.

Like most young boys who are large for their years, Jim was strong though not particularly coordinated; his body was growing at two different speeds. We were sometimes merciless with him, but his resilience was second to none. He worked hard, made steady improvements, and showed up every year. He became a regular fixture at our place; he *earned* that. Jimmy was living proof that good attitudes matter greatly in life. Jim's work contributions became as big as ours, and at times he became indispensible. And it's fair to say he became as much a part of the fabric of our history on the farm as we ourselves did.

Inevitably, some of the local farmers got to know him. It was common practice, even a necessity, to share certain equipment from farm to farm and to help each other out, whether it formed a part of the local circle of commerce or amounted to sheer neighborliness. Consequently, Jim got exposed to people like Malcolm Hamilton, Joe Scully, Jim Buckley, Ralph and Danny Thomas, Winfred Pfeifer and Stanley Mehling. Others, too. Characters all. And then there was Ben English, who seemed to take a particular liking to Jimmy. Ben played a sort of mentor role with him.

I think Ben was downright entertained by Jimmy's rawboned newness with farm tasks and also saw something good in him, some potential beyond farming. It seemed like Ben had decided to help Jimmy grow and to thoroughly enjoy his mistakes along the way. His motivations seemed part entertainment, part kindness. I think he delighted in the awkward anticipation of wondering "what crazy thing is that kid gonna do next?!" Jimmy and his mistakes were fun for Ben, as everything in this world seemed to be. Ben would roar in laughter and deliver both derision and helpful coaching at the same time. He had the uncanny gift of letting you know that he was on your side, even while he was making fun of you. A part of this was that his laughter seemed directed at the thing that just happened, not at you, the person. And to say that he laughed is an understatement. He literally roared with joy.

All farms have their own "rules," their own standards for who does what, and those rules are as unique and distinctive as the farmers themselves. As an example, tractor-driving was a hard-earned badge of honor in my family. It meant you had achieved a mastery of all the lesser farm tasks and had demonstrated a certain level of responsibility, and this rite of passage was bestowed upon the new driver with an unspoken yet unmistakable reverence. This was not necessarily the case in other farm families, where tractor-driving was looked upon like many other farm tasks: a dangerous but necessary task that had to be done, just as riding a combine or sawing wood or packing a wagon with hay. This is how Ben English viewed tractor-driving, and Jimmy Shanley, who had only rarely been allowed on our little Massey Ferguson, found himself atop Ben's big Farmall-H, assigned duties that would soon stretch his abilities a bit too far.

Just as the farms and farmers were different, so were the intricacies of the various tractors that forced their will on the farms they roamed and the fields they tamed. John Deere A's and B's had their characteristic hand clutches and distinctive pop-pop that sounded like nothing else. (I never drove a John Deere. I know I have missed something extraordinary, and I count this as a life opportunity missed.) Our little Massey was similar to the classic Ford 8N, with a low-to-the-ground profile that made handling easy. Farmall H's and M's had controls like the Massey, but handled more like the taller John Deere tricycle styles. No power steering. Learning to properly handle one wasn't easy, and trying to learn a completely unfamiliar one on the fly was a sure way to do some damage. Jimmy Shanley was trying to learn a completely unfamiliar one on the fly. And Ben English, "Old Sink-or-Swim," was his coach...

Jimmy was at Ben's for the day, "on loan" as a sort of day laborer, to help with a number of tasks. He was thrilled to be there, and Ben was glad for the help. Ben had him start early that day, handling some hay and feeding cows. He bagged some corn and cleaned heifer pens. "Take the H down in back and get the wagon; bring it up here," was Ben's idea of thorough guidance and specific instruction. He knew Jimmy had never driven a Farmall, but he also knew that doing was the better part of learning. Jimmy didn't ask questions, as he was elated about the assignment and unwilling to provide any reason for Ben to rescind the order. He got on the tractor, quickly figured out how to start it and get it in gear, and the adventure was on!

If he had taken his time, if he had first explored the operation of the H's gears and brakes and throttle and clutch, Jimmy would have been better prepared to operate this completely alien beast. But he might also have invited Ben's impatient banter. Regardless, it was already too late. The thing was rolling, and fast. Too fast. What should have been first gear was apparently third, and the H's abrupt, rough launch sent Jim into a mad scramble to find the lower gear, to brake but not so hard that it stalled the engine, to ease the gas and clutch a bit... Oh no! This darned thing is so hard to steer! Where is that clutch?! What gear... WHERE IS THAT BRAKE PEDAL!?...

The jarring thump and the loud, sharp crack startled him. He knew instantly that it wasn't good; the cracking sound had come from something far too close. Jim, stunned and wild-eyed, looked up... he had driven the H directly through the wall of Ben's empty, wooden silo! He didn't bump the wall or dent it or crack a few boards. He literally drove *through* it. Jimmy somehow got the H to stop, but the nose of the thing was already fully inside, like an out-of-control, hungry, red-iron Hereford bull that just had to get some silage right now.

Ben watched all this from a distance, and when the silo was punctured, he gasped. Then he erupted in volcanic laughter and roared his boisterous roar. Eventually, his bellowing eased into a jolly, chuckling disbelief. Others might have had a coronary right there and then, but not Ben. These were the kinds of things that happened on that farm all the time, and he handled these mishaps in stride. He knew that these were actually life's little problems; he only feared the truly big ones. This particular silo problem didn't warrant much concern. A few boards and nails later and all was good as new. Jimmy's embarrassment lasted a while, but the fact that he later piloted B52's for twenty years in the Air Force suggests that he overcame any awkwardness about operating large machines. He was our Ringer, our City kid, and we were proud of him. So was Ben. And Ben loved to tease him with the story of his air-conditioned silo.

Runaway Rig

"Every disaster screams for humor."
                                    Sylvia Millecam

(My age: 12)

There is a farming ritual, a rite of manual labor that so springs from the breast of the worker that I am convinced it must be practiced the world over. At the end of a job well done, at the end of a physical exertion that leaves you spent for that day, working hands gather and relax. They breathe easy, drink a tall glass of water or iced tea and share a fellowship of story as they reflect on what they had just done, not as individuals, but as a collective group, an unorganized, un-uniformed team. This is done on the spot, spontaneously, without cleaning up. You find a stump or a rock, a thing to sit on or lean back against, wet your whistle, and revel in the group's acceptance that one feels rather than hears. Peer respect, well earned, is a deeply gratifying thing, and this rite is where such awards are handed out on a farm.

We gathered behind the English's house late that afternoon for just such an iced-tea ritual. Seven hundred new bales of hay sat in jumbled repose in Ben's barn. And all of us had pushed ourselves to the limit getting them there. That was how work was done at his place. Ben English knew no measured steps. He attacked work with an intensity and a frantic pace that was always contagious, sometimes dangerous, and always exhilarating. When you were there, you worked hard – period. And all that made the iced-tea ritual that much more satisfying. Jim Shanley was there, and my dad, Casey and me. Red English and Merritt Herrington. And of course Ben. We were pooped, proud, and pleased.

Farming at Ben English's pace meant that there was seldom time for routine repairs to equipment. I can't recall a single piece of his equipment that wasn't dented, banged up or otherwise in need of some more permanent fix to a hasty field-repair. Ben was all about function, and his stuff worked, but it was seldom pretty. For tractors, that meant that batteries were sometimes dead or missing, headlights may or may not have worked, and minor functional elements, like mufflers, may or may not be in place.

That was exactly the case for Ben's Farmall M that spent the day pulling a baler/kicker and hay wagons and was now parked about three hundred yards from where were sitting, enjoying our iced teas and reflecting on our day's work. The M was parked where it had toiled that day, in the distant, newly shaved field, on a downward slope, so it could be roll-started when it was next needed… the battery had been removed and was awaiting repairs. The entire rig was still attached, and the whole thing was pointed in such a way that it faced directly at us, as if the M was part of our circle of farm hands, it too reveling in all that was accomplished that day. It looked at us and we looked at the M, all of us proud.

Suddenly, the M made an abrupt, halting lurch forward, giving a shudder to the entire train of equipment behind it, the wooden racks on the wagon wobbling noticeably. The brakes, no doubt, were maintained only slightly better than the battery was. We stared, transfixed, as if the lights had just gone down and the theater curtain had been drawn back. Then a second rumbling quake shook the whole long chorus line of metal and wheels and wood. Ben choked out a disbelieving bark and three long seconds later the entire parade began to roll downhill, completely unimpeded, as if it was a series of tied-together sailing sloops heading down the Colorado River rapids. The brakes, like the battery, had become nonexistent. It gathered astonishing speed and the whole spectacle was a fantastic, frightening sight. No human was endangered, nor were any livestock. But the sheer size and speed and reckless, uncontrolled flight of the monstrosity took our breath away – it was as if we were watching an enormous, empty, unpiloted airplane plummet toward the earth, a few hundred yards in front of us. The impending, rampaging wreckage, the carnage of twisted metal, the imminent, shrill wail of utter destruction was all any of us could imagine.

But we never heard that terrible metallic screeching. The sound we *did* hear was even louder and more spectacular and more engulfing. Ben English's roar of marvelous, colossal laughter hit a new high that day. It was more than loud. It was monumental revelry with a prodigious volume. I've never seen anyone more delighted and in greater, joyful astonishment than Ben was at that moment. And I'm certain I will never, ever see anyone so completely amused by an impending disaster that involves his own property, his own means of livelihood.

Somehow, the gangly caravan of farm equipment simply rolled itself to a gradual stop, and not a scratch of damage was done. To this day, I'm not sure what I find more amazing – the fact that there was no damage, or the fact that Ben English found such delicious humor in an event that so terrified the rest of us. Regardless, on that day, the iced tea and the ritual of farm fellowship tasted better than ever.

Red and the Governor

(My age: 11)

Arlene always called her son Donald, but to the rest of us he was "Red." Think of everything "Ben" and add youth and exuberance and even more full-throttle living. That was Red. And by *governor*, I mean the fuel and throttle adjustment on Ben's tractors, not the state's elected leader in Albany. It seemed that every one of Ben's tractors could fly along the road like a Pontiac or Plymouth road car, and legend attributed this to Red's illicit manipulation of their governors. The tractors went fast and Red, being young and impatient, liked speed. I remember Red delivering a loaned elevator at our farm once and then pointing that Farmall toward home. I watched in wonder as his speed approached implausibility – like a jet fueled horse and rider heading across the prairie and over the horizon. It was a breathtaking and magnificent sight. And it scared me a bit. Tractors just weren't meant to go that fast.

Jim Shanley remembers riding on the back of the governor-loosened M, with Red driving, as they headed west down English road, down that hill that was as steep as any dirt road can get. The tractor had no fenders, so "riding" meant standing on the drawbar and holding on to the back of the driver's seat. Jim said the speed was positively hair-raising and knew that if Red had needed to stop that 3-ton beast, it would have first skidded for half a football field.

Apparently they made it to wherever they were going, and luckily, no emergency hill-stopping was necessary that day. Thank goodness.

Death-by-Hay-Bale

(My age: 11)

I once had hay mow duty at English's, which meant I was the guy inside the barn with the job of distributing bales of hay into corners and away from the elevator that fed the bales up to this mountainous perch. It was the dog days of summer and the mow was nearly full, so hay, hornets and I were quite close to the insufferably hot roof. There were only a few feet between the mouth of the elevator, the nail-spiked roof above, and the growing mound of deposited bales around my knees. It was smothering and closed in, and it just got tighter and hotter as the work went on.

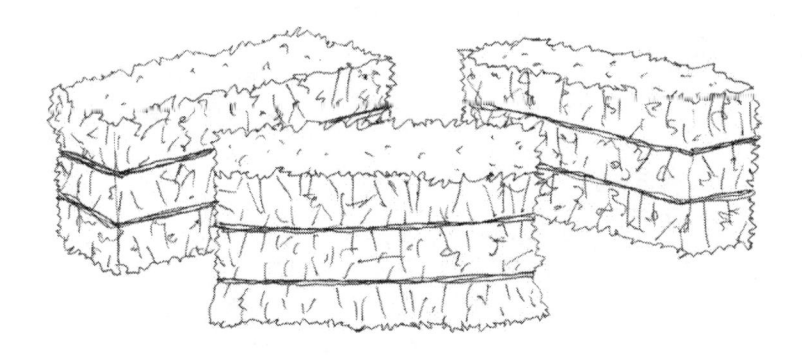

Also helping out that day was Dave Jeskie who was Red's brother in law. Both Red and Dave were older than me, bigger, stronger and both hell-bent on outworking each other. It seemed they were a mile away. They worked the wagon end of our assembly line, out in the open air, feeding the elevator that delivered an endless, unmanageable supply of bales to me. I'm not sure if they were deliberately trying to entomb me up there, or if they were just competing amongst themselves without giving me a thought. Either way, the result was the same: I was frantic and panicky and had to push myself as hard as I ever have had to, as the alternative was to become trapped in the bales, buried, and dehydrated. The shrinking place became relentlessly loud and dark and hot, and it was stiflingly humid. And those endless bales... those bales just kept coming. I worked at a delirious pace until I finally reached my limit. Enough was enough; there just wasn't room anymore. It *had* to end! I yelled in frenzied desperation for them to stop, but the rattle of the elevator and chains and gears and motors smothered my cries of alarm. For the first time in my life, I thought I was about to die.

Yet somehow the god of hay elevators allowed me to survive this harrowing experience, as my surrender erupted just as those last bales darkened the hay mow's hatch. It was over. Regardless of their motives, Dave and Red got a big kick out of my expression when I finally emerged from the barn, when I finally stepped out of the heat and pressure and darkness, and into fresh air and daylight, into my liberation. Like Ben, they roared.

I was just glad to still be alive.

Ben, Me and the Midnight Run

(My age: 9)

It was time to sell some sheep, and Ben had to get them to the buyer in Pawlet, Vermont, which was a good distance away. Because the man with the scales could only be there early in the morning, the mission was to deliver the fifty sheep before 6:00 a.m. Ben needed an extra hand, somebody to help control and contain the sheep during transfer, and I was the guy. I was nine years old. It was cold and dark and ridiculously early when Ben arrived to pick me up, his truck already loaded the night before and the sheep bleating as they do. (It's interesting to me that sheep sound like bad imitations of themselves, half bleating and bah-bellowing, like rejects from the sheep-casting for a Hollywood epic. Real sheep just don't sound like real sheep.)

The trip there was probably only an hour or two in Ben's red and white International truck, but to me it was like a trek with Genghis Kahn, traversing unknown and unheard of, far-away places, smelling coffee and sheep and nibbling on food rations Mom had packed for me. Toward the end of our work, I distinctly remember Genghis asking me to lift the last and smallest of the sheep to the scales for weighing, a sort of reward he bestowed on me, as this task seemed somehow the "task of honor" in this process. As I was still small, I staggered under the weight but got the sheep on the scale, slid the measures into balance, and called out the weight with the certainty and authority of a grizzled, old ranch hand. The place erupted with laughter, Ben the loudest and most joyful, as usual.

Night wasn't over until we had finished our work in Pawlet. As Ben guided his iron workhorse home, I drifted off to sleep, slumped in the corner of his cab, those first rays of daylight warming us both.

Chapter 7

Animal Farm
Personality in every Pen

In one sense, living on that rural farm was like living at the intersection of ethnic neighborhoods in a New York City borough. I was surrounded not by people, but by four legged characters with personalities as big as buildings. They were everywhere. The farm was at once silent and serene, yet belching with beings who asserted their will and made themselves known to the world, coming at life under full sail, self assured and unabashed. The farm's animals spoke with quirky behaviors and head butts and expressive eyes, sometimes with childlike playfulness, and at other times the seriousness of soldiers. Without ink they wrote like Shakespeare. Without language they thundered on the stage of life, bellowing their lines with passion. The place was a hullabaloo of voices, a loud commotion of characters, and they filled the farm like it was an old west saloon on Saturday night.

Despite all these personalities, the farmer maintains a unique relationship with animals. He sees them as peers and co-authors, for they are fuel for the farm and the object of so much effort. He bestows an arms-length respect and a certain professional appreciation. There is much care and general dignity, and there is even a little room for guarded affection. But it is a tough business that demands all of their fruits and eventually their very lives. Farmer and animal are in it together, fully committed. It is a way of being for them both.

Cow Cravings
what cows want

All dairy cows desperately want two things: a clear sense of where they fit in, how they rank within the herd; and an unchanging, predictable, daily routine.

The hierarchy within a herd of cows is so clearly defined that you might think they have political parties and primaries and proper elections. You almost expect to see purple ink on one hoof of each mountain-dwelling, tribal cow, indicating her vote to select a leader has been cast. But their elections are won instead through the force of fierce fighting and physical prowess. Bovine leaders emerge because they are tough, because they are instinctively driven to it, and because they sense challenges even before the challenger does.

There is a settling-in period when new cows arrive into the herd. The newcomer seeks to know its status, to know whom it ranks above, and to whom it must concede. Among cows, females, these things are established with some degree of intimidation, a measure of jarring head-butts, and an occasional skull-to-skull showdown. Amongst bulls, these all-out duels are full of life-threatening ferocity; they are violent and unnerving, sometimes sickening to watch. Amongst milking cows, the battles are still somewhat dangerous, but the side to side sloshing of their milk laden udders paints a surprising awkwardness that gives the battle a flavor of vaudeville, like two inept fighters in a ring, more furious than they are frightful, more comical and klutzy than deadly dangerous. Regardless, the battles are fought and things are finally resolved. And because of the clarity these battles bring, cows move on, content in knowing their place.

Sheila and Five-Twelve
bosses and cross-eyed followers...

(My age: 9)

I wasn't even born when they walked the first cows over from Winfred Pfeiffer's, from Archdale in 1955, but I am positive that when they did, Sheila was in the lead. She was always in the lead. Wenda, Polly, Gay Lady, Maggie, and five other cows followed Sheila. I have never seen a leader like her, four legged, two legged, or otherwise.

She was the undisputed herd leader, first to the barn and first to the pasture. When the herd moved from place to place for better grazing, she determined the destination and charted the course, led the way. She kept the peace and quickly put down all challenges. Sheila ran a tight operation.

One day Dad bought a milking cow at McLenithan's Auction Barn, a Cambridge institution that served farmers for hundreds of miles around. Cows of all ages and types were sent there and auctioned every Tuesday night (this has been going on every week since 1942). When the cross-eyed, black Holstein with the white forehead arrived at our farm the next day, she sported a chain collar with a tag, indicating she had come from a very large herd somewhere, a place where there were so many cows they were managed by number, rather than by name as they were on our tiny farm. The number on her tag read five-hundred-twelve, and that became her name, "Five-Twelve." She proved to be a good cow, despite her rough start at our place.

The day after auction, the poor thing came off the truck ramp and walked right into a new herd in a barnyard she had never seen before. No doubt she was disoriented from being moved from her original farm, staying at McLenithan's, and being moved again to our place. Now, here she was, unsettled and uncertain, anxious to belong and desperate for the stability and mundane predictability that cows love. Sheila would help her find it.

Five-Twelve stood in the midst of her newfound herd, sniffing and wondering who was who, no doubt sensing who was threatening and who would be a pushover. At the same time, Sheila spotted the arrival and began making her way through the crowd, moving in a deliberate way straight for Five-Twelve. You could see her sense of purpose, but Sheila was businesslike and methodical, unhurried. Though it was clear that Five-Twelve had not given offense in any way, Sheila walked right to her, declined any sniff-greeting, and delivered a shocking head-wallop to Five-Twelve's midsection that made her back bulge up. She turned, the two cows exchanged sniffs, and that was that. It was as if Shelia had said, "Welcome, Five-Twelve...I'm in charge here." Three minutes later the cows were heading for the pasture, Sheila in the lead. Right behind her was Five-Twelve, visibly relieved and comfortable that she knew who was boss, and delighted to have somebody to follow. Five-Twelve fit in fast, and picked up the rhythm and routine of the place almost at once, thanks to Sheila's greeting and guidance.

A year later cross-eyed Five-Twelve had squared off with Corrine, an older and sour-tempered rust-red cow whom none of us favored. The tussle had started at the water trough, where both cows apparently sought to stand in the same spot. The two went at it with a bumbling ferocity as other cows moved back for their own safety and became stadium spectators, watching with interest. After a few jousts and furious charges, Five-Twelve seemed to be emerging as winner, with Corrine's body language suggesting early surrender. But even before it was over, Sheila had arrived and delivered a plowing head ram to each. She first hammered Corrine, where it seemed to me that she was piling on the loser, bullying. But then she immediately turned to Five-Twelve and walloped her with even more skill, dispatched her to stadium seating with the rest. I realized then that Sheila had restored order in a few short strokes, that she would tolerate no bickering among her subordinates. She was the keeper of clarity when it came to herd hierarchy, boss to all, and this fact made for a contented clan of cows, a thing we all appreciated.

But just as she was sheriff and deputy, just as she kept order, she could be the mistress of mischief, the gang leader in revolt.

Cow Chow
*one dead, one drunk,
and one who couldn't stand to watch...*

(My age: 11)

Once a cow has secured the two essentials of knowing where she stands and having a daily routine, her remaining consciousness is focused on food. Her days are largely non-stop eating sessions, interrupted by the occasional need to move to where the pasturing is better, or to be milked.

About once each year, our cows would escape their gigantic hillside pasture, not out of any necessity for more space or grass, but drawn by the irresistible smell of fresh corn, the perfume of clover, or sweet alfalfa. The lumbering and clumsy giants would sometimes lean against a fence, craning their necks into the adjacent field, getting themselves drunk on the idea of some forbidden crop. The craning and leaning could overwhelm an old fence, and the jail break would be on. Sheila, like always, in the lead. They would gorge with delight and a burst with a newfound sense of satisfaction, while we farmhands would scramble and respond to the crisis. Too much of this good thing could kill a cow as its eating had no limits.

It happened to one of Danny Thomas's cows on the farm next door. Ralph, Dan's father, had called us for help, and Dad and I went immediately. Dan's cow had escaped from their pasture into an adjacent field of sweet clover. The bloated beast lay on her side in the lush, purple flowered clover, the digestive gasses from her three stomachs combining forces to stretch her gut to the point of debilitating pain. Her mouth was frothing, and her eyes bulged as she lay motionless and swollen. In desperation, Ralph stuck a knife in her lower belly, hoping to release some of the deadly gas, and it came out with a wet, poofing belly fart that gave her some fleeting relief. But it was not enough to save her. She died there before us, the victim of verdant legumes and the biological curse of a relentless, tri-bellied appetite. They talked about taking the meat, but it was all wrong. Animals had to be bled correctly and butchered immediately, and there was no time to do that now. The men got tractors and we dug a ditch, dragged her corpse there, dragged her from herself and from her unbounded instincts, from her own unrestraint, dragged her, back hooves chained together, and buried her in a gouged out gash in the hillside that would swallow her like so much clover, sweet on earth's palette. It shook me. It was a sad lesson for me. But I was now schooled in the dangers of escaped cows, and I treated it henceforth with alarm.

That is why I became so unnerved one afternoon in September of 1967. I was eleven. School had just started a few weeks before, and I had just arrived home after getting off the bus. I was celebrating the end of the school day with a visit to our McIntosh apple tree, where I had climbed to a large upper limb, picked myself a perfect red orb, and lay cradled in branches, like a Greek god supined in splendor and surrounded by perfect fruit. It was a daily ritual for me in the fall. It was my private cocoon, a delicious daydream of a place where my imagination floated freely, and cares evaporated in the Indian summer sun. On this day I imagined camping with friends, being independent and self-sufficient, freed from farming, drinking from streams and catching fish to eat. In my mind we roasted morsels over our fire and celebrated with our contraband of smuggled beer, forming a new bond of brotherhood and sharing our first taste of the adult world.

A few cows wandered to the tree, which was in the pasture, just a few feet from our back yard. I was fifteen feet above them, watching them from this peculiar perspective, able to see their substantial width which I had never before recognized. As a farm boy I was completely comfortable with cows and so their presence was unremarkable to me, almost irrelevant. More of them drifted into the scene, like ghost-spirits, cow apparitions, that gradually replaced my daydreamed friends one by one. The cows were placid and docile, drawn by the fallen, fermented apples they picked from the ground, consuming the treats effortlessly and appreciatively.

Among them was Twinkleberry, a brown and white Ayrshire that seemed to us to have less sense than the rest, not that cows anywhere are known for a remarkable intellect. In the spring of that same year Twinkleberry apparently decided to leap through the forked trunk of our cherry tree for reasons I will never know. She didn't make it. My cousin Jim and I found her trapped in the tree, her front legs suspended beneath her long neck, which was wedged tightly between the twin trunks. She was frantic, but because her front legs couldn't touch the ground, and because her head was restrained by the tree, she was quite immobile. We tried to lift her up and out, but she was far too heavy, and our efforts only panicked her further. We finally got a saw and cut one of the trunks, freeing her but at the same time terrorizing the poor dimwitted beast. She lived a life of anxiety, seemed always to be filled with fear, and the trauma of the cherry tree incident only made her worse.

She was beneath me now, unaware of my perch, my presence far up in the branches. She swallowed apple after apple, appearing to favor them even more than the others did. Then she surprised me, humbled my harsh judgment of her, as she learned something none of the others seemed to learn, taught herself and applied the lesson quickly. Twinkleberry began plucking apples straight from the tree, from those low limbs that were laden with weighty fruit. She sniffed an apple out, mouthed it gently from its stem, and took it in, then another and another. She had discovered a source of apples that became hers alone, since no other cow seemed to comprehend this new concept. Like a one cow vacuum cleaner, Twinkleberry cleaned the lowest limbs thoroughly, left them barren and well picked.

After a few minutes of this I perceived a subtle change in her, a nuance of imbalance, and a mild development in demeanor that suggested a rising but still restrained attitude, a loosening inhibition. Twinkleberry seemed to live a moment of newfound freedom, a moment without fear; she seemed confident and comfortable, perhaps for the first time ever. It brought forth in me an uneasy anticipation, an uncomfortable foreboding, knowing that I was witnessing the beginning of something significant, but I was unaware of what it was. I sat up now, roused from daydream into this equally surreal scene. It finally dawned on me…

Twinkleberry was drunk! She stumbled to the trunk of the apple tree and leaned against it, trying to force herself back to balance. She staggered a few steps and stopped, pointed her head far toward the left and then swung it around hard to the right, nearly toppling herself over in the process. She exhaled hard, snorting with effort, as if trying to expel the beguiling cloud that distorted her mind. She lunged forward with a few more labored steps, her legs wide, trying to broaden her base and stabilize herself against the spinning world. She twisted her head desperately now, shook and wrung it from side to side the way a wet dog does, trying to force things back into their familiar order.

The other cows took notice and gave her space, unfamiliar as they were with a drunken boozer in their midst. They seemed distinctly troubled, their routine now smashed by unexpected bovine behavior, teetotalers condemning the lush in their midst. They watched the scene with postures that spoke of alert awareness rather than with their normal indifference. This fact distressed me as much as Twinkleberry's actions did and convinced me that I was in the middle of an all out emergency – I must get help! It was suddenly all up to me. I had to come down from the tree and navigate my way past the inebriated monster, get adult help, and fast. But what would happen when my feet hit the ground, when I arrived within Twinkleberry's striking distance? What crazed attacks might an intoxicated, apple-drunken cow make upon me?

I had no choice. Having seen Danny's cow die from forbidden food, I couldn't allow myself to be cornered, couldn't stand by helplessly now. I swallowed hard and carefully made my way down the tree, keeping one eye on the dangerous and unpredictable beast. I was now at the lowest limb, ready to jump to the ground when Twinkleberry noticed me – I froze. For a few nerve-wracking moments, the cow and I locked eyes and stared, neither of us backing down from this unspoken shouting of wills, this unflinching showdown of determination. Continuing to stare forcefully her, I slowly put my left foot tentatively on the ground and Twinkleberry…did nothing. She simply stared and stumbled back two steps, her eyes now appearing glassy and empty, like she was looking through me to something far distant. I dropped fully to the ground, crossed the few feet of pasture in a flash and jumped the fence, landed safely and raced for help.

When Dad returned with me a few minutes later, Twinkleberry was standing among the herd, and within a few more minutes seemed almost back to normal. But she did stagger now and then, validating my story and providing enough evidence so that Dad didn't think I was imagining it all. He said he had heard other farmers speak of this before, and that she'd be fine shortly. That gave me comfort as the minutes passed. She gradually came around, much to my relief.

I was glad to know that I wouldn't have to relive the scene with Danny's cow, wouldn't have to punch a knife in her and relieve her inner pressure. I was washed over with the kind of relief that arises from an adverted disaster, a muffled joy that's mixed with a mild sense of anger, resenting this goofy cow for having put me through that flood of anxiety. Most of all I felt disbelief. How many kids get to be around a drunken cow? Who would believe that apples could do such a thing?

We sat on our porch after dinner that evening and talked about the day's events. "No more fruit trees in the pasture," Dad said. We couldn't help but laugh at our hard drinking, cherry tree hanging, ever nervous cow, Twinkleberry.

For quite a while a part of me wished I had not seen this drunken cow episode, wished I could have avoided being drawn into what turned out to be an unnerving but harmless panic. I'd have had no knot in my stomach, no alarms in my head sending me into crisis. Things might have been easier had I just turned my head and looked the other way. Like McCart used to do.

McCart, our black and white Holstein cow from a farmer with that name, was taller than the rest, though as gentle and soft spirited as any. She made an odd sight, as her hind legs were noticeably taller than the front, and her overall size far exceeded the others, a sort of eighth grader embarrassed by an early and uneven growth spurt that left her unrefined and inelegant, yet polite in her bashful insecurity. Her tall back legs gave the line of her back a comical sort of downhill slope and her head to tail length was greater than it should have been. All this made her the kind of cow people had to notice. Part of her was always sticking out somewhere, too tall here or too long there, calling unwanted attention to her when all she wanted was to be average. She was anything but that, and not only because of her size.

Cows fill a barn in regular order, each of them having their own stanchion, lining up in parallel like cars in a parking lot, all facing the same way. Each of them learns its spot and heads there instinctively and without oversight, like salmon returning to the exact spot of their spawning. This arrangement leaves a regimented row of cows, heads all along a line so that they can be fed easily, and rear ends all leaving manure in another line, which makes for easy cleaning. Beyond this, cows live by simple custom and habit, and they derive great comfort from knowing their place, from having their same stanchion, from regular routine.

Barns are the domains of socialist economies, places where rigorous equality is carried out in all workings of the place. Though individual cows are different, they are fed the same, milked the same, watered the same, and handled the same, for it can be no other way. And poor McCart, though she was a full third larger than some others, received the same rations as they did, the same amounts of food and hay and consideration. It wasn't in her to complain, but the average sized rations nevertheless left her ravenous by the time the next meal hour came around. She loved to eat, and her oversized frame needed the nutrition. But like every other cow, McCart had to wait her turn. And that was the problem.

Because she was so big, when in her stanchion, her hind legs stood where manure should have gone, and she manured where people needed to walk, sometimes she even manured into the next row of cows. All this meant there was only one place our barn could accommodate her, and that was at the far end of the longest line of cows. She anchored the end of the line, adjacent to the barn wall, where there was no need to walk behind her. Our routine was such that when cows were fed, her stanchion was last in line. And so, the biggest, hungriest, nicest cow had to wait until all the others had theirs, until they had first been fed, then she got hers. It was more than she could stand.

McCart developed an ingenious way of handling this incredible anxiety, of waiting for silage and corn and grain and hay when others were already filling their maws: She didn't look. She turned her head. With incredible self control she turned her long neck leftward, toward the wall, and forced her had in that direction, missing all the activity to her right. Cows to her right rattled their stanchions in anticipation, bobbed their heads up and down with frantic enthusiasm as the tasty delights were brought to them one at a time. It was a chorus line of gusto, each cow yearning for her turn, preoccupied with the prospect of her own serving, and the gratification of gorging, satiating their ample appetites.

But McCart made it easy for herself, ignored the obvious, refused to look, and in doing so, found a way to endure the unendurable. She must have indulged in a self imagined wonderland, some far away phantom of a place where all was good and nothing mattered, where hunger didn't exist and patience was never needed. We couldn't help but laugh at the old girl, and to appreciate her way of coping. She was a great cow, a lover of her cow chow, a captive of her own body, sentenced to wait, but not to watch.

Franklin
speed demon and angel food mogul

(My age: 12)

I had never seen anything so fast! He zipped across open spaces like he had been shot out of a cannon, with bursting starts and abrupt stops that seemed to defy Newtonian physics. His panicked, high pitched screeching added to the pandemonium and all this made us hysterical with laughter. The brand new crème colored piglet was smaller than a football and undeniably cute. But his cuddly appearance belied his energy; he was anything but docile. He had wriggled out of Dad's arms and was now loose in the barnyard. We posted Dad and Mom as sentinels at each gate as a way to contain him while my brothers and I assumed chase-and-capture duties inside the contained area, our now barnyard-piglet-corral. We didn't stand a chance.

We were new to pigs and this fellow was new to us, but in all our anticipation of pigging, we never imagined this scene. It never occurred to us that it could all be over before it even started, that a jet fueled piglet you could easily hold in one hand might escape in such an explosion of furious speed and shrill shrieking and could literally be gone forever. This was all so suddenly thrust upon us that it startled us into an adrenaline pumping episode, full of desperate urgency – but at the same time the sheer ridiculousness of it, the shocking explosion of speed and sound from something so small and cuddly delivered an unexpected punch line that was inescapably hilarious.

Our desperation drove us into the chase, but every time we were undone with laughter before we could get close enough to grab him. In each instance, our inner urgency was thwarted by a joyfulness that arose from something so deep in us that it had us actually rooting for him, wanting to see him once more dazzle his pursuer with his remarkable athletic brilliance choreographed to his clamorous, piercing squeals. He was splendidly speedy and took the whole thing so seriously that we were overcome, at one point all three of us chasers were on our backs howling with uncontrollable laughter, completely outmatched by this wee wizard of speed and ear splitting sound.

We eventually seized on a plan in which we used long boards to create an ever decreasing space, trapping him in a corner that was bounded by boys with boards on one side, a barn on another, and a board-lined fence to complete the corral. We fashioned a hole for the piglet between two boards along the fence line; this hole was to be his only means of apparent escape. My brother Joe, who was four at the time, went behind the fence, behind the hole, where he could not be seen by the piglet, and held open a burlap sack against the opening. The rest of us would charge the little fellow, drive him through our makeshift funnel, through the hole in the fence, and Joe would bag him once and for all.

We charged, and he immediately screamed and tore a scorching path straight for the trap – it worked! But that little pig hit the hole with such fierce velocity that those of us inside the barnyard heard a "wuuummphff!" and saw Joe topple over backward, saw the brown burlap bag still tumbling in wild disarray several feet away from him. All the action was outside the confines of the barnyard now, and if the pig escaped there, we would never catch him. It seemed to all happen in slow motion... We ourselves were now trapped inside, watching it all from the helpless side of the fence, unable to grab the throat of the bag and close it off, sealing our catch inside. Joe's tumble dazed and disoriented him and the bag, now a living thing itself, just continued to convulse and roll farther away. But like a bloodied boxer after a moment of being stunned, Joe willed himself up from the canvas and crawled to the still squirming, still shrieking bag and courageously pinned it down, sealed it off, and finally held our captive high, triumphant.

And so our raising of pigs had started.

Franklin, fresh from his burlap snare, was our first pig, and he was a character. We raised one pig at a time, as a sort of supplement to the dairy cows that were the focus of the farm. There were three pigs over the years, Franklin, Calvin, and Lyndon. They were named after Presidents, more for the irony of it than to make any sort of statement. I found them cleaner than I had ever imagined, provided one distinguishes between manure, which the pig abhors, and dirt and mud, which he wears like a Gianni Versace blazer. Franklin was more social and personable than most other animals I encountered. He was appreciative of his meals, and often downright chatty with grunting, seeming to ask me all about the day's news and discussing at length the goings on of the farm.

A pig on a mission is a daunting thing. As Franklin grew, he seemed to go in and out of rutting stages, occasionally demolishing the oak planks of his pen and even breaking through the concrete floor as if he was armed with silent jackhammers and other tools that he secretly broke out at night. We never quite knew how he did it, but he could tear apart almost anything – old bicycles or sawhorses or fiber drums. He seemed to enjoy these occasional props which we tossed to him like Romans to a lion. It gave him something to do, something to focus on and obsess about, and his destructions were utterly complete, magnificent in their thoroughness. He would meet our eyes the next morning with a sort of self satisfaction and a smiling pride that seemed to say "look what I did," the bicycle corpse in pieces behind him, placed as so much nuovo art in his trendy apartment.

Franklin would eat almost anything. He delighted in leftover greens and vegetables and would mangle meat with an effusive gusto. He would consume cardboard and corn and fish remains and crayons, old boots and plastic and tree branches. But he loved slop, a simple mixture of water and any kind of grain, especially if it were served in a low, shallow pan that he could stand in while he was eating. To him, this was heaven. He was so enthusiastic in his dining habits, that it became a real trick to distract him long enough to get the bucket of slop into his pen, lest he go at it before I could even set it down, causing a massive spill that bothered me more than him. Once it was on the ground, I'd next have to tie the bucket in place because he'd otherwise drag it off after his meal, demanding it yield more for him, and roughing it up when it failed to produce. We would occasionally find a battered bucket, broken free from its lashings, looking like it had been in some terrible subway collision. He had a voracious appetite and an ugly impatience.

One spring day Mom learned that the local A&P grocery store in Cambridge had a large shipment of expired angel food cakes on hand, having outlived the "sell by" date stamped on the packages. Each cake was in its own box, a powder blue and bright yellow cardboard encasement with a large cellophane window that showed off the tasty contents. There were two complete shipping pallets full, two hundred fifty-six cakes in all. As the A&P couldn't sell them, they were happy to be rid of the whole shipment, and those cakes made for a happy Franklin for several weeks.

At first, we carefully removed the cakes from their boxes and set them inside his pen, alongside a bucket of water, and it was obvious that he was thrilled with this new side dish. He snorted more loudly and attacked the food with even more vigor and even began to call to us when he heard us approaching the barn, still distant. Over time, he began to grow impatient with us, grunted more and more vociferously, demanding with his rutting and head butting that when we arrived that we hop to it and get him a cake – NOW! So soon after, the cakes, boxes and all, went into the pen, right into the shallow water bucket that was his wading pool and dinner plate. Franklin snorted and danced and devoured with relish. His tone of voice, if a pig can be said to have one in his grunting, boasted an air of satisfaction. He loved those boxed delights, and our work was made easier as we now had no need to put the packaging in the trash; it was mere condiment to him.

On one occasion, Franklin, the marvelous miner of concrete floors, the appreciative prince of angel food cakes, seemed to us to return the favor, to compensate us as best as he could for his meal, to offer a sort of piggly praise. On this morning, we found his bucket lashed in place, just as it had been left the night before, the vessel for water and slop and cake. But this time, inside the emptied bucket, he had somehow placed an enormous new chunk of concrete flooring. It was as if he wanted to show his thanks, to offer what he could in return, a quid pro quo designed to keep the cakes coming. How he performed such feats was a mystery, but his resourcefulness and enterprising nature impressed us. Moreover, it seemed to me that he interacted with us in a sort of knowing exchange, a partnership and co-authorship of farming, with us doing our part, and Franklin, our first pig, doing his.

Franklin, angel food cake king

Edward A. Baah
"starting at left tackle, number 72, a sixty pound sophomore from Vly Summit, New York..."

(My age: 12)

There is a reason for the stereotype. A brand new baby lamb is deliciously delicate, affectionate and soft, as light as feathery down, and as fresh to the nose as lavender. These things, plus his clear desire to be with other beings, make him simply irresistible, a delightful and marvelous creature that cannot but disarm us, soften us in every way. So it was with our tiny newborn lamb that my grandfather brought to our farmhouse. He weighed only five pounds, and it seemed most of him was soft woolen curls. We named him Edward.

Pop set him down on wobbly new legs, inside a makeshift wire mesh pen in the backroom of our house, the room where we kept coats and work boots, where our washing machine sat, and where cats were sometimes allowed on frigid winter nights. This room was half barn and half house, the middling ground from which we ventured toward farm work, and the place to which we returned at the end of the day, ready to shuck off shoes and odorous work clothes. Edward's pen was square, three feet on a side, and lined on the bottom with newspapers. Ironically, it sat where it was warmed by the freezer's condensing coils, the thing that made the freezer frozen, the thing that kept our meats in storage, at first made tiny Edward warm.

We mixed formula for Eddie twice a day and fed him from a large glass root beer bottle with a black nipple stretched over the opening, just like an enormous baby bottle. He drank enthusiastically and feeding him was great fun, a rewarding thing for a young farm boy. There was no fussing or cajoling like a real baby might need, no need for handling him just so or being careful to not bump him too much. Eddie charged for the bottle when he saw it and forced himself into our laps, bucked his head in affirmation when drinking, and slobbered liberally on himself. You couldn't make a mistake feeding him if you tried, other than to let him yank the nipple clear off the thing, creating a gush of wasted formula, which did happen once.

He soon began to bleat and ba'ah at us whenever we were around, and he loved to have his head scratched, to which he responded by butting us with his forehead. It was play for him, butting things and head-ramming us and anything that moved. He was too small to hurt anyone and so we encouraged him, got on all fours and literally got head to head with him at times, and rolled on the floor in laughter, Eddie still butting us with all that he had, which just tickled us even more.

He eventually outgrew his small backroom pen and graduated to a larger area in our cow barn, at the far corner of the place, right in front of McCart, his new roommate of sorts. The two of them got along famously, with McCart stretching out far to smell him and Eddie, dwarfed by the oversized cow but unaware that he was overmatched, butting her nose as if he was laying down the law.

Edward A. Baah was now his name, having been formalized somewhere along the way, bestowing a certain dignity to him, acknowledging him as a force in the barn and in the lives of all in that place. But he was Eddie to us, especially when we would play with him. He was tethered now, not penned in, and that meant we had direct and easy access to him; there was no barrier between him and his keepers. So our wrestling with him continued, even expanded. He butted with more force now and it was beginning to hurt a bit, which somehow made it more fun and more hilarious than ever. We even got to where we'd stand against the wall and call him so that he'd charge our knees, intent on ramming us for good measure. Just as he was about to deliver his blow, we'd bow our legs, open them at the knees and Eddie would ram not us but the barn wall behind our legs, sometimes causing quite a loud whack, making us glad we didn't have to take the actual pounding he delivered. I don't think he ever figured it out. Regardless, we all loved this little game, Eddie included, and we always shared a laugh with him when it was over.

Naturally, all this roughhousing made him comfortable with people and made us comfortable with him. We'd wrestle and exchange head-butts, and we'd even sometimes put little kids on his back for a rodeo ride that never lasted long. It seemed that Eddie got the idea of it, easily making himself available to accept a rider, but then, when released, sprinting this way and that so the rider would fall off. After each ejection, Eddie would return to the starting place, almost begging for another cowpoke, ready to bronco his way into the winner's circle.

One day my brother Joe had Eddie out on his rope leash, walking him for some outdoor exercise, when my cousins were visiting. Justin, our cousin who was Joe's age, walked with them. The older kids were playing touch football nearby and Joe, Justin and Eddie watched with interest. They let Eddie off his leash, as he seemed content to be near us, watching us with Joe and Justin.

Casey and Edward A. Baah, head-butter and football player

"Huddle up!" I called, self-appointing myself as team captain. It was our ball, and we had just marked the boundaries with our sweatshirts, not needed now that the August sun was high.

Casey and my cousins, Jim and Janet Shanley formed our circle of bent forward heads, confident we could advance the ball against the others, against my older brother Rick and John Shanley, my Uncle Jim and Dad. I knelt on one knee and outlined a simple plan. "Jan, you hike it to me and block for just a second, then go to the left on a delay. Jim, you line up right and buttonhook in front of Rick. Look for the ball right away. Jan, I'll throw to you if Jim's not open. Case, line up left, but stay in to block. I'll move behind you for protection – Okay!"

The huddle broke and we lined up, ready to run the play, which we took more than just a little seriously. (We lived for these games, dreamed about them, bragged or sulked for days afterward.) Everyone was still just before the snap of the ball, which released us all like a starter's pistol, springing us every which way. Somehow, Eddie got caught up in the stop and start of it all and went wild with us, sprinting and zagging on every play and freezing when we were in huddles and before the ball was snapped. We roared with laughter and found that we couldn't complete a single play because no matter how determined we were to stay sober, the sight of Eddie, mid-play, zigging and bolting abruptly among us brought us to our knees with uncontrollable laughter, tears in our eyes and full of joyous disbelief. He even began to join us in our huddles, as if he too would receive an assignment…and we'd always give him one. "Eddie, you go five and out, look for the pump fake, and then go long!"

I cannot say that he followed the play that was called, but Eddie could always be counted on to be in the huddle, to freeze before the snap, and to take off in some crazy and frantic way when the play began. And if the defense tried to hold him, Eddie would butt them hard, like a pulling guard looking to spring his running back. Our football games were never the same, and Edward A. Baah, our special pulling guard and downfield blocker, gave color to our play and to our summers, gave color to the whole place.

Sweet Lou
love is in the air...

(My age: 13)

We named our brand new Hereford bull "Louis E'fombrasio;" I have no idea why. I suppose there was no reason other than we liked the sound of it. We rolled the "r" for effect. He was a gentle little guy we could each easily lift when he arrived, all new and clean smelling, a soft, thick, red, furry fellow, agreeable and of good nature.

He was playful and enjoyed jousting with us kids. But as he grew, something in his DNA took over, pushed him toward procreation, toward needing to assert his maleness at every opportunity. If we walked in front of him, he'd leap up and try to mount us, humping, which was at first an entertaining oddity. But that soon became dangerous as it evolved into serious business for him, and he was growing rapidly. He was still good natured, provided we were on the other side of whatever fenced him in, but now we had to be wary. He mounted grain bags and bales of hay, tractor tires and anything that moved – or didn't move. "Sweet Lou" was becoming a nuisance, and was now big enough to cause real damage if he decided to. Dad wondered out loud about how long we should keep the growing lad.

His undoing was on a February day when Dad was plowing snow in our barnyard. Louis was out there getting some air, free to walk where he wanted within the fenced-in barnyard. After a few frustrated attempts at mounting the tractor tires, he gave up. But something sparked in his macho, male, bull headed brain, and Louis could suddenly see the real enemy, his real rival, the thing that prevented him from his all out romancing of that desirable tractor tire. It was the snowplow blade that tried to outdo him. The snowplow was the thing that challenged his mating supremacy. The snowplow blade, Louis had decided, had cavorted with the tractor tire, moved in unison with it, in a disgusting, dancing display of public affection, taunting loveless Louis by ramming some snow into a pile and impressing Lady Tractor Tire, making her swoon with passion. It was more than he could take!

Rebuffed by the Tractor Tire of Desire, Louis attacked the snowplow blade with a sudden and frightful vengeance. He squared off with it and menacingly raked his front hoof in the snow, head down and determined. He charged, battering it so brutally that Dad felt the tractor lurch. Louis bashed the thing again, lifted it with his ferocious hammering head and made the metal plow creak with pain, made the bolts on the plow complain loudly. Again he pounded, so hard this time that the tractor tires slid in the snow. That would teach the thing! That would impress the tire, would make her fall helplessly in love with him. He smashed the snow blade again. Again and again and again, until Dad drove the thing off, escaped from this mating ritual of death, parked the tractor and puzzled plow in the barn, and closed the door behind it.

Louis had outgrown our ability to manage him, and he had an ever growing and overwhelming desire to love something, anything. His size and his hormones had mixed into a sobering cocktail, one that could kill us. And as much as we all liked Sweet Lou, his time had come. He was a good bull, doing the only thing he could. We told his stories often and we missed him. Most of all, we hoped Louis E'fombrasio finally found true love.

John Dollar
from car attacks to stumble stick to three legs...

(My age: 10)

Just as Louis E'fombrasio loved a good tire, Honest John Dollar hated the very same thing. Tires weren't Johnny D's love object, but rather they were his nemesis - the one, single thing he simply had to defeat, the thing he was born to destroy. John Dollar was our only dog, a Beagle mixed with something larger. He was as loyal as any dog ever was, but it seemed to us that he was as brainless as he was loyal. We tried to train him, to teach him some modicum of manners, to have him respect the master's command to heel or stay or to come. We did our best to teach him to follow *any* command. We clearly failed and we knew it. Still, we somehow expected him to behave in certain ways simply because we willed him to, and we were guilty of blaming him when he did the only thing he could do, which was to be a dog and live by his instincts. And John Dollar was 100% instincts. Thought, training, obedience, a doggly desire to please – none of those things entered into any equation of John Dollar's life or actions. It's not that he didn't want to please us. It's just that he couldn't help himself; he was all instincts and nothing else. One of those instincts, the ancient canine instinct to attack and destroy car tires, ruled his very being.

John Dollar launched for cars like a greyhound after a mechanical rabbit. He tore after cars with reckless abandon and with the single minded focus of a cliff diver. Those cars represented all that was evil to John, all that was wrong with this crazy world, and the universe had given to him the entire, global burden of removing those vile vehicles, and especially the things that made them go, tires. When John did catch up to a car, his work had just begun. Now the real task, the real calling that pulled him forward was to kill the tires. He bit them and barked at them and dove into them and ripped away at them with every ounce of himself. His emergency take offs were stunning things, but they paled in comparison to the thunderous, ferocious combat he waged when he got up close.

He chased cars with such terrible tenacity that drivers often swerved to avoid hitting him, which my parents deemed to be a danger to us kids. We would sometimes be near the road, on our bikes or working nearby, and the cars did indeed come close more than once. And so my grandfather, always the smith and inventor, withdrew one day to the confines of his tool shop, his reclusive kingdom of table saws and drill presses, vices and grinding stones. He emerged a few hours later with John Dollar's custom collar, to which he had fastened a short length of chain that suspended a wooden dowel the thickness of a broom handle and about ten inches long. It hung from his neck, and the dowel, balanced in the middle by the chain, dangled in front of John's front legs so that his knees banged into it when he ran. It was like a loosely tied wooden bow tie. Full out sprinting was no longer possible for him.

The stumble stick collar didn't deter his tire passions, but it caused a sometimes pathetic, sometimes hilarious scene when John chased cars. He never made it very close to a car with that contraption on, but the resulting summersaults and flips could be spectacular things, like cartoon scenes with a furious commotion of dust and dirt clouds, a tail or dog's nose or stumble stick occasionally popping out of the cloud before it was immediately snapped back into the tumbling blur of fur and fury. "No, John! Stay!" we'd shout whenever a car approached, but he couldn't hear us, his ears already disconnected by instinct. Off he'd go and we watched, mesmerized, waiting to see the inevitable canine train wreck that always caused us to laugh and shake our heads in sorry disbelief. It took years of wearing his knee blocking bow tie before he relented, before he mellowed a bit and moderated his instincts, slowed his wars into skirmishes more filled with the sounds of barking than the sights of self destruction.

In later years Johnny D. lost half of his left front leg, so the collar and bar were mercifully removed. We don't really know how it happened, but the prevailing theory is that he got caught in a trap in the woods somewhere and gnawed it off. Or perhaps he waited it out and the leg disconnected itself somehow. All we really knew was that John disappeared one day without a trace, and after a few days we assumed the worst. We looked along the sides of the road, assuming some car tire may finally have taken him down, martyred him in his religious war. But we never found him. Two and half weeks passed. Worry and wonder turned into sadness and resignation. We did our best to move on, but he was often in the back of our minds, saddened if no longer hopeful.

Then, one morning, there he was, lying in our front lawn, licking the stump that used to be his upper leg. It was messy and unsightly, but the bleeding had already stopped. He was still in pain and found himself quiet corners and took food we'd bring to him, and eventually, surprisingly he turned the corner toward recovery.

At long last our three legged dog finally declined to chase cars with any seriousness, choosing instead to bark and make a show of himself, a sort of statement to the universe that he was still there, still carrying his hatred for tires. He still got himself into serious scrapes with neighboring dogs who had their own territories to defend, their own wars to wage. Despite our trying to convince him otherwise, he'd follow us to distant fields and take whatever poundings three legged dogs take. It never seemed to bother him much, and Honest John Dollar, ever loyal and resilient, seemed happiest whenever he was in our midst, provided there were no cars!

And the Supporting Cast...
aggression, fright sight, hockey practice and more

There were other characters too, other personalities that surrounded us. Goz, our first and only goose, seemed to mind only my grandfather but found all other humans offensive. He chased me and pecked at me and terrorized me as a small child, made it clear that his territory was wherever he decided it was and that mine was nowhere but the house. I don't remember much about him other than he bit me and bullied me. I was glad to see him on our Thanksgiving table one year, found him as unpalatable on my plate as he was in our barnyard. I did not like him and am convinced he did not care for me.

Goz, that terrible goose, with my grandfather

Our cat, named only "The Old Lady" was a master mouser and mother of our full feline staff of seventeen. She was smart and affectionate yet didn't push herself on us. She came when called and then went back to her domain, preferring her ample hunting grounds to household luxury. She could often be seen dragging a carcass of some unwanted rodent twice her size, taking it to her collection of kittens and keeping them well fed. "Tom" was her sometimes husband, a real bum of a fellow, arriving out of the clear blue every few months, strolling in from who knows where like he had just stepped out for a brief cup of coffee. He seemed shifty to me, a guy not to be trusted. He probably told the Old Lady he loved her and wouldn't leave again, that he was changing his ways and was serious this time. He'd be around for a few days and disappear as silently as he arrived, off for strange, unknown places. She tolerated him, but somehow remained in charge, always made it clear that he was a visitor under her benign jurisdiction. She was a great animal; he was an absentee father.

"Upstate" was an unremarkable cow in every way, except for a horn so crooked it curled right back into her head, and gave her a look that frightened whoever saw her. We delighted in showing her off to cousins and visitors who found her downright scary, like something in a house of mirrors at the county fair. I felt bad for her in a way, as the poor thing was an easy going cow, never intending to frighten anyone.

"Kate" was a brown and white yearling heifer that ran loose, along with five others, during winters in our heifer barn. The six of them shared this chilly space, protected from the sub-zero elements only by a single layer of barn boards, with burlap bags stuffed into large cracks to slow the breeze that came through. Though not any bigger than the others, Kate ruled the place, was the alpha-cow of this frozen pen. She'd frequently hammer others into the wall when they tried to take food she thought was hers.

The others learned from her, and it soon became a contagious thing with slammee turning into slammer, and heifer after heifer would bounce off the walls. But then they'd go right back to eating like nothing happened. A flurry of action and board-rattling body checks, then normalcy. We'd feed them hay just before we retired for the night, that being our last task of the long day. When finished, we'd walk toward the house after doing this, our boots crunching the snow covered ground as we made our way in moonlight. Suddenly we'd hear a rush of heifer legs and hooves through hay, then... Wham! Kate had just plastered somebody into the boards, like an enforcer on a hockey team, marking her territory and letting all puck handlers know she was a force to be reckoned with. There would be one or two other rushes to the blue line, followed by some fierce sounding board action, and then all would be quiet. Hockey practice was over for the night, and they'd go at it again tomorrow.

And there was "Jersey Cow," who was as sweet and gentle as could be. Another Kate won the prize at the fair, and Noel did too. Hearts was McCart's daughter and danced for her food. And the others too, all the others. So many of them. Personalities in every pen.

Chapter 8

Hard Work

Farms are physical places. They are relentless and unforgiving, intolerant of any farmer that might catch a cold or break a finger or come down with the flu. Farms are immune to holidays, ignorant of vacations, unconcerned with electrical power outages or shortages of fuel. They are dismissive of broken down equipment, or deaths of the farmer's relatives, or the vagaries of brutal winter storms. The mainspring of the farm clicks always onward, mechanically issuing demand after demand after unending demand.

Farmers must milk cows twice a day every day without fail. They must feed their animals and care for them when they are sick, regardless of the day or season. When spring comes, plowing and planting must be done. In summer, the farmer is focused on cutting hay and baling and storing it away. Fall means harvesting corn and oats and making final preparations for winter which brings its own demands of feeding and barn cleaning and snow removal. Along the way, the farmer has to build whatever needs to be built, repair what is worn, secure feed and fuel and materials, sell milk and cows and rent equipment, can food and mend clothes, and manage the rest of household and family life.

Behind the more apparent work, the stuff of raising crops and animals and producing milk, lay the more obscure yet equally toilsome tasks of maintenance. In addition to cutting and baling and stowing hay, the farmer has to repair broken mowing machines and shattered mowing blades; he must unplug clogged hay conditioners and replace broken rake tines and baler shear pins; he must adjust baling machine knotters and fix flat tires and replace exhausted bearings. Plowing brings broken plow points and chopping corn means plugged slio pipes and broken power belts. "Farming" means wrenches and screwdrivers, makeshift tools and perpetually bruised knuckles, jammed fingers, bruises and cuts.

The work is hard and there are no days off. Ever. Yet only farming so directly ties one's labor to one's subsistence. Therein lies both the smothering burden and the inexplicable, irresistible attraction of farming.

Potatoes
("B'dayduhs")

(My age: 5 and 16)

It was the first real work I remember doing. Dad befriended a Vly Summit local named Hank Zielinski, a Polish immigrant and survivor of World War II. The war was their first bond, my dad being a Navy veteran, but the conversation soon turned to potatoes, which to Hank were like underwear: something incredibly close to you, something you needed every day, something you never wanted to be without. "B'dayduhs," he called them. He loved those spuds that were his mainstay when he lived in the old country, and which kept him alive during the wartime period of homeless horror. He spoke of their magnificence and their reliability, waxed on about their capacity for lasting through long winters, swooned about their resilience in the face of bad weather. Hank adored potatoes, and he made my dad fall in love with them.

It was quickly agreed. Hank would provide the seed potatoes and the wisdom of his potato-ing experience; Dad would do the plowing and provide the boypower to manage the crop. It was hard work, but great fun, as it was a hands-on, up-to-your-elbows-in-dirt kind of work. And I was a five year old boy who loved dirt as much as Hank loved spuds. We made two potato fields, one near Hank's place and one close to our farm. We worked them both: plowed and planted the seed potatoes, hilled them up and weeded them, hilled them again. In the fall we rooted through soft dirt and took our rewards, found the buried treasure of potatoes that were stunning in size and quantity, a bountiful and magical yield, more than both families needed.

Along the way I worked beside Penny, one of Hank's daughters, who was exactly my age. I generally took no notice of girls then but found her to be a decent worker and a satisfactory playmate during breaks in the routine. Four of us kids were playing tag during a break in one of our potato hilling sessions and were running helter-skelter, laughing. I ran smack into her and stunned, kissed her. I have no idea why, but some wire in my five year old brain connected to some other wire, and the kiss was over before I could think. I didn't think much of it and was ready to keep running, but Penny wasn't. I could see her face scrunch up, trying to decide if this was nothing or if it was something – or if it was something enormous. She chose the latter and went off screaming. I continued playing until adults were summoned and arrived. It then became clear that, upon stealing my very first kiss, I had committed a great offense, a terrible transgression, my own personal war crime for which there could be no forgiveness. I was directed to a corner of the field and sentenced to stay there until I was allowed back to work, which at the time seemed to me to be a colossal punishment, an injustice of great magnitude. Regardless, I finally got back to hilling potatoes and kept my head down for the rest of that humiliating day.

That field produced plenty of potatoes for us. I did my best to dig them out without damaging them, to fill them into baskets which the adults dumped into our little green wagon, hitched to our tractor. I remember riding home that afternoon, sitting with my brother Rick, atop a huge mound of potatoes in that wagon. Once home we re-loaded baskets, and the potatoes were delivered to their resting place in our dirt cellar, just beneath the stairs that led to our kitchen. We would eat potatoes every evening for almost all of the next twelve months, and every day, I was reminded of the close connection between the simple earth and the work of our hands. It was so very literal.

Mom must have prepared almost twenty thousand home grown potatoes over the years. Potatoes had become a way of life for us, something that Hank was proud of and Dad was glad to have. Aside from plowing, much of the work was done by hand. It was tough, tedious stuff, and our potato fields grew larger each year.

One August morning when I was sixteen we once again found ourselves hilling potatoes with hoes and shovels. My brother Casey and I had transitioned from little ones into awkward adolescent teens. And being adolescent boys, we believed we were gifted with much great advice to offer our father about how to do things better, whether it was cleaning barns or haying or hilling potatoes. Sometimes Dad handled it well, but at other times our juvenile arrogance got the best of his waning patience. This was one of those rare days when both were true. He was fed up with us, angry at our endless criticisms and thoughtless, bombastic proclamations – and at the same time he was entertained by us, amused by our youthful foolishness, that special naivety that has no self awareness. Being a bit older than Casey, blessed by just a few meager years of maturity, I sensed Dad's fuse shortening, and I backed off.

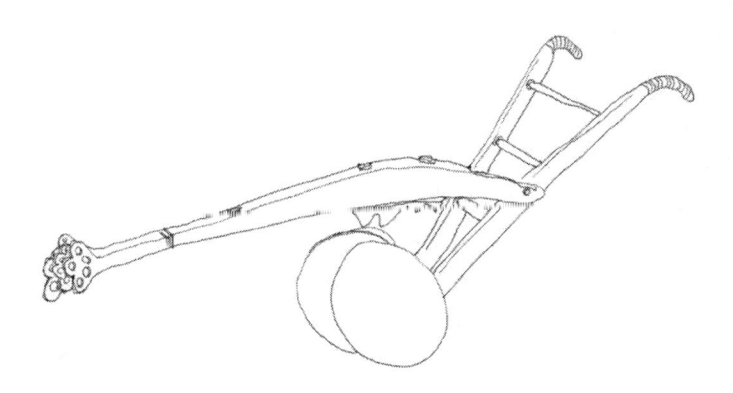

But Casey, oblivious to such cues, charged straight ahead, offering unsolicited and half baked ideas, more criticisms than they were suggestions. I stepped back even farther now, aware that sparks would soon fly, and not having to be in the middle of it, could be entertained by it if I could stay invisible. It was always a great delight to see a sibling get in trouble, that universal kid entertainment that bettered movie theaters or clowns or magic shows. Dad goaded him further.

"And just what would you do?' Dad asked, feigning sincere interest, acting as if he genuinely thought he might be wrong and that Casey might have a great idea or two to teach the aging, feeble minded farmer.

"Get the darn hiller is what I'd do" Casey snapped back, referring to our horse-drawn potato hiller, a two hundred pound behemoth we had not used in years. We had indeed pulled it with a tractor once, and it performed reasonably well, but on much younger potato plants where little damage could be done. This was not the case today. It was a bad idea, and I knew it.

Dad replied, gentle and reasonable sounding as ever, inviting the oblivious Casey into a corner from which there would be no escape. "Gee, Casey I don't think the tractor can pull that thing in here. It will be too rough on the plants unless we pull it more gently, slowly, like a horse would…and I don't think you guys can pull it. It's just too heavy…"

"Aww, c'mon!" Casey retorted. "I can pull that myself!" He made no attempt to mask the disgust in his voice. Casey was big for his age, and had been muscling-up to get ready for football that year, but I knew he was biting off more than he could chew. His machismo and his hormones were doing the talking now.

Dad set the final trap and placed the sweetest bait inside. "Oh jeez, Casey, you can't do that. I know you've been getting ready for

My brother Casey and Dad: "Labor and Management reach a tentative peace"

football, but you're not ready for this kind of work. This is real man's stuff, and you're just not ready..."

"Like crap! You bring that thing here and I'll show you how it's done!" Casey fired back, wanting to tag "Old Man" on the end of his sentence but checking himself just enough to hold it back. That did it; Dad had him. Casey was clearly agitated and felt confrontational, so confrontational that I felt momentarily cheated. Dad didn't have to be tricky or clever, not crafty or enticing. There was no intrigue, no game, no display of manipulative skill. Casey was ready to leap full force into whatever trap was set, almost willingly, and Dad had simply laid it out there for him. Casey was now already fully inside the trap, engulfed by the thing, about to be bitten by it. Yet, blinded by adolescent hubris, he still couldn't see the teeth clamping down on him.

Dad was already half way to the barn and his tone suddenly changed. He released the anger and frustration that had been bubbling beneath his artificial politeness. "Get your smartass up here, you overgrown halfwit!" came harshly from over Dad's shoulder toward Casey, who responded with vigor and determination, certain of his invincibility in this battle of wills. The show was on, and I did my best to blend into the scenery, to watch but not become part of the coming feature program.

It was a delightfully entertaining drama. Dad demanded Casey strap in like some draft horse, and Casey did so with relish, bursting with anxiousness - he couldn't wait to show up the old man, to prove his male maturity, to establish himself as co-ruler of the place, an alpha male in the making, a future boss of bosses. I was absolutely dying. I wanted desperately to burst out laughing, to howl like never before at the sight of my horse harnessed brother trying to prove his manhood and my hardheaded father determined to break the spirit of this brash young colt, this draft horse, still unwilling to obey the master. I was twitching with swallowed joy, shaking with suppressed laughter, but I bit my lip hard and stayed mum, stayed in the audience, stayed well out of the line of fire.

Casey dragged the thing with a fierceness that surprised and impressed both Dad and me. My God, he's going to do it, I thought to myself, as I watched him drag the thing to the potato field, the bulky hiller sent gravel scurrying every which way from under its oak and iron frame.

Dad was loving this, shouting at him now like he really was a horse. "Heeyah!" he called out. "Hiyu'up! Left, Boy! Go now!" This made Casey even more furious, feeling his manhood was being discounted by the lighthearted banter. He pulled even more furiously now and this in turn made Dad even giddier, more vociferous in barking instructions to his one-boy team of horses.

He was doing it! One foot at a time, one leg-cramping thrust at a time, Casey, our new workhorse, our new plow beast, was actually pulling the hiller, actually hilling potatoes, his horse face full of desperate determination, while Dad worked the handles on the back end, grinning with delight and guffawing loudly. They were both making a horrific noise, yelling and cursing and teasing and encouraging. It was half teach-him-a-lesson, half marvelous entertainment, and half football training. Yes, it was more than a thing; it was a thing and a half – it was that big. I was positively thrilled, wanted to freeze this absurdity in time, so I could pull it from the fridge now and then, savor the tastiness of this scrumptious scene, and set it back inside for later. It was simply the most deliciously entertaining thing in my life – better than Broadway plays, more wonderful than a World Series game, more memorable than a helicopter tour of Hawaii. Nothing compares. Nothing.

The divine scene on stage finally collapsed into a rousing, rolling on the ground, unguarded, collective whoop of laughter. Dad could no longer play his role; he was so amused by the whole thing. Casey could no longer take himself seriously, finally having the entire vision come in to focus in his mind, seeing himself as plow horse and bellowing teenager. And at long last I was liberated from any need to stay on the sidelines. The three of us howled with delight and choked out huge yelps of laughter. We were sweaty and our skin was dirt-caked, but our spirits were high. We celebrated the theatrical production with wonderful applause and unbridled merriment.

We went on hilling potatoes. (Casey completed that row, but not the many others that needed hilling.) Potato-ing was part of life on that farm. It was hard work. It dried our hands and toughened them, and more than anything else we did, forced our hands directly into the soil, into the earth that nurtured us. And somehow, that was a grand thing, a thing for which I am still thankful.

Whenever I order potatoes at a restaurant, I still think of our potato farming days, of Hank and Penny, of Casey and Dad and that horse drawn hiller, and of the mound of "b'dayduhs" beneath our cellar stairs. Memories make the potatoes taste better, full of flavor. I savor the first bite, and wonder if that particular potato was hilled by a hoe, or was it hilled by some early-teen boy, lashed to some horse drawn contraption, driven by the half-crazed, blustering hormones of adolescence.

Corn
fury and serenity...

(My age: 9)

It was old, even then. Our ancient Papec corn chopper and blower was all iron, right down to its wheels. Iron chain conveyor, iron fan paddles, iron drive wheel, iron control levers, iron guide rails. Iron everything. It was about ten feet long and weighed slightly less than a modern aircraft carrier. Our tractor strained audibly when moving the thing. It sank slowly but perceptibly in our muddy barnyard, right before our eyes, one fraction of an inch at a time, until each wheel was six inches down and the additional iron surface area that met the earth finally stopped the sinking.

I hated that that Papec. Hated it because I feared it, found it daunting and terrifying. Hated it because it was frightfully loud, one of the loudest things I have ever heard. It roared and screamed so I could feel the sound batter my body. Hated it because it was unbelievably dangerous, with a thirty feet long, one hundred pound, leather drive belt that traveled at 30 miles per hour, and sometimes came undone right in front of us, flew like an unguided leather missile. Hated it because it took Malcolm Hamilton's finger and never gave it back, tore it from his hand and obliterated it and blew it into his silo like so much silage.

That thundering, roaring machine took stalks of corn and carried them along toward its wicked, whirling, bladed iron paddle, spinning at twelve hundred revolutions per minute, where the force of the blade and paddle was so severe that it chopped the corn and instantly blew it straight up the forty feet of pipe to the top of our silo. There was nothing sophisticated about the Papec, no elegant physics at work, no fluid dynamics to create air flow or reduce friction. It was pure violence, pure force, and it did its work loudly and with eye popping brutality.

As a young child I watched it from a hundred feet away, from within our house, from behind a window and from behind a heavy chair that I hoped might somehow give me protection if the angry Papec ever came undone. As I entered the farm's work force for real, I still did my best to stay clear of that bawling, raging, ominous behemoth, tried to find work where the belt wouldn't fly if it came off a pulley. I kept my hands well away from the thing, preferring to be teased and called chicken than to take a chance with that monstrous, angry, screaming machine. I didn't care. It terrified me.

Malcolm Hamilton, Papec victim and neighboring farmer, helped us chop corn each year. His presence always meant it was fall and it was corn chopping season. He was large and loud and bombastic but had a heart of gold and worked as hard as any man I have ever met.

"Jesus, the sonnuvabitch can't jump up there and bite ya!" screamed Malcolm over the roar of the thing, teasing me. He said it in his unique voice, high pitched and whistling, laced with cusses so magnificent and artful that Mark Twain would have marveled.

Malcolm could have provided source material for the *Sailor's Manual on the Art of Cursing*, if they were ever to publish such a thing. I was five feet away, on the wagon, hand delivering stalks to the Papec, where Malcolm was standing.

"Put that goddamn bunch right here! Jeeseaychrisse, I wondered if you got lost going all the way back there!" he came at me again, taunting now, but serious too. He pointed right where he wanted the next few stalks, pointed with his finger stump, did it on purpose so I could see the mutilation this Papec had caused him. Winked at me from under his broad brimmed, straw hat – his way of saying that he'd continue to harass me but that I was right to fear the thing.

The chain conveyor dragged stalk after stalk into the malevolent maw of the gluttonous, mechanical beast, where it ferociously pounded it to pieces, shredded it, and knocked it to kingdom come, screaming at the top its lungs the entire time. Tractors roared at full engines; the Papec howled; Malcolm barked instructions nonstop and loudly jabbered friendly taunts; huge belts whirled on the edge of control; and before one wagon had emptied its stalks of corn, the next one arrived from the field, overloaded and sagging, pulled by yet another tractor, adding to the clamorous bedlam of the barnyard.

Toward the end, as the silo neared being full, my job changed. I wasn't there on the ground feeding the Papec, I was inside the silo, frantically shoveling the chopped corn away from the mouth of the delivery tube, keeping it from becoming clogged, racing against time and relentless, furious flow of silage, my ears rattling from the fantastic noise of the thing which reverberated around inside the silo with no place to go.

My cousin Tom shared those inside-the-silo duties with me one year and I can still remember meeting his eyes with mine in what we feared was our slio-coffin of cacophony, both of us wondering if we might die there. My eyes asked him to save me if it came to that and his spoke the same to me. From that moment on we have been bonded in a brotherhood of battle, survivors of our silage war.

* * * * * *

Months later, in the deep of winter, I found myself in that same silo, same fork in hand. But all was stark silence now. Pitch black and peaceful. The outermost ring of silage, the outer twelve inches, the part that rested along the silo walls, was frozen solid. Like silage-ice castle walls, protecting me in the empty, cold night. I felt that frozen silage wall in the blackness and whacked at it with the fork, loosened enough of the stuff to collect and send it down the long chute to the cow barn. I took another forkful, this time from the floor of silage under my feet, that being easier. I thought back to the September silo filling, to the fury and frightful havoc, to the overwhelming noise of it. I couldn't believe I was in the same place, so completely transformed now.

I took a break in the silo, rested and caught my breath, alone in the utter darkness, leaned against the fork and let my mind wander back to the cornfield, to the hand held sickles we used to cut each stalk and throw them on the wagon, the beautiful fall colors of the place framing the field. I'd gotten blisters from so much sickle handling, was glad I wasn't sickling now, though I missed being out in the September sun.

Another few forkfuls and I was done, having delivered enough silage to feed the cows that day. I entered the chute and climbed down the ladder, then delivered a shovelful of silage to each of the cows, McCart last, her head turned toward the wall. That single act made all the work worthwhile, because it told me how important that silage was to her, how fantastic she thought it was. She appreciated it, and it showed.

* * * * * *

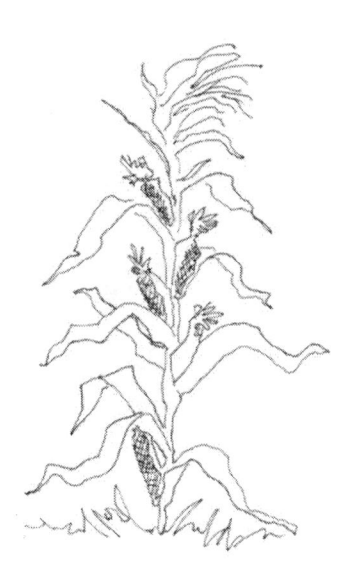

    We didn't pick all the corn when it was green. Some stayed in the field until the stalks turned a yellowish brown, shriveled up and dried out. The ears were hardened now, and we'd husk them, harvest the ears for making grain. We could get mechanical pickers on some fields, the drier ones. But other fields, the wet ones, we'd pick by hand. Dad would drive us there with the tractor and green wagon after we arrived home from school. We'd pick and husk and toss each ear into the wagon until it was full. We'd pass the time by talking or by listening to a New York Jets game on the radio if were a Sunday, or by chatting about anything that came to mind.

    When we got to the corn crib, we'd unload the corn, use shovels to get it onto an elevator or a makeshift trough that got the corn into bins for the winter. Then once a week during the winter, we'd bag the corn and some oats as well, set them out for the General League of

Farmers truck or the Agway truck that picked it up and delivered grain back to us. It would all end up in front of a cow someday.

Corn. It came at us with relentless regularity, arriving at times with a calamitous, terrifying racket that absolutely unnerved me. And at times it came to us softly, gentle in its silent serenity. It was always hard work. And it never ended.

Route 66
it was no highway to heaven...

(My age: 12)

There is one thing more regular on a farm than potatoes, one thing more endless and eternal than corn, one thing which is always waiting when the dairy farmer wakes and when he finishes each day, one thing that just keeps coming, more predictable than milking, more interminable than haying. That one thing is manure. Cows are prolific eaters, and all that intake eventually has to go somewhere. Manure. Manure in the barns and in the barnyard. Manure in the pens. Manure in pastures and in fields, waiting to be plowed under as fertilizer. Always manure.

"Why aren't we going to use the manure spreader?" Rick asked with surprise and resentment when he returned to the barn, having just dumped the wheelbarrow full of manure on to the wagon. Dumping manure on the wagon meant we boys would have to pitch it off again, and it was bitterly cold out, below zero on this January morning.

"Because the spreader's chains will freeze in this weather" Dad answered. It was apparent that he was pleased with himself, pleased with his decision to not test fate and not have to face the daunting problem of frozen manure spreader chains. Boys were more reliable, and much easier for him to deal with.

"Well *we're* gonna freeze if we go out there" I shot back, equally pleased with my comeback. "I'd rather see that thing freeze than me freeze!"

"Don't talk foolish talk!" This was Dad's standard reply when he had run out of patience.

"I'm not!" I said.

"When that darn thing freezes I have to come all the way back in here and get a fork and shovel and then empty it, then bring a bucket of hot water to thaw the thing, then I have to lay under that freaggin' thing and hammer out links and insert new ones – it's a freezing pain in the ass and I'm not going to do it today!" Dad was adamant. He was unshaven and his sweat-soaked cap hung over to one side, his cigarette dangled in the other direction, and his face was determined. I knew better than to antagonize him when he got like this.

"Why not dump it?" asked Rick.

"Whaddya mean?" asked Dad, puzzled but clearly growing impatient with this conversation.

"Let's just dump it off to the side of the diving board and we'll get it in the springtime" Rick explained. The diving board was our name for the platform that rose above the manure spreader (or wagon) from which we would dump wheelbarrows full of manure; it was a sort of perch of a place that extended for fifteen feet or so out the back of our barn.

Dad didn't reply, and I took that as a sign that maybe he was open to the concept.

"Yeah" I said, adding on, "that way you don't have to deal with that unreliable spreader, and we don't have to be out any longer than we need to in this freezing cold."

"We'll get it later" added Rick. "It won't be that much. Plus, it'll freeze solid, so it won't stink, and it'll give us a spring project."

Dad didn't care about the stink. This was a farm, and it always stunk; it was like background noise to him. But I could see that the idea of a spring project intrigued him. He liked having projects to keep teenage boys engaged and busy.

"How many winter days do you think will be too cold? How many days would we just pile manure out back instead of spreading it?" Dad asked, for the first time directly signaling that he was actually considering the idea.

"Ten," I popped back, not having any basis whatsoever for the estimate, but knowing that ten was a light number of days and would therefore help our case, would help keep us out of the brutal cold weather that day. Rick shot me a look as if to say I had made an error, that I should have set Dad's expectations differently, but he didn't say anything. Was my number too high? Too low?

"When in the spring would you guys clean it out?" Dad was really considering it now, really thinking this idea over.

"We'd all get it done in a single April weekend" answered Rick. "You wouldn't need to do any of it."

"Just you guys?" said Dad with a smirk of disbelief.

"Yep!" Rick and I replied in unison.

"We'd all get it done as a team" said Rick. "Me, Gerry and Casey, just the three of us."

"One boy, full boy. Two boys, half a boy. Three boys, no boy at all..." This was Dad's way of saying that when he had one boy doing a project, things went well. But when a second boy joined in, the two boys ended up distracting each other to the point where work output was actually halved. And when a third boy entered, the work result, the fruits of labor, were reduced to nothing. It was an exaggeration of the truth, but Dad was right to a certain degree, and we knew it. His reply let us know he was considering the idea further, but our "we'll do it alone" plan felt thin to him, felt weak.

"We'll get it done" I added, feeling the need to take a stand on the issue, to declare good intentions in spite of Dad's concerns.

Dad took the next wheelbarrow full and handed Rick the shovel, an unspoken signal that Rick was to clean off the walkway while Dad did the dumping. Rick and I looked at each other, pleased that we might be nearing some compromise with Dad, that we might be avoiding the miserable task of pitching manure off wagons in the bitter cold of deep Upstate New York winter. Dad came back and none of us said a word. Our sense was that we might get him to concede if we just kept working and let Dad get to the decision on his own.

What we didn't know until a few minutes later was that while Dad was out there, he had slipped on the frozen diving board and the wheelbarrow had dumped to the left, spilling the load right where Rick had suggested, and Dad had quietly endured the incident. He took it as a sort of cosmic, manure-god sign that he should dump for now and wait until spring. Rick's idea had been adopted, and it had become policy in Dad's mind, but he kept it to himself until the final wheelbarrow load was to go out that morning. He nodded toward Rick to take the last load out.

"You'll see where it should go" was all he said to Rick. It was clear to me later that he enjoyed being cryptic about it, about the fact that he had begun the dump-until-spring practice but wanted us to discover this fact on our own.

Rick came back with a smile but remained equally mum, which intrigued me, but it also irritated me a bit. I didn't bother to ask, and instead went to see for myself. I popped my head out of the tiny door to the diving board, the dwarf-like opening in the back of our barn, to see the beginnings of our winter dumping mound, already beginning to freeze. We made quick work of the little bit of manure on the wagon that day, and that marked the end of our winter manure spreading for some time.

The rest of that month and most of the next was frightfully cold, and what started as an emergency solution – to dump manure only occasionally and only on the most severely cold days – instead became our everyday norm. Instead of daily spreading, we piled manure behind the barn, wheelbarrow after wheelbarrow after endless wheelbarrow. It quickly made a mound that we had to traverse, as it completely surrounded the diving board. The only place to take the next wheelbarrow was out over the top of the frozen manure mound, to the edge of it, and dump the new load at the far end of our manmade mountain. We laid boards down for the barrow wheel to ride on, one board after another. We fashioned a path, a sort of frozen manure highway that just kept going – we named it "Route 66."

The construction of Route 66 became an annual practice when the severity of that year's winter settled in. Some particularly cold years the mountain of manure would run for forty feet, topped by our sleek wheelbarrow highway that always made the next wheelbarrow trip possible. Building it was the easy part.

When spring came, when the warm weather finally defrosted Route 66, it had to go. Day after day we'd shovel thawed mounds of pungent manure into our manure spreader, take it to a distant field, and do it again. It was never something that could be accomplished in a single weekend. And on more occasions than I would like to admit, when I was there with my brothers, we proved Dad to be a wise philosopher and sage: "One boy, whole boy. Two boys, half a boy. Three boys, no boy at all…"

Eventually finally, we'd finish. At last we'd take a deep breath, and enjoy the sense having accomplished a big task. The next morning, back inside the barn, we'd be at it again. It was hard work. It never ended. No days off. Ever.

A view of the diving board, wheelbarrow and manure spreader, taken after the farm became inactive. The site of our Route 66.

Chapter 9

Visitors

We were blessed with a steady stream of visitors who brought vitality and enthusiasm that always renewed us and freshened our spirits. They inoculated us against the dreary, sometimes painful isolation of farm living. Energetic visitors came with eager, working hands, and they celebrated the hard labor of the place, bathing themselves in the gratification that can only be found by straining muscles in honest, physical work. Few were tourists.

All were couriers of companionship, bearers of new insights and perspectives, proof and regular reminders that there was a bigger world beyond ours. I waited anxiously for them to arrive and kept my vigil, a dirt road sentinel as I scanned the distance for that cloud of signal dust that heralded an approaching car. I was saddened when our visitors left, saddened to tears at times by the sudden loneliness. Their absence was made that much greater by the enormity of their recent presence. Our visitors weren't temporary or transient wayfarers; rather they were a permanent part of that place and time, part of the farm itself, and like the place, they are in me.

They came to our little remote farm, our isolated simple place, precisely because that's what it was. Relatives and friends flocked there for company, to socialize with the Preeces. Moreover, something deep within them hungered to reconnect with the rightness of simple living, which was disregarded in their suburbia, ignored in their worlds of city office buildings and factories. They came as pilgrims and as visitors to a sort of interactive museum, anxious to engage with beings who carved today's meals from a rocky chunk of earth. They wanted to experience, however briefly, a certain cow's milk on their morning cereal, green beans from our garden or pork chops from the pens in our barn. Some relished the physical work of the farm. Others were more concerned with escaping, not so much being at the farm as not being in the snare of suburban sameness. All were great company. All talked late into the night. With each of them, we planted ourselves on our porch through long summer evenings and gathered around our kitchen table when winter raged beyond our humble door.

Mom and Dad – a lighthearted moment

Part of the attraction was the magic of my mother and father, who were some of the best hosts I ever witnessed. When visitors arrived, Dad came alive in a new way, bursting with unrestrained interest, wanting to know everything there was to know about them, and he rarely took up any time talking about himself. The spotlight was on the visitor exclusively; Dad visited a Labrador-like focus on those who came, and his attentiveness was genuine, something the visitors could sense and which reacquainted people with the fact that they were indeed, truly fascinating. Mom was tireless in her kitchening, and despite the weight of her work, was always able to transform our farmhouse into a sort of comfortable tea parlor, the perfect place to simply sit and chat, privately and unrushed. Unjudged. My parents met people without airs or expectations, showed their raw delight in having company, and without setting out to do it, made visitors feel wonderfully welcome.

Having company, having visitors was the norm for us, not the exception, and it made our place different than most of the farms around us. Our visitors brought ideas, opinions, stories and gifts. But more than that, in their coming, they brought their implications. And inch by inch those implications changed my life. In their coming, I felt a lifeline to a world beyond my own. In their coming, I saw the farm and Cambridge through their eyes as much as through mine. I saw it as a wonderful place which I was temporarily visiting, a transient farmer-boy on his way to somewhere else. I didn't see it so much as a place that entwined with my veins and spoke to my soul, not then. That would come to me only later. I saw it then as a great place to have been to, to have started from, a great place to be leaving from on my way to wherever it was they advised I go next. They voiced their suggestions, many of them. Some even tried to press me into service as surrogate, insisting that I lead the life they wished they had led. Others were more selfless. All were filled with good intentions.

But the words not spoken rattled my ears far more than ones that were. The words not spoken shouted to me through each of them, through the example of their lives and their visits. They shouted to me that there were endless possibilities, that anything was possible, that the world beyond mine was a wondrous one, just waiting for me. Our visitors arrived like well-tooled tinkerers, who repeatedly reshaped the lens in my life's telescope and constantly tweaked my compass dial. They made mine always a bit different than the navigational tools of people around me, which made me different than my friends in ways I wanted to be and in ways I hated. They didn't do this in secret or somehow against my will. Rather, I ran wholeheartedly to our visitors, attracted by parts of them that I wanted to make my own. I brought my scope and compass to them and opened the guts of the things, asked them to change my bearings with their talents and their tools of perspective. Tinkerers together.

Lord of the Battenkill

(My age: 39)

Dan McPeek was Dad's best buddy from the Navy, a shipmate who was with him when Dad went into the salty Pacific off Okinawa in 1945. Dad was riddled with shrapnel after a kamikaze attack. Dan helped as another sailor fished Dad out of the water and carried him across the gun tub, lugged his limp body to Sick Bay, where they brought him back from the edge of death. Dan came to the farm every year, and my father was thrilled about each visit. Because Dan was mechanically inclined, because he had a knack for engineering and project management, and because my father found these things positively baffling, our greatest, most ambitious projects were always planned around Dan McPeek's visits. My father thought of Dan as an absolute mechanical wizard, perceiving him as some affable, bearded sage with a cone shaped hat marked with crescent moons, holding in one hand a wand with a star on the end of it, and in the other a wrench. Dan McPeek, in my dad's mind, was a magician, a genius seer and marvelous mystic of all things mechanical.

We built a milkhouse, poured concrete, ran electrical lines, built sheds and oil tank storage systems, reclaimed swamplands, repositioned gates, redesigned plumbing, constructed stanchions, dug ponds, hayed our largest fields, built a swing and baseball backstop, removed massive trees and tore down barns – all scheduled around Dan McPeek's visits. To my father, Dan was Frank Lloyd Wright, Andrew Carnegie, Leonardo DaVinci and a marvelous, permanent friend, all rolled into one.

To me, he was a wonderful man, but more importantly, he was always my ticket to a fabulous fishing trip.

It hit me as soon as I parked the car and opened the door. The distinctive smell of the Battenkill River rushed forth and welcomed me back. It engulfed me at once and danced its delicious greeting. Clear, cold water cruised smoothly over the modest dam before us, spilled and churned with the August air around it. The shallow, rocky-bottomed, trout-filled river sent off an unmistakable, tasty mist that made gentle love to my nose. The vaporous air was clean and cool, filled with the earthy smell of moss-covered rocks and the sweet, patient decay of maples and elms. It carried hints of the ripe, green slime that makes camp where water meets granite, where river water ebbs and flows and gives life to delicate lichens, where damp air lilts along with musty mushroom spores.

The gentle, endless, soft spill of the river filled my ears. The falls were only a few feet in depth, and the flow was pleasant. But the falls were fifty yards wide, and compounded only by width, the easy, tender roar reverberated off the steep bank that rose up on the far side of the river. The result was mellow and pleasant, a muted, life-filled rumble, soft on my ears, and perfect mood music for the sights and smells that accompanied it.

Site of our fishing expeditions on the Battenkill

"Is this the place, Dad?" Brian asked. He was ten, the oldest of my three children. Andy was eight and Beth five. They were here with me and my wife, Sue. We had come to see a few old friends, to revisit Cambridge, to experience the Washington County Fair.

The quest was mine, really. I wanted to share it all with my wife and kids, of course. I wanted them to see and feel what I did when I was a kid. But I also wanted to grasp it back for myself, to recapture some of those lost days of my youth. I wanted to relive nuggets of my childhood fishing junkets here with Dan McPeek and re-experience those sublime summer moments on this pastoral patch of river.

Fishing expeditions with Dan were always to this exact same place, and they were glorious times in my youth. Those half-day excursions were filled with natural wonders and were always abundant with fish. This spot was my Yellowstone, my Niagara Falls, and I came as Daniel Boone and Mark Twain, as outdoorsman, riverman. I remembered hauling in feisty bass and sweet little trout, plucking countless bluegills from this spectacular river. As kids we were delirious with our fishing success, and our fishing trips to this river positively thrilled me. I wanted to do the same today, to again be a little boy on the Battenkill, to feel the thrill of fish on my line as Battenkill water sloshed through my sneakers. I wanted to haul the fish in and bring that work of living art close to me, to catch glorious glimpses of my hooked fish, flashing streaks of silver in the water near me.

Dan was an avid trout fisherman and he loved that beautiful river. To me, he was the Fisherman King, the Lord of the Battenkill. He was endless in his patience with us kids. Dan helped us with every conceivable part of the fishing experience, from prepping poles and digging worms, to untangling lines, to attaching lures, to hooking worms and removing fish. It is a wonder there was any time left for him to fish for himself.

"Yes, this is the place, Brian," I replied a bit absentmindedly, preoccupied with the nostalgia that washed over me upon seeing the old, familiar scene for the first time in almost thirty years. "Not much has changed... I think you're going to catch a few fish today, buddy."

We unpacked the poles and bait, the cooler with our sandwiches and sodas, and a few towels to dry our inevitable plunges into knee deep river water. I could tell that Brian was anxious to get to it, excited about fishing. But the others seemed listless. They had grown tired of my prattling on about the beautiful Battenkill and the bounty of fish I had promised. My guarantees carried little weight with them when it came to fishing, as I had failed to deliver against earlier promises, Ohio promises.

I had fished the region around our Cincinnati home and occasionally had successes here or there. But I could not reproduce hook-hungry fish when I came back, when I dragged my reluctant family to river spots or lakesides that had been fruitful the day before. I ordered my gang once to the banks of the Little Miami, an Ohio River tributary, where fish bit hungrily the day before. But the poor kids only endured hours of sweltering heat and unrelenting mosquitoes, fishless. They suffered the further insult of retrieving their lines, time after time, still laden with fat bait. Whatever fish were there couldn't even be bothered to steal a worm from the kids, to send the hook back empty, to tease the novices with their presence, and at least thereby make themselves known. They were gone. It was as if, overnight, the fish had evolved into quadrupeds and had walked right out of the river, abandoned it for some high hillside meadow. I did not blame my kids for doubting me, for doubting they'd catch any fish that day.

"It's pretty," said Sue, making an effort to keep things upbeat, and noting the hardwoods that rimmed the little river valley with green. Upstream there was still a steamy, morning fog that lifted off that perfectly glassy patch of river.

"It is," I agreed. "I wish you could see it in October when the leaves are changing." I thought of how the river took on the color of the sky. When fall colors were at their peak and when fortune provided a clear blue sky, the scene was so perfect that it looked artificial. It conjured up the thought that nothing in real life, nothing so completely natural, so completely unaided by man could be so beautiful, so colorful, so pleasing to the human eye.

We made our way toward the concrete bulwark that marked the near edge of the dam that formed the falls, and we walked along the crest of the thing until we reached the lower section of the river. The concrete structure seemed so much smaller to me now, thirty years later. The abutment presented itself today as just an average thing, a normal retaining wall, completely unremarkable. But as a kid, when I was the age of my own kids who were with me on this day, that wall was a colossus. It was, for me, a Sphinx guarding entrance to the Nile, to our own Angel Falls. It was a forbidding guardian, a sentinel of mammoth proportions, and it marked the very edge of a remote, watery wilderness.

"Whooah," said Beth as she traversed the thing, tentative with each step, her anxiety apparent. "This is high, Daddy… I'm a little scared." She inched along with great care, her eyes fixed on the sloping concrete leviathan beneath her. I took her hand and she clung close.

"That's where we're headed, Beth" I said, pointing to the granite outcropping twenty yards in front of us, hoping to give her some comfort. We stopped so she could fix her eyes there without having to walk on what felt to her like a concrete precipice. I could see her taking in the narrow section of river that separated us from the fishing spot.

"How are we going to get across that?" She was frightened by the prospect of crossing the rocky stream. It looked bigger to her than to me, rougher and more dangerous.

"We're going to have to cross *that*?" Andy interjected, disbelieving and concerned as he eyed the rush of water. "That water's moving pretty fast. What if we fall in?" He had raised his voice to be heard over the rumbling roar of the falls which filled his ears and made the river appear somewhat furious to him.

"It's okay," I assured him. "We'll take our time and be safe, and I'll help each person across. We'll go one at a time."

We got to the end of the concrete abutment and I stepped down, finally stood on smooth, rounded river rocks that marked the area of Battenkill flow. I was here again, a boy at the Battenkill.

"Dad, can you help me down?" It was Brian, ready to go but a little intimidated by the height of the drop, uncertain whether he could safely jump down by himself.

"Sure!" I answered and lifted him down. Andy came next and then Sue helped Beth down. I was still helping Andy get comfortable on the slippery shore rocks when Brian yelped from ten yards away, having crossed part way through the flowing water, trying to reach the granite on the other side that was our fishing destination.

"Dad! Yikes!" He had slid off one slime-covered rock and was shin-deep in river water. I could see he was safe, that he simply needed to take a few more soggy steps and he would arrive. But the rocks were slippery and Brian's face showed a trace of fear. I could sense his anxiety as he held his pole high over his head and nervously searched the flowing water for a place to take his next step. Each watery hole, being black with slices of rushing river, was unfamiliar to him and so each suggested potential danger. Yet I knew what he couldn't know, that every spot was only inches deep and harmless.

I walked atop dry rocks to Brian and then led the way from there, deliberately stepping in watery holes as a way of demonstrating for the kids that the dark holes need not be feared and that getting wet was part of Battenkill-ing, even something to be embraced. Andy plunged his way along and Sue took Beth's hand as they sloshed ahead. One by one we reached the broad, dry granite rock at the edge of our little island. I studied their faces briefly, and I saw signs that their comfort level was growing and even perceived the subtle signals of new enthusiasm.

Just as the last of us arrived on our granite fishing platform, Brian tangled his fishing line around a scrubby, wild berry bush among the trees. I helped him clear the line and showed him how to carry his pole to avoid future entanglements. He immediately applied the lesson and finessed his line around the next bushy hazard. Meanwhile, I rigged up Andy and Beth with hooks and bobbers and bait. They plopped their lines into the river while I talked Brian through the process of baiting his own hook with a worm. Sue got the cooler situated and pulled the camera out of a small daypack to capture the scene.

The fish catching frenzy started immediately.

"I GOT ONE!" Andy was nearly beside himself with delight. His eyes were large and he was singly focused, fixed on his red and white bobber that had been yanked a few inches under water.

"Reel him in, Andy!" I shouted, excited for him.

"He's right here!" Andy took a step back, thrilled with having hooked his fish, but not yet wanting to be up close and personal with the thing, not sure what to do now that the fish was only three feet away. "Look at him – there he is!" He kept both hands on the pulsing pole as he nodded to the quick little bluegill that darted in the water.

"AAGHHH! I've got one, Daddy. I've got one too!" I could tell from Beth's line that she had a bass, as it was jerking furiously and the tip of the pole was bent far over. She was hanging on tight, and I could see she was determined. Beth was on dry granite with plenty of foot room and leaned against a large log for stability.

"Hold on, Baby-D!" I shouted to her, using her nickname as a way to provide the encouragement I knew a five year old with a small bass on the line would need. Knowing she'd be fine for a few moments, I scrambled to Andy and held his line, then lifted his bluegill out of the water while Andy's eyes popped further, and Sue clapped and cheered her applause.

"Wait, let me get a shot. First fish of the day!" Sue said, as she navigated over slimy rocks to get into position to snap a photo with a Battenkill background. Andy was happy to hold the line, but reluctant to handle the bluegill, so I did the handling for him and talked him through my steps, teaching him how to handle a fish and unhook and release it back into the river.

"Dad! Help!" Beth was still fighting the bass and the feisty little fellow still had plenty of energy. She had done well to hang in there with this underwater bronco.

I made my way toward Beth, but before I got there yet another fish tore into an underwater worm attached to hook and bobber. "GOT ONE, DAD!" Brian barked.

"Way to go, Brian!" I shouted back as I helped Beth turn the crank on her reel, pulling the fighter closer to us. Beth was thrilled and let out an involuntary scream of delight, "Yeeeeahhh!" She looked at me and smiled one of those genuine-joy smiles that only kids can smile, unpretentious and unfiltered, raw and pure, and fiercely jubilant.

I handled her bass and after a photo, we sent it back to its river home. She wanted no part of fish handling but was quick to thrust her hand into the can of worms and bait her hook so she could do it all over again. I helped her by casting her line to a likely spot. A fish bit immediately and took the bobber under, but I acted like it didn't happen, said nothing, and handed Beth the pole. A few short seconds later she screeched again in triumph.

I talked Brian through the landing and handling of his elegant little rainbow trout, and we marveled at its beauty, a living canvas painted in pale pinks, soft yellows and gentle turquoise-blues under speckles of deep brown.

We spent the next hour doing more of the same. The kids tried different areas, and I taught them how to cast so that the river floated their tackle to the places they wanted to reach. This new skill opened up possibilities for them and they began to roam the river's spots more freely. Along the way, we all got soaked to one degree or another, but it didn't seem to matter. A wet tumble, which earlier might have caused great distress, was now mere inconvenience.

After an hour we broke for the brunch we had packed. I grabbed a towel for each of the kids and we made our way to our rustic riverside lunchroom which Sue had prepared so nicely. We sat on a mossy clump of a cushion that welcomed us to a more intimate connection with the granite mound, surrounded by white driftwood that had washed up to the spot during the spring thaw. As we did, I stole a few glances toward the kids, watched them in secret and noted that they were taking in this scene of river falls and granite clumps, scattered like icebergs amongst the churning flows of fish-filled waters. They saw the beauty of the place, they were appreciating it, I could tell. The sun was well up now, and it dried our pant legs and the wet seats that had fallen into the river. The falls rumbled on in the background.

Lifting a bass from the Battenkill for Beth

We wolfed down our brunch of sandwiches, donuts and apples that we consumed together, seated as family, as if we were around the dining room table.

"This is awesome!" Beth offered. "I caught my first fish ever!"

"Did you see that bass I got?" Andy chimed in. "That guy was fighting so hard I was afraid he would break the line!" His face radiated a warm, summer glow that was contagious.

"You guys are doing great," Sue said. "This place is amazing."

"I want to try over by that big log. Is that okay, Dad?" Brian pointed to a large, bleached out log that hung out a few inches over the bubbling water, close to the falls area.

"Sure, but we'll have to be careful," I replied.

For two more hours the kids fished. Sue gathered up our things and took photos and cheered them on. And I did what Dan McPeek did for me and my brothers thirty years ago. I untangled lines, and baited hooks. I offered guidance and encouragement and occasionally provided instruction. I lifted fish from this beautiful little river and squatted low for photos, holding live trophies in front of thrilled children with fishing poles in their hands. I suggested that a line be cast here or there and watched hopefully. I bathed myself in the delight of children as they felt a surge in their line, saw their bobber pop and lunge in the water, and reeled glory toward themselves. I had no time to fish for myself, no time to recapture those boyhood days with a pole in my hand and a trout on the line. I no longer wanted to. I was no longer a boy on the Battenkill. I was, on this day and for my children, a Fisherman King.

I finally came to see this beautiful little river and this glorious fishing hole of my youth as Dan McPeek must have seen it three decades ago. I drank in the smells again, feasted my eyes, and felt my soul confirm that this was perfection – the way things are supposed to be. I marveled at the magic of childhood and the power of place, at how this simple fishing trip was, in my kid's minds, an adventure into the rugged, glorious wilderness. I was struck at how this river, for them, was a faraway, exotic, wondrous place. I could tell it would become for them a place of their dreams, just as it had been for me. I came on this day to fish and recapture perfect pieces of the past. I caught those pieces but not in the way I had expected. I caught them because my children caught them for me. I realized that I had become my kids' version of a Battenkill Lord, and in that moment, I was one with Dan McPeek. I stood in the shallows and again felt the Battenkill sloshing through my sneakers. I saw it all through Dan's soft eyes, and that made my own eyes watery with appreciation.

Thank you, Dan McPeek, for having brought me here. Thank you for introducing me to the world of fishing and to the banks of the Battenkill, the sweetest, most glorious little river I have ever seen. Most of all, thank you for being so selfless, and for introducing me, thirty years later, to the joys of fishing with children. You will always be my Fisherman King, my Lord of the Battenkill.

Dan McPeek, Lord of the Battenkill, and me, 2009

Gentleman Jim, Tractor Thief

(My age: 6)

He had been just one day away from being ordained as a Catholic priest. He took seriously the idea that the priesthood was a calling, and because he ultimately felt called elsewhere, he walked away from the starched white collar and the way of life it required. The St. Bonaventure graduate and fully seasoned seminarian would have made a fantastic priest. In the end, he was true to his discernment of the spirit and lived a life full of integrity and good example. He brought people to faith in a different way, but he did it nevertheless. My Uncle Jim Duffy, my godfather (and later, my wife's godfather), was one of the finest men I have ever known.

He was tall and big-chested, broad shouldered and handsome. He was a serious professional and a civic-minded man who ran for local office and won elections with overwhelming margins. He always did the right thing, stayed on the high road, even when politics got nasty. "Gentleman Jim" the newspaper called him. He knew the Connecticut State Troopers and city council members, rubbed elbows comfortably with the men in suits in the boardroom and the guys on the shop floor. Uncle Jim wore a necktie, every day – even at home, even on Saturdays. The only exception I know of is when he visited the farm, when he wore tee shirts and khakis and sturdy work shoes. He kept them at the farm, permanently. My mom would launder them after he'd leave, and she'd fold them neatly and place them in our attic, where Jim, expressing much appreciation, would retrieve them upon his next visit. He was steady and easy going, clear minded, certain of his values, and not afraid to roll up his sleeves. Jim was a statesman, a quality guy, and he was authentic.

He was also a relentless teaser.

To be teased by Jim was to know that he liked you. It was his love language, and it was the love language within most of my family. To have Jim yank your chain was an unmistakable sign of his affection, a clear statement that shouted his approval. We all wanted to be his target. One summer day I was just that, his clear target, and I'll never forget it.

The Duffys had been visiting for a few days and were now packing their Ford station wagon for the trip home.

Dad and Rick on the Ford 8N tractor

It was high haying season, and I was a youngster of six, too young to really do any work, but old enough to go the fields with Dad and ride on the tractor with him as he cut hay or loaded bales onto the wagon. I was very much aware of farming, very much around farming, but not yet a direct participant. I knew all about it, though, or at least thought I did. At least I knew that the tractor was the core of farm machinery, that it was the essential centerpiece. I knew that without that tractor, nothing could be done, that all would come to a stop. And it was clear that Jim Duffy thought our little tractor was fabulous.

"Nice little tractor, Don, niiiiice" he said after he drove it into the barn earlier that morning. I was standing next to it as he rolled it in and jerked it to a stop, too sudden in his braking. I could smell the exhaust and feel the warmth of the thing as it radiated the heat it had collected while out in the bright sunlight. "That's a real sweetie, that one is. Nice cornering, smooth engine, plenty of power, Donny. Plenty of power. I really like this baby." And the day before, when he had been driving it in the hay field, he gave a long cat-call of a whistle, and declared it "the perfect machine, just the thing to make any farm really hum." I thought he liked it too much.

"Yessiree!" he declared when he was backing the thing up to the manure spreader the previous night, and he gunned the engine for show which I thought was unnecessary and a crime of tractor abuse. "I feel like I'm one with this dream of a machine! I can just think left and it goes left. It's like it was made just for me, Donny." I didn't like that he called my dad 'Donny'. I sensed he was manipulating Dad somehow, sweet-talking him. I was disappointed that Dad didn't seem to mind or notice that Jim was up to something, and I worried he was about to get duped. I wanted Jim to remember it was our tractor and it belonged to my father, wanted him to respect that more. "Um-hmm! This is what a farm needs!" He was pouring it on thick.

Jim had been going on all weekend about "his own sweetheart of a farm" in Milford, Connecticut. I had been to Jim's house. It was a small, neat as a pin place, right in the thick of the suburbs, near the city and nearer to dozens of other semi-urban houses. I had played wiffle ball in his back yard, which was small and tidy, just big enough for a six year old to play ball in. Bobby Shea lived next door and came over to play with me and my cousins. That helped because the yards were small, and the ball often went into Bobby's back yard, so his playing legitimized our frequent trespasses to the Shea's property, trim and compact as it was. There was no way Jim could have a farm at his place; it was just too small.

"Yeah, I'm hoping to expand the place – expand my farm, ya know," Jim now declared to my Dad, as they both stood in front of me. Jim was speaking at Dad, but really to me, indirectly. "Been thinking about buying Shea's, ya know, a way to stretch my property out for more crops and some pastureland." Shea's plot of land was tiny. I knew it wasn't enough to make a real farmer's field. I thought to myself that this guy, my uncle, didn't know what he was doing, didn't know what he was talking about when it came to farming.

"Oh," said Dad in reply. "Planning on cows?"

"Yep. Milk's the thing down there, Don," said Jim. "Got a contract with the school system. Greased the palms of the state boys and scratched their backs – told 'em now they had to scratch mine. Six thousand cartons of milk a day for the kids in school. Contract's all mine, Donny, aaaalllll mine. Five cows out to get that done. Going to put a barn in the back yard, put the rest of it to corn."

I was dumbfounded. I had no idea how much milk went into six thousand cartons, but I knew five cows wouldn't come close to getting the job done. He's nuts, I thought to myself. I also knew that "greasing palms" wasn't honest, that bribes were wrong, and hearing his pompous claim of ill-gotten gains made me angry inside. And "put rest of it to corn'?! What, the twenty square feet of it?!

"Got a few cows now, do you?" asked Dad, who seemed to be showing real interest. This alone irritated me further. Why would Dad entertain this crazy conversation? Why didn't he tell Jim that he didn't know what he was doing? That any farm that could possibly fit in his postage stamp of a yard wouldn't be big enough to produce anything. This was insane!

"Yeah, three. An Ayrshire, a Holstein, and one Angus. Angus gives the most milk of the herd. I keep them in the basement for now. Got a small field of oats down there, too. I like the idea of the field inside because I don't have to go out there in the hot sun or the cold winter; it's just better that way." Jim tipped his nose up as he said this, stated it with confidence and arrogance, with a sense that seemed to suggest he knew more about farming than my dad did, and that really irked me. I'd been in Jim's basement and so had Dad. It was far too small, ridiculously small for a field or for stabling cows! And I knew an Angus was a beef cow, not a good milker – and 'herd'?! THREE cows made a 'herd' for this crackpot?!

Uncle Jim (L) and Dad (R) with the Ford 8N, "one sweet machine"

"Hmmm, I see." Dad was agreeing with this buffoon! What was he thinking?

"Yeah, I need the tractor for a while, Donny. Not long. Maybe a month or two. I'll have it back by September…"

September!? This madman was going to borrow our tractor for MONTHS?! Was he crazy? This was out of the question. Absurd! September? He had to be stopped. If he took the tractor, our own farm would be brought a standstill. I was beginning to panic.

"Gee, we'll probably need it before then" Dad said, thankfully. I was finally relieved to hear my Dad stand up to this whack job of a wannabe farmer. Field in his basement!

"Okay, Don. Okay – I'll have it back before September."

"Sorry, Jim. Can't do it – we just need the thing is all."

With that Dad shook Jim's hand and wished him safe travels back home. Dad promptly pivoted and headed for the barn, said he had manure to clean out.

Jim stood with his arms folded across his broad chest and waited for my dad to enter the barn. "He'll never miss it," Jim said out loud, seemingly to nobody. He headed straight for the tractor, which was parked in the barnyard. He got on and started the engine. It rumbled to life, shot a soft puff of dark exhaust out the back and then hummed at an easy idle while he checked the gas level in the tank.

"A little low for the trip to Milford" he muttered thoughtfully to himself, yet loud enough so I could hear. "Maybe I should top it off… nah, I'll just tow the thing."

I was beside myself. I was coming unglued. I was witnessing this man steal our tractor! Not only that, but he was stealing it in order to work on his ridiculous farm in his ridiculous basement! All because he cheated to get some milk contract that he could never fulfill with five cows – which he still didn't even own! I felt dizzy, panic-stricken and alarmed. This whole thing was outrageous!

Jim Duffy put our grey and red Ford 8N tractor in gear and drove it right up to his station wagon's back bumper. He gunned the tractor's engine again, which further infuriated me. He was going to tow the thing to Connecticut! Then he was chaining it to the car. The chains clanged loudly as he flopped them over the tractor's front axle, as they thudded, heavy on the dirt road beneath his bumper. I nearly peed my pants! I *had* to stop this!

"Nooo!" I finally howled. The words came gushing, "YouCant'tTakeThatTractorrrr!!!!!" I was running at him now, furious and determined. "Stoppp!"

Just before I got there, just before tears started to pour out, Jim Duffy smiled and winked and promised he wouldn't do it.

"Okay, okay. If you really feel that way, well, okay then, I'll leave it here."

"I *do*. I *do* feel that way! That's *our* tractor and you can't take it to your stupid farm!"

I could tell by the explosions of laughter all around me that I had been duped and that flustered me more, brought tears welling up, but I fought them back, choked them down. In my zeal to keep Dad from being bamboozled, I was blinded to the fact that I was the target. I was angry and embarrassed. Yet, at the same time, I was so very relieved. Our beloved tractor would be staying; my uncle was indeed not a thief; and this stressful gag was over.

"Come here," Jim said softly, easing me with a large, protective hand on my shoulder.

Jim helped me up into the tractor seat and unchained it from his bumper, then slipped into the seat behind me. We drove our little Ford tractor back to the barn, and he let me steer the whole way, thanked me for the help with driving and promised he'd never take the thing again.

"You don't really have a farm, do you, Uncle Jim?" I asked him, hoping to confirm my understanding of the whole charade.

"No farm, Gerry. Not a single cow or a single stalk of corn – and no milk contract, either. *This* is the place for a farm, not down there." His smile was big and almost apologetic.

"Good" I said. "When are you coming back, Uncle Jim?"

He smiled again. "September. Got to help you and your Dad with the corn."

Dad had appeared near the car once again and was smiling at the whole episode, amused by Jim and me, tickled by the teasing. It made me smile, and in the relief of it all, I coughed up an involuntary gulp of a laugh from down deep. It felt good, and it finally allowed me to join the whole gang in one last round of collective laughter.

I looked up at Jim as we said our good-bye's. For the first time, I saw - and felt - the playful twinkle in Jim Duffy's eyes that told me he loved me and that told me his teasing was a rite of passage I had somehow earned. It was a wonderful feeling and it lifted me high. Gentleman Jim had gotten my goat, and it made me love him all the more.

Frank Seymour

The Brotherhood Meets at the Storm Soaked Gridiron

(My age: 10)

Dad sat alone in our little, white '62 Rambler station wagon, watching the end of Cambridge High's football practice as the September rain pounded down fiercely. Daylight was fading. It had been raining all day, and it had produced an earthy, leafy, fall smell that pleased and cooled the nose, a cozy, chilled, organic perfume that that came up from the mud below and hinted at the coming of winter. He turned on the engine and started the heater as the flying beads of furious rain rattled the car and thundered on the roof.

Practice would be over soon, and my brother Rick, now a freshman on the team, would be out of the showers and they'd be on their way back to the farm. Dad still had milking to do, and he needed Rick there to help with an unruly cow that required extra handling. The heat in the car began to loosen the pungent scent of cows that was embedded in his jacket and the traces of barnyard muck that lingered on his work shoes. The rain kept pounding as Dad lit a Viceroy cigarette in his dry cocoon of newfound warmth.

As he waited and watched through the cascade of water running over the windshield, Dad's mind drifted off. The blurry scene in front of him was soft and dreamlike. The vibrant colors of football uniforms, abstract splotches through the current of water, were set against pale, distant hills. Indistinct voices and the occasional popping of pads were interrupted by coaches' whistles, muffled through the steadily drumming rain. In his daydream, he thought of his own football playing days, and how wonderful sports were for boys. He was grateful that his boys would have the chance to play. He felt the concept, perceived the idea more than "thought" it:

Nothing can touch a boy's life quite like the experience of sports. It shapes a place in the boy's very heart and it helps settle the jumbling of teen turbulence, eases the confounding befuddlement of adolescence, helps clear the foggy veil that obscures self. The teenage boy has no idea who he is. Sports can give him part of the answer, even before he knows it's a question. The teenage boy's head is full of unsolicited advice, loaded with "should's," overwhelmed by bewildering possibilities, and he is on fire with hormones that prevent him from even acknowledging any of these things. At the same time, he lacks the life machinery to process these messes, to

work his way through them and find answers. The machinery will not arrive until much later. The boy is there, still in charge, but he is leaving. The man is at the doorstep but has not yet arrived. The boy is still "becoming."

It is against this backdrop that sports work their magic. It is here that sports thrust answers into the boy's lap. Coaches and teammates and scoreboards tell him who he is and where he fits in. His own experience on the field or the court makes it even more clear what his strengths are and where he is weak. It points out where he has failed in courage and where he can soar beyond anything he thought himself capable of.

The sport itself does this by speaking the teenage boy's own language, his native tongue. It is a language marked not by words, not by vowels and verbs. It is a language of the body, a completely physical language that the boy feels rather than hears. He senses it as he dodges and deceives a competitor in the open field, feels it in the burn of his legs, fully spent, when he is outrun by another player. He feels it in his fingertips when he fumbles a ball, and in his shoulder when he makes the perfect tackle. The boy's fingers talk to his soul when the bat he holds strikes the ball solidly, and when he is off the mark. His chest feels the message when he sacrifices his body for team. The teenager's body hears what his ears cannot. His body **is** his ear, and it hears what the sport tells him about who he is. In this way, sport shapes the boy, settles and clarifies some of life for him.

Sport helps him meet himself, allows him to gain some early comfort with who he is, and sends him more confidently toward the door, where he can usher in the man he will become.

"Hey, that kid of yours ought to be a guard! I don't know what the heck they're doing with him as a darned wingback – he aint no wingback! Geez!" The straightforward voice erupted forth from a short, squarely built man that appeared out of nowhere and had yanked open the Rambler's passenger door, barged into the seat, and slammed the door behind him, leaving the rainy mayhem behind. He had started talking at Dad before he even had the door fully open. The intruder was unapologetic, composed, matter-of-fact in both his speech and his eye contact. He wore a wool newsboy cap back far on his forehead in a way that showed his full face, round and honest. Dad, was reeling inside, struggling to recover from his daydream. He had never seen the man before.

"They got whatchyacallit at guard now, over on the right side there, but that kid's only gonna be there one more year and they otta be gettin' another one ready – play him on the left side so's he can learn the system and he'll be ready for next year on the right – most important position on the team. That's where they ought to put Ricky." Dad was still dumbfounded, completely taken aback, off kilter and unsure how to respond.

Who the heck is this guy? What is he doing in my car? How does he know my son? Dad thought to himself, still spellbound. And yet he found himself already liking this man, already felt the earliest bonds connecting them. This oracle stranger, whoever he was, was right: Rick should be a guard, Dad agreed. Dad instinctively liked the man, though he couldn't fix in his mind why. Liked him without even knowing his name, without saying a word, without even a 'hello.'

Dad had met Frank Seymour.

* * * * * *

High school football shaped my Dad and shaped Frank Seymour, too. Dad was undersized but tough, full of heart and courage, and through football he learned of the incredible power of determination. It defined who he was forever. One of his old Shelton High teammates would often visit the farm. He would sit on our front porch on summer nights and tell tales of Dad's long ago fierceness and outright willpower as a player – still telling Dad who he was, decades later.

Frank was shaped by captaining a team that made an incredible second half comeback, a historic and legendary final drive that earned his team a league championship, and for which he is still remembered today. Frank believes he can win anything, no matter what the odds. It is not a wish or a hope, but a profound conviction that was etched deep within him fifty years before on a high school football field in Whitehall, New York.

Dad and Frank both played the position of guard.

They both were in love with the role of that player, the guard, as it not only shaped them – in a certain sense it *was* them. So, when Frank burst through the rain and stormed into Dad's car suggesting Rick should be a guard, he spoke to something deep and enduring in my father, something permanent and fixed, something at Dad's core. It was more than the fact that Dad had agreed with Frank's declarations; it was bigger than the facts about Rick's physical capabilities, talent and aptitude. It was that on that rainy day in September of 1966, Frank and he immediately became kindred souls, bonded in the brotherhood of football guards.

Over the next ten years Frank Seymour and his family became regulars at the farm, visiting often. They were wonderful friends. Frank proved to be as selfless a man as I have ever met, and he had the self-assurance to walk up to anybody anytime and say anything that was on his mind. He gave me a 1950 Ford pickup truck when I was in high school. Gave it to me. No strings. No brakes, either, but they were fixable, and I was soon in great shape – a high schooler with his own wheels, which was a rare thing in those days. A few years later I sold it, but the adolescent me failed to recognize the real value of the thing, and I let it go for a paltry price. Down deep, I know it hurt Frank, but he never said it. My blunder quietly torments me still.

Frank donated property and secured pole lighting and built a ball field, giving Cambridge and her kids the gift of a Little League program, the first in the area. He appropriated pole lights, built dugouts, harangued others and garnered support. And never told a soul where any of it came from; he never took credit. He conspired with a few other Cambridge residents to give selflessly, and he did it all the time.

Beyond that, Frank was a part of our personal lives, made himself that as he barged into our teenage lives like he did with Dad in that rain-riddled parking lot. And we loved him for it. As teens we complained loudly of his forwardness and pretended to find offense with it, but down deep we loved that somebody cared and that somebody was paying attention to us. As the years went by, his house in Cambridge became a second home for us kids, a safe and welcoming place we could go to whenever we needed. It was a great place to watch a college football game (Frank had color television!), or to wait out a winter storm while we tried to make our way home to the farm after practice. Frank, being remarkably social, was "in the know" and heard things, picked up every rumor and every nugget of knowledge about the town's people. He'd hear things about me that my parents wouldn't hear, and he would then pull me aside, get in my face a bit and challenge me on some misbehavior, call me a "punkinhead," and he was right. But the bigger thing was that he never went to my mom and dad with these things. In a sense, Frank was a self-appointed third parent, and he handled behavioral issues in private, kept things "in the family" so to speak.

I loved that about Frank, and so did others, like Dad and my brother Casey.

An Arctic Rescue - All in the Family

(My age: 21)

One cold, winter night in February of 1977, my brother Casey, a high school senior, had use of the family car to drive himself to and from a friend's party in rural Center Cambridge. Two days earlier, he had received word that he had been accepted at West Point, so Casey was celebrating that special elation and relief a teen feels when fog lifts and the future finally appears in clear view. He'd be the third of the Preece boys to go the Academy, and at long last he was on his way. On top of that, he had the car for the night and a relaxed curfew of midnight, both gifts of lenience for the soon-to-be-cadet, a signal that parents were letting go and giving him his much desired space. He was feeling large.

Casey arrived at the party and was greeted by all with hearty hoots and congratulations which only made him feel bigger. He soon discovered that David, a friend who lived in the village, needed a ride to get there. He was considering picking David up, giving him a lift when word came that the food was almost gone, a near crisis among his classmate partiers. So Casey, large with a car and a future, seized the chance to save the day and headed for David and a fresh supply of pizza.

Snow was and is a part of life there, and it was everywhere in the winter months. Wise drivers adjusted their driving accordingly. Casey was not yet a wise driver. He was inexperienced and overconfident. He flew too fast over Center Cambridge Road, the beneficiary of luck, not skill. The fact that he arrived at David's without incident convinced his subconscious that he was a master of the road, just as he was now master of his future. David already had the pizzas, and Casey chauffeured David and their delicious smelling cargo back to the party, too fast again on that same road. Luck worked for him one more time, as all went well. In a special way, Casey enjoyed the reality of life on that night, took it in with singular awareness, a rare teenage experience. He felt on top of the world, and didn't want to miss a moment of that feeling, which he had learned was fleeting.

Soon it was past midnight, past his curfew, but he didn't yet have the self discipline to abide by that parental rule. He knew he'd be punished, but he expected a reduced sentence given his West Point ticket, still newly minted and fresh with the rich scent of printer's ink. So he hurried David home and flew along the same road yet again. As before the trip was without incident, the car gripped the icy, snowy road as it had no right to, telling him one final lie.

At 1:00 a.m. he finally headed for home, pressing speed even more as he wanted to minimize the damages due to his curfew violation. Physics caught up with him on this trip. Physics overpowered luck. His tires finally lost their grip and slipped along the ice, slid along the snow that covered the road, and the Oldsmobile F85 headed for the deep snow bank on the side of Center Cambridge Road, ignoring the curve of the asphalt. A body in motion tends to stay in motion...

Casey's eyes widened as his universe seemed to slow to a crawl, as the car began its gradual, unstoppable whirl to the left, smooth and steady as a gentle dance, still carrying far too much forward speed to be stopped by the snow bank at the side of the road, which was approaching relentlessly, steadily, inescapably. He watched the headlights illuminate scenery as if they were lightly twirling spotlights searching the landscape. Everything was utterly quiet. The only sound was that of the gliding tires which gave off the gentlest "uusshhh." He even had time to acknowledge the smell of the remaining pizza that sat in the passenger's seat and wondered to himself how about how it would go flying, how badly it would collide with some part of the car's interior and what kind of mess it would soon be making.

He hit the snow bank head on, and the burst of noise brought everything back to real speed. Everything suddenly felt wildly chaotic and loud, and frightfully rough and dangerous. It all happened so very fast. The shock from the snow bank shuddered through the car and through Casey and jolted him hard. Snow exploded in front of the car as a monstrous wave of white washed over the windshield, furious and close in the crazed headlights.

Still rattled from the impact, the car flew, airborne, ten feet into the field. The snow was so deep that the landing wasn't harsh; it made everything mushy and sluggish and it gave out a loud "puumphh" as the car walloped down. It finally plowed to a stop, came to rest on a cushion of waist-deep snow, thirty feet from the road. Once again, there was complete silence. Casey was shaken but uninjured. He rammed the door through heavy snow several times before he could exit, but finally got out of the thing and circled it, looking for damage. His legs plunged crotch-deep with every step. He couldn't find any dents, but the car was half submerged, like a half-sunken vessel in a harbor, resting too deep in the water, gently buoyed by silt and sand against her hull.

He made his way to a tiny house nearby, a humble ramshackle of a place, knocked persistently and finally woke the inhabitants. A dingy, yellow naked bulb came on just inches above Casey's head.

"Eh?" from the unshaved man at the door, groggy eyed and on guard, untrusting.

"Can I use your phone, please sir? Slid off the road up there and need to call for a tow."

"Wha?" the man was still waking up.

"I slid off the road in my car, sir. I just want to make a call so I can get the car pulled back onto the road."

"Uhuh. Phone's right there." He nodded to the little table right beside them. "Icy out there."

"Who's that, Daddy?" came from the darkness behind the man.

"G'back ta bed, sweetie. It's nothin'."

Casey dialed and Dad answered. Dad told him to stay with the car and said he'd be there soon. Casey hung up and looked back up from the phone. The man and his wife and daughter were huddled there staring at him, wondering what they should do with this intruder and whether he was there to somehow harm them. The tiny room was overcrowded with old furniture and empty cereal boxes and musty carpets. Their frightened eyes hurt him; he didn't want to be a bother to anyone and knew he was already creating plenty of inconvenience for others.

"Thank you," Casey said softly, setting a dollar near the phone to cover the toll call. It didn't feel sufficient to him, the dollar. He pulled out a second one and set it on top of the first as he thought of how these people were living, as he felt guilty for crashing into them, for thundering into their solitude without warning. "I'd better head back there." He didn't want to go back to the dark coldness, but he hated seeing the look on the faces in front of him. He only wanted them to not feel distressed, and he knew his being there was the cause of great disturbance. It was not the kind of place that was used to visitors.

"Thank you" again as he slipped out into the black silence and empty chill.

At the farm, Dad called Frank Seymour, who worked for Niagara Mohawk, the power company, and asked for his help.

At 2:30 a.m. Casey saw the lights of rescue coming along the road. Dad had arrived on our tractor, wearing a cold-weather, thermal suit and armed with towing chains. It had been a long, cold ride for him. Casey was relieved to see the lights and hear the distinctive clanking of the approaching diesel engine and the wop-wop of tire chains on the tractor. Within minutes, more lights came, as Frank had now arrived driving a Niagara Mohawk utility line truck, equipped with a winch and fully provisioned for night work under any conditions.

With yellow lights spinning, Frank backed the truck to the edge of the road as the truck beep-beeped loudly into the blackness letting the nighttime know that it was shifted into reverse.

They had the car back on the road in no time, and Frank flipped on a powerful spotlight that now illuminated the car like it was sitting on an operating table. After pawing packed snow from the wheel wells and the grill, from under the muffler and axel and engine areas, they could see that no damage was done which was a huge relief, especially to Casey. They headed back to the farm, Dad with the car. Not only did he want to drive it so that he could inspect for any change in the way it drove, but his sending Casey back on the tractor was fitting punishment. Frank drove to the farm too instead of heading home. He wanted to be there in case anything further was discovered.

Casey watched Dad and Frank leave in their vehicles. He watched as the vehicles and their lights faded into the moonless night, now suddenly still and silent again. He started the engine and pointed the tractor toward home. The high school senior wore only a light jacket, and he had a fifteen minute, frigid tractor ride ahead of him. For what felt like an eternity he watched the snowy, empty road in front of his headlights, felt the rhythm of snow chains beneath his tires, and felt the cold air relentlessly pour through his clothing and wash over his skin. It was so cold it hurt, but he wouldn't complain. He was too humbled for that, too ashamed of his poor performance on this night.

It was 4:00 a.m. when Casey finally walked into our kitchen and took in the warm, homey smells of the place, full of coffee and oak logs burning in the fireplace. Frank was there with Mom and Dad. Casey joined them all at our kitchen table. He could read no anger in their faces; this relieved him.

At last it was over, and the adults talked easily.

Dad recapped the whole thing and concluded that they were truly fortunate.

"Casey's okay. We're all okay, and we didn't have any damage to the car whatsoever" he said in relief, as if he had realized it for the very first time.

Casey kept mum, but he thought of Frank Seymour's selflessness. He thought of how this man was rousted from his sleep and from his family, how he saved the day, of how he now sat with them all instead of collecting overdue sleep that had been stolen from him.

"Geez, could have been worse," said Frank. "Could have broken bones – or could have been killed even..." Frank's voice trailed off as he said this. "Heck, could have punched out the radiator or bent a wheel or broken an axle."

"God, yeah…" Dad was pensive, grateful. "And the best part of the whole thing," Dad said half to himself, "is that we didn't even have to bother anybody…"

Frank exploded, "Didn't have to bother anybody? Who the heck am I? What am I doing out at 4:00 in the darn morning?" He was irritated, felt taken for granted and was hurt.

"Oh hell, Frank," Dad responded dismissively, "you're family… I mean we didn't have to bother anybody that wasn't one of us."

Frank just stared at him.

"Aww, c'mon, Frank. You *know* you're family," Dad repeated, stating what he considered to be obvious.

It was as if Frank Seymour had been awarded the Nobel Prize, as if he was called into the Oval Office and presented with the Medal of Honor. His eyes lit up and he absolutely beamed, sparkled with unexpected mirth. He took on those words as if they were laurel wreaths, wore them as trophies of unconditional acceptance into our clan. Frank held his shoulders just a bit more squarely and lifted his voice the slightest octave.

"GeezKrise!" Frank bubbled out, giddy with delight but simulating anger, "You call me at 2:00 a.m. an' get me outta bed to come out in the freezing snow and pull him out, and you say you aint bothered nobody?!" Frank's counterfeit anger was obvious, his all-out smile, his irrepressible joy betrayed his act. He couldn't suppress his smile, though he tried mightily. Frank went on and on about this, masquerading madness and fabricating an affront, yet undeniably jubilant about his being favored as family. The night had turned into a sort of celebration for Frank, and he loved being "inside" with us, loved how Dad bungled the message by taking him for granted.

Frank never forgot that night. He still carries on about it every time we see him, even today, more than thirty years later, still one of us, still honored to be taken for granted just a bit, still honored to be "family" – and he is just that.

Sunday: *"Frank and Josie here."*

Wednesday: *"Casey got a phone call from (Congressman) Pattison's office. Appointed to W.P. 4:15 p.m. Frank and Josie out here in the evening."*

Friday: *"Casey had an experience with the car. Frank was a great help. 1:00 a.m."*

Don Preece's diary entries
February 20, 23, 25, 1977

Dad, Casey, and Frank Seymour

And All the Others, Especially the Women

I could never name them all, not all the others, yet I must mention at least a few. But first I must say a few words about the women I have not mentioned and do not mention in all of this. I drone on about uncles and men-folk-family-friends and farmers as if women were not part of this narrative, as if they are somehow not a part of "me." They are.

My mother, my lifelong standard of duty and perseverance, has shaped me in every conceivable way. My grandmothers, Gertie and Eva, were women of incredible strength and quiet determination. Aunts and women family friends showed me joy and love and the unstoppable power of conviction. Local farm matrons ran civic groups and drove tractors, milked cows and held jobs that made family farms solvent. They also worked from morning till night without many of the household appliances we take for granted today. Garbage disposals, automatic dishwashers, clothes dryers, crock pots, and even food blenders did not often find their way into dirt road farmhouses of that place and time. Those selfless women were teachers and cashiers and tellers and nurses and clerks and business owners. And they were tireless wives and mothers too. I have no idea how they did it all.

I have not written more about those remarkable women who so influenced me only because of economy, and because the men were so much more in front of me. So many more of my hours were spent in the presence of men, simply by nature of my being a boy on a farm. I hope those wonderful women understand that their pivotal and colorful contributions in my young life remain with me and speak to me always. I ask for their forgiveness on this topic and for their indulgence as I continue to prattle on about the men.

* * * * * *

Ray Beinkowski played high school football next to Dad (Ray was the tackle who lined up beside my dad, the guard) and came to our place every year. He was always a favorite with us because he absolutely loved physical work. Our place reminded him of his uncle's farm in Derby, Connecticut, where Ray had interned each summer as a kid. His uncle farmed with horses and Ray, a big guy, did a lot of heavy lifting there. I think something deep in Ray desperately wanted to recapture something from his youth; I hope he found that magic on the farm with us. We certainly found magic with him. Ray worked with a ferocity that could make others feel small, if only because he was such a large and powerful man and because he threw himself so fully into labor. He introduced me to the joy of working hard. Ray was also a self-taught accordion player, and he was a remarkably good one. Nothing could compare to a few tunes from Ray as we collected on our porch, all spent after a long day's work.

My uncle Dan Teevan introduced me to the wonderful game of golf, but he did so much more than that. Dan taught me about playing life consistently down the middle, not over-swinging or overreaching and how that simple strategy allows one to relax a bit, to enjoy the journey, and to win. I have been a lousy student. Still, Dan's message was a great one. He was not a big man, but he loved the farm, loved gardens, and never shied away from dirty work. Without saying it, he told me that consistency and courage meant more than might.

Uncle Howard and Aunt Gert came with generous gifts and with slideshows of their trips to places like Taiwan and Hong Kong. To a rural farm kid of that era, it was like hearing from astronauts about Saturn and the Andromeda Galaxy. These were far way, exotic, barely imaginable places – but these people were living proof that you could go there.

Occasional nameless escapees from the city would arrive at our farm with hang gliders and ask if they could soar from our high hill. I would hike the hill with them and watch and listen. I would imagine and dream as I observed them lift off gently and soar serenely over our farm. People could indeed fly.

Bill Bergen, Joe LaCoursi and Andy Kaiser were wonderful neighbors who showed me what it looked like to be kind and joyful. Howie Schmitt gave us more than a few pieces of baseball gear and lived life with a vibrancy and energy that was contagious. The Foxes came every year and kept us acquainted with Connecticut and the world of business. My cousin, Jim Shanley, and his family, were perhaps our most frequent out of town visitors, and Jim was there so much he is a sort of second-brother to me. The whole family was smart and mannered and hard working. They still are. Then there were the Carlsens and Walshes, Buckleys, O'Connors and Guidons, all wonderful people, and wonderfully unique. Teachers and ball coaches were marvelous mentors, and characters all. As I said, I dare not try to name them all.

Then there is my Uncle Dean, who… well, he deserves his own chapter here. And he shall have it.

Chapter 10

Uncle Dean

My dad's brother, my Uncle Dean, was the greatest performer I have ever known. DeNiro and Newman had nothing on him. And unlike the Hollywood icons, Dean was a real, in the flesh genius whose lap I could sit on and whose breath I could smell, sometimes winter fresh and sometimes stale with cigarettes or sweet with scotch. He was an incurable method actor who spontaneously went fully into character, often moving well into the scene before you even knew the play had started. Dean left you delighted when you finally discovered that all was theater, that you were somehow part of the set, on stage under his direction. At the same time, he was a delightful and creative character actor who thrived on the give and take with whomever might join him. He was a gifted story teller with a delicious sense of humor and a near pathological appetite to entertain others. It was his way of honoring those around him, gifting them with what God had granted to him, and he shared it generously. Uncle Dean made us cry with laughter and always left us wanting more.

He was an artist in every sense, and his talents went beyond just acting. Dean was an accomplished painter and pen and ink artist who dabbled in poetry and crafts. He was also a sort of human artist, a Connecticut salesman by profession, and he won clients over with wit and care and irresistible charm. And he was the tender guy whose eyes teared up when he spoke about losing his daughter Annie, when he shared his regrets in private, and when he told me how much he loved me and my dad, how he loved his wife and kids, when he blubbered about his failures as a father and husband and as a man. A part of his wonderful gift for connecting with the deepest part of people was a connection with the deepest part of himself. I think that brought him both magnificent joys and profoiund knowledge of the human self-disappointments every one of us carries. Our gifts are our curses too; his were no different.

Dean's visits to the farm were always exciting and always included some over-the-top acting that left us stunned and breathless, like delighted zip line riders, newly provisioned with spectacular stories, anxious to share the tales of our recent ride with whomever would listen.

I miss him. I hope that he is smiling as he looks down on us, and that his elusive Bluebird of Happiness is perched lightly on his shoulder.

> *Most Entertaining – Dean Preece*
> *Best Looking – Dean Preece*
> *Best Dancer – Dean Preece*
> *Funniest – Dean Preece*
>
> *Senior Superlatives, 1944*
> *Milford High School, Milford, Connecticut*

How Do You Like Them Bananas

Oysters "R" in Season

> *Dean Preece starred in these two 1966 short films by filmmaker Lionel Rogosin, whose works included an Academy Award Nomination and other honors.*

The Y. U. Barn

(My age: 5)

Every barn, every building on the farm had its own name. The Dodge barn, the field barn, the woodshed, the turkey barn, the milk house, the corn crib. But one name stood alone in distinctiveness: the Y.U. barn. It has been called that for as long as I can remember, and the name traces directly to Dean. It was the barn in which Henry Thomas stabled his horses, which must have made it a very special place in that era. For very different reasons it was special in our era too, always a very special place for the Preece kids and our visitors.

"Why you, dirty rat...why you, sidewinder...why, you..." The words were mumbled and slurred as they slowly slipped out of the side of his scowling mouth, slid down by the toothpick that dangled from the edge of his lips. The western vest he had found at Goodwill fit him perfectly, and his black cowboy hat from the same place slung well forward over his face as he dozed, standing upright but motionless, thumbs hooked into the front of his denim jeans. He was leaning back against the barn, one foot propped on the barn wall behind him. He had been stationed here by the open barn door all along, since the moment we left the house, and we immediately spotted him.

My older brother Rick and cousins Kathy and Janine were all exactly the same age, nine, and they slithered past him, afraid of his ominous presence but giddy with playful anticipation. They said nothing but stared at him as they entered into the barn. Being four years younger, I stood back a bit, too afraid to pass, but unwilling to miss what was coming.

My Uncle Dean, fully in character, sensed my presence and thumbed his hat up slowly, uncovering a drowsy eye that sneered at me from its shadowy cover. "What, boy?" he asked with a disgusted drawl. "Git in there, fella!" he snapped, giving a tilt of the head that aimed me toward the barn door. Too terrified to disobey, I dispatched myself to the barn, scooted past him with anxiety and fear. I heard him mutter toward me as I passed, "Why you, good for nothin'..."

As my eyes adjusted inside the darkened barn, I discovered that I was the last to enter. Dad was there and all my visiting cousins – Leslee, Tom, Sue, plus the others. I felt the door behind me darken and I whirled around to find my Uncle Jim Duffy, arms folded across his huge chest, had emerged from the shadows and taken up his position as bouncer, an imposing door-guard whose body language made it clear that none of us would be allowed to leave. And yet his presence was somehow comforting to me, as he lent credibility to the whole affair. Dean was a known madman, and I was suspicious of his every move. But Jim was somber and solid, not given to tomfoolery as Dean was, and Jim's being there put me at ease a bit.

His hat now severely tilted to one side and still forward, covering one eye, Dean rounded the corner and grabbed my cousin Kathy by the arm. In a moment her expression changed from playfulness to terror and she let out a shriek that triggered a sudden explosion of wilding chaos.

"Why you, gunslingin' little skunk!" cursed Dean, staring right at Kathy, as he flung her toward the enormous mound of soft hay that had been staged there. Screaming erupted everywhere and we scattered like ants under a rock that had just been lifted. Instinctively, Rick dove at Dean's legs, trying to protect his cousin, but Dean made short work of him too. "Why you, sneaking snake!" and off went Rick, helicoptering into the landing pad of hay. He screeched with delight, and I suddenly got it. In that instant I realized that this was play and it was all to be acted out, scripted thespians on a stage. Tom was next, then Sue, then me, Janine and Leslee. Without instruction we had formed a queue, an orderly line of lemmings, each of us dancing with anticipation as we all immersed ourselves into our roles, flinging and being flung, all with the cry "Why, you!!"

Dean relished his role and feigned a great anger, loudly yelping out his lines. "You kids are gonna pay! Tha'ss the lass' time anybody gits near my ranch! Why, you lousy kid!" and off would go another actor, spinning wildly through the air, screaming and laughing her way into the soft mound, pretending great offense and protesting with all her might and with all the vocal cords she could muster. Dad was throwing whomever he could catch, and the bigger kids were tossing the smaller ones, all dizzy with delight, all howling at the top of our lungs, "Why you's" everywhere. It went on for several heart-pounding minutes, and I found myself sweating a clean, sweet perspiration, sweating in the way that only hard-playing children can.

At one point, my younger cousin Tom became intimidated, and being smaller than the rest, tried to make his way toward the door.

I watched as Uncle Jim took a step to block his path, glowered an expression that stopped him in his tracks and rumbled out his own "Why, you... where do ya think you're a'goin' mister?" Tom pivoted and screamed and ran right into Dean, who instantly sent him flying like the rest.

This act by my usually stoic Uncle Jim so stunned me, that I perceived it with alarm, sensed that the world had suddenly gone crazy, and I too felt frenzy sweep over me. As I did, I realized that Dean had scooped up my feet and Dad had me by the arms, and they swung me with deliberate intent now, arcing me forward toward the hay but not letting go yet. "One!" they barked out in unison as they swung me back for another go. "Two!" as I came forward with momentum now, fearing the great fling to come, screaming with a joyful fear. "THREEEE!" and I went soaring, unable to breathe, adrenaline freezing me motionless as I flew... "WHY YOU!" they all barked out at once, as I approached the hay mound, somehow having become the grand finale of the whole thing. I had become the closing act and exclamation point on our play, with the curtain closing as I pillowed into my easy landing.

Everyone was panting when I regained my senses, when I crawled out of the hay and looked around, armored against any "Why you" onslaught that might come my way. But none came, and I could see it really was over. Our staged scene had ended, scripts complete. We bunched like actors after the play, caught in that timeless moment after the final curtain has drawn, but before erupting in celebration and congratulations. Dean had lit a cigarette and had gently resumed his original position but now inside the barn. His hat drooped over his eyes and he leaned back, one foot propped against the barn's wall behind him. He started it softly and one by one we all joined in, joyfully singing the lines that had become a part of our shared childhood, our collective memory, our song of the Y.U. Barn that we still sing when we gather together, fifty years later:

I was standing by a bank in Arizona,
Never thought of doin' anybody harm,
When along came the Sheriff of the county,
He flipped his badge and grabbed me by the arm.

He accused me of the robbery of a mail train,
Said I was the leader of the gang,
I was tried without a judge or jury,
And the verdict was that I was gonna hang.

Refrain: *I'll be hanged if they're gonna hang me!*
I'll be hanged if they're gonna hang me!
I aint talkin' like no smarty,
But there'll be no necktie party,
I'll be hanged if they're gonna hang me!

I sent wire to a friend across the border
Asking him to bring a .44
But, instead he brought a gun for shooting water
That he purchased in a 5 and 10 cent store.

Refrain

Wrote a letter to my sweetheart on the prairie,
Asked her to help me make a prison break,
She sent a cake and inside put a hacksaw,
But, she forgot to send an axe to cut the cake.

Refrain

"I'll be Hanged if They're Gonna Hang Me"
Recorded in 1936 by the Tune Wranglers on the RCA
Bluebird label (as modified by the Preece family for
exclusive use in the Y.U. barn)

Dad and Dean would have been about ten years old when this song came out; I imagine that it may have been a part of their repertoire at that time, but I am only guessing.

Y.U. Barn (on left)

Halloween

(My age: 5)

My brother Rick and I had just finished attending a Halloween festival at Cambridge Central School. I was in kindergarten; he had just entered fourth grade. The event was a late afternoon affair, and it was dark when the festivities ended. There were games and treats and contests of all kinds. It was a big deal for us, as these kinds of events were rare, and Mom had sprung for the occasion by purchasing "real" costumes for us, not the homemade kind we normally wore. We each wore an outfit that had come from the local Five and Ten, prepackaged flimsy gowns matched with plastic masks, each with a thin elastic band that went behind your head to hold it on. Rick was a red-suited goblin with bulging eyes. My gown was black and the mask featured horrifying, angry eyes and the red buds of new horns. We thought ourselves spectacularly fearsome.

Being early evening, Dad was busy milking cows and Mom was preparing dinner, so Uncle Dean was the one who was there to take us home after the school affair ended. We chatted on the way to his car in the parking lot and he sensed our excitement over the Halloween holiday, over the sense of fun and fear that seemed to be everywhere.

"You boys hop in the back" Dean said. "I've been having car troubles lately – a bad engine problem that scares me a bit… and I don't want either of you up in the front seat in case something terrible happens." We were oblivious to the bait, and completely accepted Dean's concerns as being genuine. It was a bit troubling to us to see an adult so concerned, and it created an ominous sense of foreboding in both Rick and me. We suspected Dean was up to something, but we failed to connect the dots in this case. We just didn't see it coming.

"It's been weird," Dean said to himself, out loud and for our benefit. "I drive all the way up here from Connecticut, and everything's fine. But as soon as the darkness came, everything with this car started to go wrong, almost as if this darned car is haunted…"

The "rough engine problems" started soon after we left the lights of the village and entered the blackness of farmlands. Dean continued narrating out loud throughout the trip, talking to himself, but loudly enough so we could hear every word. There were times when the car lights went out altogether, times when the car stalled and rolled silently, engineless. As we proceeded on our journey, the engine seemed to become increasingly erratic, with herky-jerky stalls and jolting starts, sharp swerves left and right.

By now, we had become aware that Dean was acting, that all this was fantasy, but he had us on edge, nevertheless. And we loved it.

"Damn ghosts," he muttered. "You won't get us, by God! You might be haunting this car and this engine, but you won't get us, no sir…" Again the car went silent; the engine was dead. "Don't worry, boys," said Dean, clearly intending to worry us out of our minds.

I curled up a bit tighter in the back seat, edged a bit toward Rick, whose eyes were getting wider by the minute.

"I see you out there!" Dean shouted out of the driver's window into the blackness that was hillside and woodlands, illuminated only by the full moon, low on the horizon behind it. "Leave us ALONE! We're just going home; that's all. Leave, dammit!" He was clearly becoming more agitated and concerned, and it felt like we were headed for some shadowy showdown with haunted spirits. I was delightfully frightened now, and could tell Rick was, too.

"I'm gonna… What did you say?!... I said… Hey! … Stop that" Now the car was rolling slowly, there was no engine, and the lights were out. It was pitch black and it was clear that Dean was doing verbal battle with spirits on Cobble Hill Road. We were powerless passengers, observers, completely at the mercy of these beings and the war they waged with Dean. It was adrenaline-pumping stuff now, and we were leaning forward on the edge of our seats, beginning to whine and shout our own complaints. Acting or not, this had gone on long enough.

"No!" Rick barked, trying to act tough, but I could feel the false bravery.

"I want to goooo hooooome!" I whimpered, frightened almost out of my skin, even though I secretly wanted more.

Suddenly Dean threw open the door of the darkened, gently-rolling car, and jumped out. He yelped at the ghosts and seemed to be in some terrific and brutal battle out there, filled with tussles that had him rolling the ground, and the sound of punches and bodies bouncing off the side of the car. It was fantastic stuff!

He jumped back in and restarted the engine, gunned it hard and finally got the lights working. "You won't get us, you lousy spook-faced bastards!" he shouted into the blackness.

Just as suddenly, we came to another tire-chirping stop.

"Nooo," I whined.

"Uncle Dean!" Rick pleaded.

But Dean was already out of the car again, and this time, because the lights were on, we could see his furious fighting, his leaping at spirits near our headlights and his tackling of ghosts behind us. Dean's coat had been yanked off by one of the attackers, and he swung it wildly as he was thrown across the hood of the car, right in full view of the front windshield. It was a horrifying battle that had our hearts in our mouths. We were spellbound.

"You boys drive home without me! I'm not going to… make… it!" This sent Rick and me into our own orbit, screaming and hollering and wailing that we couldn't do it, that weren't big enough, that…

"Ahhhh!" Dean was trying to escape from them now, howling at them and yelping when he suffered their fierce blows. From out of nowhere he leaped in through the front seat passenger's door, rolled down the window and screamed, "Take that you bastards!" He slid quickly to the driver's side and punched the engine, sending tires screeching. Rick and I were nearly out of our minds now, shaking with fear and amazement and thrill.

Twenty yards later the car had slowed again but was still rolling slowly, engine idling and lights on. "I thought I told you! Son of a…" Dean promptly squirmed out of the driver's window and went onto the roof of the rolling car – ONTO THE ROOF OF THE ROLLING CAR – and battled the evil ones up there, pounding and howling and rocking the car furiously. He dropped from the roof, swung his legs in through the passenger's window, and in a jiffy was back in the car, behind the wheel. This time he left them behind for good. He raced the engines, spun tires, skidded around corners and drove at a reckless pace for the remaining three miles.

"You guys check the back window – look to see if they're following us!" he commanded Rick and me. We did as we were told, frightened even more by the notion that they might still be chasing us, haunting us further.

A few minutes later and we exploded out of the car and raced toward the house, bursting with our story, our fear, our delicious thrill. Dad heard it all and seemed visibly concerned. He was serious-minded and troubled, said that there were odd things happening during milking, strange sounds in the barn, too. Said he got out of there fast, but now that he had the whole group of us, wanted to go back and see if we could discover what Halloween-weirdness was happening down there.

We quickly formed a sort of posse, Rick and I still in our costumes and the rest of us, cousins and family members. All the adults were there, except for my Aunt Joan, Dean's wife, who was "upstairs, asleep." We headed straight to the barn doors and walked into the darkness, straining to see. We were all wonderfully scared but had comfort in numbers. We knew we were going to be frightened, scared half out of our wits, and we both feared it and yearned for it. Suddenly an unfamiliar light came on, a light in a place where one didn't previously exist, focused high on the rafters above us. And just as suddenly a heavy rope swung in front of us, swooped straight toward this new spotlight, creating a momentary awareness that "it" was about to happen...

I literally shrieked when the skeletal corpse swung into the spotlight, the heavy noose around its neck. The dead man was wearing jeans and a jacket, boots and gloves, yet his head was that of a skeleton, white and toothy and eyeless. Kids screamed, adults gasped, and we tore out of that barn like we were on fire, didn't stop until we were near the house.

The adults finally corralled us there and calmed us down a bit. They steadied us as we swung wildly between giddy joy and helpless terror. We were all panting and breathless, bursting with contradiction.

We were thrilled, wanted it all to stop, wanted it all to continue, wanted to go safely to bed, wanted it to never stop scaring us.

"Let's settle down and enjoy this beautiful, moonlit night," Dad suggested. We all agreed, and made ourselves pliable to his suggestion. "C'mon," he said, "let's go to the back yard where we can see the moon more clearly."

He led us to the back yard, and we gathered around him, standing exactly where he wanted us to stand, and gazed toward the hillside there. Finally, we were all settled and still.

"Look how that moon is resting just over the horizon," Dad remarked.

As if on cue, as soon as Dad said this, Dean lit a cigarette and agreed, "Yes, look at that moon," he repeated. We were all staring at it now, a perfect yellow globe that looked huge next to the earth.

Just then, we heard a distant howl, a sort of woeful wailing. It was long and drawn out, sad sounding and distraught. "Ooowwwwhhhhhhhh!"

"What was that?" Dean asked aloud, acting alarmed, re-lighting his already-lit cigarette. Then another long, agonizing wail came from the hillside as we stared. "Hoooooohhhhh!"

As we stared, a human figure moved across the top of our rocky outcropping, one hundred yards distant, silhouetted against the bright moon! We were transfixed. The wailing continued, and it was clear now that the howling was from this remorseful figure, womanlike in her long gowns and flowing wraps that blew in the wind behind her. But we could also make out that she was witch-like, as she wore a tall, pointed hat with a broad brim, barely visible in the silhouette. Dean lit his cigarette a third time, and she passed again in front of the brilliant moon, backlit by it as she paced in the opposite direction, lamenting in her loud cries. "Eeeyoooww!"

It was over as suddenly as it started. We were absolutely amazed, spellbound by the wonder of it. Because the mysterious figure was so distant, we were emboldened, unafraid and ready to suggest pursuit, to press for exploration and flashlights. Yet we all secretly wanted someone *else* to pursue, to explore. We didn't want to be up close with this wailing witch, not after all that had happened this night.

Cooler heads prevailed, and after much deliberation, we finally decided that we should head inside to the safety of the house, have some hot chocolate and settle down for the night. Just then Joan appeared from out of nowhere and joined our circle. She said she had been awakened from her deep sleep by the noises, so she got dressed and came outside to be with us, to see what all the howling and ruckus was about. We kids all started talking at once. "You wouldn't believe it, Aunt Joan," we babbled in unison. "There was this screaming lady…"

We knew we had been duped. And yet we loved it so much, we were so appreciative of the effort and the wonderful theatrics, we honored them all by playing our role to the hilt. We adamantly claimed to have been thrilled, terrified, and amazed – and indeed we were. It was the best Halloween ever.

Dean and Dad

The Great Alonzo B'Gonzo

(My age: 12)

My cousin Sue had ordered three of us kids into service, and she directed our arranging all the chairs so that our modest living room was transformed into a sort of auditorium. All the seats were jammed into rows, facing toward the far room where Dean and Dad secluded themselves. They were behind the closed doors that divided what was now a stage from the audience. Connecticut relatives from both sides of my family and a few friends were there. Twenty eight of us were at the farm for this Thanksgiving, and the main meal, a feast, had just ended. I was twelve, gorged with turkey, pumpkin pie and companionship.

We all took our seats, but we were unruly and jabbered loudly amongst ourselves. Then my Aunt Joan, Dean's wife, who was normally quiet and in the background, stepped out of the loud, bubbling crowd of us and made her way forward. She stopped just in front of the doors that served as closed curtains, cloistering Dean and Dad. She cleared her throat and our chattering and buzzing died to nothing. You could hear a pin drop.

"Ladieeeees and gennntlemeeeeennn!" she began, taking a deep breath. She started softly, spoke slowly and deliberately. "The occult has long been studied by many ancient cultures and fascinates scientists and sociologists even in this age. There are indeed psychic phenomena that remain mysterious, that defy rational explanation, that befuddle the human mind." Joan's tone gradually picked up; her voice gained volume as she proceeded. "Yes, there are spirits... AND POWERS... from which great strength, great WISDOM can be drawn!" We were stunned at her unexpected loudness, jolted up straight in our chairs when she shouted 'powers,' and she really belted out the word 'wisdom.' "But only by those special FEW, those gifted ORACLES, whose powers are beyond what we can comprehend... those with the power to know the THOUGHTS OF OTHERS..." She was much louder, more forceful now, and her pace had increased; there was

177

palpable urgency in her voice. "There are MYSTICS and GENIES and SOOTHSAYERS from the Orient, from the sands of Morocco, from the isolated mountainous regions of the Middle East and the Baltic states. Yet NONE compares with the genius to be before you tonight! NONE has his wisdom! NONE has his powers! NONE has his mystical gifts of MAGIC!... Ladies and gentlemen... I give you... The GREAT... ALONZO B'GONZO!!!!!!"

We erupted in applause and loud cheering, delighted in the theatrical ham before us, participating in our own way by overdoing our response in the same way Joan had overstated the introduction. In that moment, we had all become actors, all immersed as one into the scene.

Suddenly the doors before us were swung open, and there in front of us stood Alonzo B'Gonzo. Dean Preece wore my Dad's oversized terrycloth brown bathrobe, and had wrapped a white towel around his head as a turban. His arms were folded high across his chest, and a red dot had been magic-markered on his forehead for added effect. To top the scene off, it was obvious that a lamp, which was hidden from our view, had been fashioned into a makeshift spotlight, and it was squarely fixed on Alonzo, center stage. Being so delightfully surprised, we spontaneously applauded, cheered, hooted and crowed, half in genuine appreciation for the effort, and half in cat-calls that signaled the cheesiness of it all. Yet Alonzo's steadfast stares, his unwavering eye contact with cat-callers and doubters silenced us, and caused a part of us to slip into the notion that maybe there really was something to the magic of Alonzo B'Gonzo. Dean had a truly magnificent power to stay totally in character, despite what happened around him, and this wordless power settled the crowd and drew us back into the act.

He was pensive, and started with the tiniest voice that caused us to strain to hear him, called us to even greater silence. He spoke in his native tongue, which turned out to be a fascinating concoction of absolute gibberish.

"Vee tresh nahani lakoom... vee tresh nahani valoota... vee tresh nahani mallo pop tumish kempa..." He went on like this for what must have been a full minute, becoming increasingly lost in his deep thoughts, occasionally looking toward the heavens and at other times closing his eyes, finding his deepest, centered self. We were mesmerized. "Krey... krey koll umplentol nehemash... krey koll AMPLA etro wejuzz emplah BETRA!!" We had become totally engrossed, fascinated by his ability to invent gobbledty-gook words on the fly and actually make it all sound like it was a real language.

Alonzo turned toward Dad, his humble assistant on stage, and quietly said "Pyanjo." Dad stared at him, motionless, numb. "Pyanjo," again from the Great Alonzo. Dad looked confused, and we momentarily had the sense something on stage was unraveling, that the actors weren't on the same page. Dad did nothing. Alonzo suddenly spun toward him and shouted "PYANJO!" and slapped my dad hard across the cheek. It was loud, and it hurt, and it stunned us as much as him. Dad bowed, cowered, then scooted to the table behind them and pulled out a cigarette from the pack that rested there. He nervously gave it to the Great Alonzo, actually placed it between Alonzo's lips, and lit it for the Great One as his own hands shook with fear. Alonzo nodded pleasantly, finally satisfied, clearly having demonstrated his absolute authority and supremacy. Dad groveled and bowed. Alonzo grunted "Oompkeh," which clearly meant a condescending 'thank you' in the strange language of his distant homeland.

Alonzo went on speaking to us. He was composed and casual, talking through lips that held his cigarette. His hands never touched the thing; they remained folded across his chest. The cigarette just dangled from his lips, as he puffed and talked in his native tongue. He turned to Dad. "Kakoi" he ordered, matter-of-fact-ly. Dad reached up and took the cigarette from Alonzo's mouth, and knocked the ashes into his hand. Alonzo coughed softly and nodded. Dad returned the cigarette to Alonzo's lips, and Alonzo went on speaking as if nothing unusual had just happened. A few sentences later he and Dad repeated the process again, and it became apparent that Alonzo was finding the cigarette annoying now, but he went on. Then, without warning and mid-sentence, without any movement of any other part of his body, the Great Alonzo B'Gonzo tongued his cigarette so it flipped on his lips, tumbled backward into his open mouth, and he simply swallowed the lit and smoldering thing whole. He continued speaking without missing a syllable. "Voriffiyo skadla rohk melpint" he went on, rolling his "R's" and chuckling softly like he had just uttered some insightful words of light levity, shaking his head as if it was something obviously ridiculous, allowing us to feel that he had just shared some inside joke with us, like we were "in" with the Great Alonzo.

He whispered privately to Dad now, and Dad called for a volunteer to come forth and sit in the chair that was on stage next to the two of them. Alonzo made a big production out of studying the various candidates, peering deeply into their eyes while Dad humbly explained that The Great Alonzo was seeking a soul with which he could best communicate, a soul that somehow connected with Alonzo's through the mystical power of spirits. At last my youngest brother Joe was chosen, and he sat in the chair facing us, nervous and delighted at the same time.

"I... can... speak your languagings," Alonzo labored out in great effort, complete with his invented accent. "These boy I have chosed... he ees of the right spirits. I will perform... my magics!" We clapped with delight, hooted and cheered our support. Joe was not so sure.

Dad lit candles and placed them around Joe's chair and Alonzo made a great show of his hands to us, making it clear he held nothing. Then, he brought his hands over Joe's head and chanted something imperceptible and knelt on one knee, laid his hand directly on Joe's head and pulled a nickel from his ear! Dad, the assistant, made a Vanna White sort of show with his arms, pointing them toward Alonzo, signaling that he deserved our applause. We gasped in disbelief as

Alonzo showed the coin to us, triumphant and proud. Someone in our midst snickered, and Alonzo took great offense, shouted the person down, and stared his magical stare of intimidation. Alonzo then held the coin up for us to see and abruptly threw it over our heads and into the darkened kitchen behind us. We heard it rattle around on the floor in there, behind Aunt Joan, who was near the kitchen door. Alonzo turned toward Joe and repeated the entire process, again pulling the coin from nothing. We knew we had been duped – but we had no idea how. We loved it and applauded enthusiastically.

Next came Alonzo's powers of mind-reading, in which he discerned which playing card, among nine laid on a table, had been selected by someone from the crowd, the secretly selected card known to us but not to Alonzo. Dad would ask him if it was this card or another one, and after great deliberation, Alonzo would finally make his choice, always getting it right. To make sure he had no way of seeing which card was being selected, we placed our own guards on him and even took him to other rooms, closed the doors and shouted to him so that there was no way he could have seen or heard the card selection happening on stage. He would stare deeply into the chooser's eyes, and read the person's "klesh," as he called it, their spiritual aura which only Alonzo could see. With great strain and deliberation, Alonzo always got it right. He would often chant and would occasionally come close to making his first mistake, but then he would suddenly sense the spirits telling him something, sending him a mystical message. Somehow, he always ended up with the right card, selecting it for his humble on-stage assistant, flawless in his powers of magical mind-reading. We were completely taken in now, thoroughly sucked into the magic of Alonzo B'Gonzo, magician and foreigner, marvelous mystic in our midst.

Finally, the adults were called forward to the stage and the doors were temporarily closed again. Then, one by one, each of us kids was called forward to the stage to participate in Alonzo's grand finale, the Great Levitation. Aunt Joan again introduced the act, explaining patiently to us that we too could share in the magic of the Great Alonzo B'Gonzo, that all that was needed was belief, that mere faith in Alonzo's powers could bring us the gift of our own magic – that we could, and WOULD… walk on air…!!

As each child was called forward he or she entered the stage. A circle of on-stage adults surrounded the wooden table leaf from our kitchen table, which now rested on the stage floor, a prop in this magic show. Alonzo, in his badly broken English, met each child, held their hand, and closed the stage doors behind them so the goings on became something the rest of could hear but could not see. With each child there were hushed whisperings and encouragement, then silence. Soon adults would be telling them that they were safe, that it was okay, that they should have faith in Alonzo, and finally in one calamitous chant in unison, that they should STEP OFF! At the same time we could make our siblings' and cousins' voices behind the door, whimpering that they were afraid, claiming that they didn't want to do it, that they COULDN'T do it, that… NOOO!! Then, there was an eruption of applause and laughter and joy that grew louder as the session went on, each victim and child actor becoming a part of the ever-larger on-stage crew and diminishing the audience by one more. The anxiety of anticipation grew steadily for those still anguishing in the waiting audience.

When my turn came, I wanted to wet my pants, to be anyplace but there in the presence of the great Alonzo B'Gonzo, to run away from this crazy family and join another one. But I was too old for that, and needed to show my pre-teen coolness to all. Alonzo had already stepped me onto the table leaf and bowed to my height, looked deeply into my eyes and told me that I was going to walk on air. He said it with such conviction and confidence and with breath only a few inches from mine that I felt I had no choice. He told me that I was to put one hand on his shoulder and the other on Dad's who also stood beside me, opposite Alonzo. He told me to place a hand on each of their shoulders, in order to balance myself as I was lifted. One adult was squatting at each end of the plank, the table leaf on which I stood, ready to lift it and me into the air. The others muttered encouragement and told me that Alonzo *really was* magical that they *really had* walked on air; that yes, it *was* scary, but that Alonzo *could* make it happen! Oh how I wanted to believe them… The blindfold came without warning, from someone behind me. It masked my fright and anxiety, as it must have for those who came before me. I could see nothing.

Suddenly I was being lifted – it was all happening too fast for me. I needed time to prepare, time to think this through, yet I could sense the height already, could hear the voices around me drop in position as I was elevated above them. Alonzo's shoulder and Dad's shoulder were down there now and I was too high too fast! I fought back the urge to show emotion.

"Too high!" one sane voice below cried. I thought it was Joan, but I wasn't sure. "He's at the ceiling, Don! Pleeeease lower him! Dean, stop it!"

The CEILING?! The fools had lifted me to the freaking CEILING!? It bumped my head lightly and I was angry now, really shocked at their lack of judgment and irresponsibility – this had gone TOO FAR! This had to STOP! I was going to get hurt and it pissed me off!

"Step off!" they were all hollering to me. "Trust Alonzo!" came from some idiot, some buffoon who might need to drive me to the hospital in a few minutes.

"Cut it out!" I shouted back. "This is too high" I bellowed. "Drop me down, goddamit!" I barked, stunned at my own language but unwilling to let myself be hurt by out-of-control nincompoops.

"STEP OFFFFFF!"

I refused! I reached for my blindfold, needing to do whatever it would take to regain some sanity but as I reached they tipped the thing, lurched it left and made me lunge out over them into the air and into the fall that would break my bones. I was out there, mid air, still blindfolded and now flailing and angry and ready to kill them if I survived this lunatic tragedy. "SHIIIT!"

It was the most awkward landing of my life. Rather than freefalling from the height of the ceiling, I touched the floor immediately and without any speed of gravity whatsoever. Yet the surprise of it, the unexpected, far-too-soon gentleness of it had my knees buckling and my arms groping for balance. Unbeknownst to me, I had been lifted only an inch, and those around me had squatted lower and lower, giving me the false sensation, through touch and sound, of being lifted. Someone had gently tapped my head with a book, which I took as the ceiling, deceived again by illusion. I was on the ground, safe, and the roars of laughter washed over me. Though I was completely safe, my heart was still pumping from fear. And now my sense of surprise joined with the rush of relief that had no other place to go, and so it burst forth in the form of my own laughter, and I joined in with the circle of family around me, delighted.

With that initiation, I became part of the stage crew and acting troupe, a thespian playing my part as the remaining brothers and cousins came forward for their part in the Great Levitation.

One by one they submitted to the turbaned, madman magician, entered the act and scene that had been written just for them. One by one they abandoned logic and stepped dangerously out into thin air, and fell in love with The Great Alonzo B'Gonzo.

The Cold War

The Cold War was a very real part of the 1960's and 1970's for me. It was real for all Americans of that era. Though there was little anybody in Cambridge, New York, could do about it, it was discussed every night at our dinner table, and was always a topic of discussion when visitors came.

It was not abstract to me. The Cold War invaded our rural little farm when new military jets, being tested in the skies above us, shook us with their unexpected sonic booms which came frequently and without warning. Those fantastic booms rattled my little body and frightened me with their ferocity. It was made personal for me when a secret military test flight out of Westover Air Force Base crashed in a field on Ben English's farm. The pilot died in the horrific explosion. The crash site was cordoned off and cleaned up quickly. Little was said, which only fed the sense of intrigue and unnerved me all the more. We went to fallout shelters and practiced air raid drills that had us diving under desks at school; we knew teenage boys who were killed in Vietnam. Woodstock was only a couple of hours' drive south. We were preoccupied with the Cold War, troubled by the seriousness of it.

Dean, on the other hand, used it as a setting for comedy, a stage prop that enabled entertainment.

Dean often brought his best friend Les to the farm. Les was a tall and strongly built man in a trench coat, a bit swarthy and dark, and aside from his theatrical performances with Dean, was quite private. When he spoke, it was with a great knowledge of foreign affairs and with a passion for American interests. Les claimed to have worked for a shipping company, which explained his frequent international trips, which were highly unusual in that era. He guarded the sense of mystery that was naturally aroused amongst us and at times was open and deliberate in his deception, occasionally changing his story about exactly why he was in Cairo the previous month, or what he was doing in Bangkok the month before that. None of us bought the shipping company explanation. We were convinced he was an American agent, a spy. He suspected this was our belief, and either because it was true or because he simply enjoyed toying with us, Les allowed the belief to grow. He even nurtured it along, played it up for our benefit.

Together, Dean and Les formed a potent pair, and they loved performing impromptu theater for and with everyone they encountered.

Cold War - Uranium!

(My age: 9)

Dad hated that Dean and Les wouldn't stop. "I *live* here!" he scolded, under his breath so he couldn't be heard by the others in the lounge of the White Swan hotel in Greenwich that night in January of 1966. But Dean and Les had spontaneously entered into a new act, one they created as they went, and there was no stopping them. Dad found himself reluctantly on the stage Dean and Les had created; the unsuspecting patrons of the place were their audience.

"So how bad do they want the stuff?" asked Les, speaking too loudly and directly at Dad, acting like Dad's recent private scolding was instead a clandestine and confidential disclosure between the two of them. "You can't trust those government bastards," said Les, again too loud. People in the lounge noticed. They glanced over and took note then looked away, acting as if they were disinterested. But Dad was certain those locals would keep listening, hearing every word just as they have been for the last few minutes.

Dad looked down and cringed, red faced and flustered. It had been funny to him at first, when it first started, a couple of minutes earlier. But it had gone too far now. Enough was enough. This was a small town and everyone knew everyone else. The idea that uranium had been discovered locally would spread through the village like wildfire and would reach neighbors by the end of the next day.

"Now Mr. Preece," started Dean, sounding and looking quite official in his bow tie, long trench coat and wing tipped shoes, his classy felt fedora, completely out of place in Greenwich. He was too loud also. "Mr. Preece, we have sampled that soil and our core drillings are rock solid, if I might say, undeniable. It's high grade uranium, alright."

"Aaagh," scoffed Les, who was playing the role of Dad's advocate, dressed in sloppy jeans and a denim jacket, appearing as a down-to-earth local, not a government agent.

Dean shot Les a hard look. "Mr. Lee, I'd appreciate being able to speak directly with Mr. Preece, here, if you don't mind," said Dean, appearing frustrated and anxious. Dean proceeded on.

"Mr. Preece, more than the core samples, your country needs you, sir. Your farm on Vly Summit Road is your livelihood, Mr. Preece, I know that. But that farm, and the uranium it holds, is more than a livelihood to your country, Mr. Preece. It is life itself!" Dean said it with a grand flourish, a great show of grandeur that was designed to catch the attention of anyone in the place who wasn't already eavesdropping.

"Make him pay ya, Don," said Les. "Uncle Sam's not sending this Congressman here for nothin'! They got dough and let them pay you big, I say!" Dad shook inside with laughter but kept a lid on it, swallowed it back down so that he didn't broadcast to others that this was just a game, an innocent piece of make-believe.

"But Congressman Craig," my father objected, "surely…"

"As a ranking member of the House Committee on Ways and Means and Foreign Affairs, Mr. Preece, I implore you to allow the mining to begin on your farm at once! The Soviets have thirteen grade seven nuclear weapons – why we've been over all this already, Mr. Preece! We need that uranium, and your farm has more of it than any place in the Continental forty-eight!"

Dean reached into his inside jacket pocket and pulled out some papers, waved them high so that others would notice and laid them on the table. "Just sign right here, Mr. Preece, and your country will be forever indebted to you, sir. Future generations of Americans will live in safety because Don Preece agreed to fuel the atomic weapons we needed as a country, Mr. Preece… and yes, we're willing to pay seven hundred thousand for those ten acres, though it's likely half the land in this town has uranium just beneath the surface."

Two men at the bar huddled for a short moment in private, then got up abruptly and walked briskly out of the place.

Dad looked down at the paper he was to sign. It was a receipt from the Riverside Motel in Wallingford Connecticut, where Dean had spent the night earlier that week. Nobody could see that detail; all they saw was some congressman demanding that he sign a document that would make him wildly wealthy. In his real life, this "congressman" was a traveling metals salesman. Dad nearly choked when he saw what the paper actually was, and despite his wanting this charade to be over, couldn't help himself, couldn't bring himself to get up and walk out, to tell everyone there that this was just a joke.

"Mr. Preece, I don't want to get testy sir, but if you don't sign this land over – and that's a whopping sum of money for just a few measly acres, you know that – then I'll be forced to convene a congressional inquiry, and you'll be subpoenaed. The United States government will have that uranium, Mr. Preece, and we'll have all of it that's under this ground in little Gren'ich, here." He pronounced it this way, the way they do in Connecticut and New York City, to indicate his foreignness to the locals, who pronounced the name of their little town 'green-witch.'

Another patron whispered something to the bartender then scooted out in a hurry. Dad had had enough; he had to find a way out of this madness.

"I'll take it under consideration," was all Dad could find to say. He stood up as if to leave, but Les and Dean stayed put. By his standing, Dad had boxed himself in a corner now and had to decide quickly what he would do next. If he walked out, there was no place for him to go. Dean had driven the three of them there and had the keys to the car, and it was bitterly cold out. If Dad stayed, who knew where these two lunatics might go with this theatrical game that was probably already spreading through the little village. He looked at Dean. "Good day, Congressman." Dad walked out.

"Poor hillbilly..." muttered the Congressman.

"Just wants what's his," shot back Les, tossing Dean a line so he could run with it, not knowing what Dean might do next.

"Well, your company did the core drillings," said Dean, "and if we found uranium on his place, we'll find it on other places, just like the Palivka mine in Alaska." Dean pulled 'Palivka mine' out of thin air. "If you find it in one place, you'll find it everywhere. You find some locals willing to sell, Mr. Lee, then sample their soil. And when you find uranium – and you *will* - you call me in Washington. I'll come up in the private plane and will meet you in Albany, then we'll come out here and settle. Money's no object, Mr. Lee. God knows we need the uranium, Mr. Lee, God knows. If those Russian bastards are successful with the SR-288-Alpha... well we know what that means, don't we..."

"Indeed Congressman Craig, indeed sir."

* * * * * *

The next day Dean and Les left town and headed back to their lives in Connecticut and New York City. Dad, shamefaced and embarrassed, went back to the White Swan and explained the whole thing to the bartender there and asked for his help in quashing the rumors that no doubt had already started swirling. The bartender claimed to have heard none of the conversations from the previous night but helped Dad figure out who had been in there and might have overheard things. "Those fellows were pretty loud," admitted the bartender referring to Dean and Les. Dad looked up phone numbers and made calls, apologized profusely and explained that the whole thing was a bad joke, a lark that had gone too far. Nobody admitted to hearing anything or taking any notice of it whatsoever. Dad didn't believe any of them but was relieved at their kindness, their claims of deafness.

Nobody ever came to the house or called about the uranium find at our place. Nobody even admitted to thinking it might be true. But every once in a while, even years later, somebody in a barber shop or hardware store would meet Dad for the first time, and they'd say that they heard a rumor once that maybe there was something special out at the Preece place, that some fancy congressman had visited once... There was something special out there, indeed.

Cold War - The "Device"

(My age: 20)

My West Point roommate, John Armstrong was 6'5" and weighed 220 pounds. He was a big guy. That's why I wasn't all that scared when the driver of the Dodge van that picked us up in Newburgh didn't stop to let us out when we asked him, when he instead started to head east along the Massachusetts Turnpike, going in a direction we hitchhikers didn't want to go. I got bigger when John was around. I was bolder and cockier and quicker to confront anybody or anything. And the driver had just frightened me.

"What the hell's your problem, dude?!" I had shouted at the van's driver, who smelled and had long stringy hair and a dirty, bearded face. He wore an old Army jacket and kept mumbling toward us as he drove, called us "man" all the time. He still ignored me. "Pull over NOW or I'm gonna kick your ass right here, at fifty five miles an hour!" He still didn't respond to me. John leaned forward, which was all it took. Scary Hairy pulled over, we got out and exchanged curses with the guy that had given us a ride north for more than an hour before hijacking us for a few miles in the wrong direction. I never hitchhiked alone after that.

Within minutes we crossed the turnpike and caught a ride going back the opposite direction and then north to Mechanicville, which was thirty minutes from the farm. That was as far as we could get with our thumbs. So, as planned, I called the farm and asked for a ride from there while John and I hung out at the Mechanicville McDonald's. We made quite a sight in 1976. A short guy and a monster, both in tight military haircuts and dressed in plaid pants, looking more like we were waiting for a ride to the nerd convention than a ride to a farm. We sipped our Cokes and then went outside to wait at the curb for whoever was coming to fetch us. They would be here soon.

I spotted the Connecticut license plates on the dark sedan before it even turned into the McDonald's parking lot. "There they are," I announced flatly to John, my voice signaling our weariness from traveling and our wish to finally get to our destination. I could see two adults in the front seat and could tell it was Dean and Les. Dean was driving. John and I picked up our bags and waited.

The sedan rounded the corner to the parking lot, tires chirped a bit, and then the car accelerated dramatically, heading right for us! Dean was going thirty in the parking lot, the engine was roaring, and just before he plowed through us and the McDonald's wall, he spun the car to the left, skidded it sideways, tires howling to a stop. At the same time, the back door came flying open, swinging dangerously and wildly toward us as the car continued to skid toward us. Taking our cue, we dove frantically into the back seat, and John and I yelped out loud hellos.

"Shut up, assholes!" came the sharp reply from Les, who had spun around in his seat and now had a pistol pointed at us. "Get the hell down, goddammit! You know better!"

Dean had the engine roaring even more now, the tires were squealing and I could feel us accelerate out the lot, could smell the scorched rubber of spinning tires. Then we swung right, turning into traffic at a ridiculous speed, John and I with our heads down, kneeling on the back seat floor, disoriented and unstable with all the speed and turning. We were in shock, stunned by this onslaught that had us badly off balance.

"Have you got it?" shouted Dean.

"Got what?" I answered, still not sure what was going on. John looked at me, confused, puzzled – and neither of us knew whether to laugh or fear for our lives.

"Don't crack wise, smartguys!" Dean barked back. I felt the barrel of the gun now pressing against my head, felt it was plastic, something they had picked up at the Five and Ten Cent Store. I knew this was a scene, an act, and I told John as much by shooting him a wink, both of us still huddled on the back floor. His relief showed.

"Have you got it?" Dean came at us again, now shouting without restraint. The tires squealed again as we felt the car swerve to the left, felt a bump, then felt it accelerate hard.

"Yes, we've got it" answered John, who wanted into whatever game this was.

"Good" said Les. "And the code..."

"Of course they've got the goddam code!" Dean shouted at Les. "Langley doesn't let these agents out into the field – not handling the device – without the goddam code! That's the freakin' point of the Stokholm Protocol!" He scolded Les with this, condescending in his tone.

"I know that," Les shot back at him. "We *know* they have the code, which is exactly why I'm asking – to see if they *deny* having it, which is what Geneva has asked of them – unless they aren't connected with Lockheed or even Moscow - in which case they won't even admit to having the device in the first place!" Our heads were spinning.

"Alright, alright," said Dean. "We all need to calm down a bit." I peeked up to see the tree limbs whizzing by. I couldn't tell where we were, but I could tell we were going far too fast for the road we were on, and I heard a nearby car honk its horn.

"Down!" screamed Les, and Dean gunned the engine even more.

"Blue Dodge?" asked Les, who wanted to know who honked their horn.

"Blue Dodge," confirmed Dean, nodding his head.

"Sonnovabitch!" shouted Les, angry with us now. He turned back to John and me, plastic pistol waving. "Were you followed? Did you use the safe house? Did you take the goddam handoff from Carlos? How MANY of them are there?" We were overwhelmed again, couldn't tell what to reply to whom, felt the car lurch again and corner hard, tires howling.

"Shit – they don't have it!" cursed Dean, angrily. "They don't have it, and the unit can't be detonated without it! Rico will have us dead for this!"

"DO YOU HAVE THE DEVICE?" Les asked emphatically, literally screaming at us.

"Yes!" John and I shouted in unison.

"Heads down!" barked Les, who now turned back toward Dean and addressed him privately. "Should we ask them about the package?"

Dean nodded and punched his horn, jammed the brakes and then accelerated hard again.

"Okay, okay," said Les, calming himself. "Let's take this one step at a time, fellas. Now we have to know – we *really* have to know if the package is complete, and if it is, what's the trigger mechanism?" he stated in a monotone voice. "Is the relay system electromagnetic, titanium or liquid resistance? Which is it boys?"

193

"Titanium" answered John.

Simultaneously, Dean said to Les, "Has to be titanium because of the Radial Corvelling Cones," inventing yet another important-sounding, gibberish word.

"Right," said Les, thoughtfully. "Of course." Les turned back toward us, visibly working to control himself. "And the Spyrell Channel – it's clear, right?"

"Totally clear," I said. "It's totally clear."

"Well, it's clear as far as we know... I mean the Ruskies..." Dean corrected me, making the point that while I thought the 'Spyrell Chanel' was clear, we never know what Moscow really knew, what intelligence they did or didn't have.

With that, Dean and Les seemed to lighten up a bit, and John and I felt it was safe to sit in the backseat, to get up off the floor, as long as we slumped low so as not to be seen by any car that might be tailing us, which Dean was obsessed about.

"And Berlin?" asked Les after a long pause. "How did you boys like Berlin?"

We didn't know what to say, frozen in our lack of creativity.

"I know the feeling, fellas," said Dean with a smile. "I do very much know the feeling... Her name was Olga. Born in Minsk and defected to Argentina. I was there making a drop for the X58 project in Berlin in '63 when, out of the blue, she walked up to me in a little cafe..."

It went on like this for the entire half hour trip – they never came out of character, not for a second. John and I played along as best as we could, relieved to be alive and not in the middle of some web of real spies and intrigue. Our improv acting skills were substandard.

At last, we arrived home safely, delivered The Device (whatever that was), and enjoyed our weekend visit to the farm. It was a Cold War trip two West Pointers will never forget.

The Cap'n and the Mutinous Scallywag

"Avast there! ...Maybe you thought you was cap'n here, perhaps. By the powers, I'll teach you better! Cross me, and you'll go where many a good man's gone before you, first and last, these thirty year back — some to the yardarm, shiver my timbers! And some by the board, and all to feed the fishes. There's never a man looked me between the eyes and seen a good day a'terwards, Tom Morgan, you may lay to that."

Long John Silver, addressing a challenger
from *Treasure Island*
by Robert Louis Stevenson

(My age: 15)

"Four bells!" Dean, seated at one end of our kitchen table, had turned to his left to issue this command to some remote character that was apparently far off. Dean's command had a long, echoing report that he whispered out of the side of his mouth for our benefit. He was acting, that was obvious, but what was this all about?

"Aye, Cap'n, four bells," Les shot back at him, quick as could be and quietly confident, business like. Les was seated at the other end of the table, opposite Dean. He was acting something out with his hands and arms, miming that he was hauling on a heavy rope that went to something high overhead.

"Half left, down one quarter," came Dean, louder now, hand to his mouth, as if sending his voice across some distance. Before he finished his sentence it came back to him, echoed by Les.

"Half left, down one quarter." Les's voice was also loud and echoing, and was strained a bit, showing the physical effort required to haul the rope he was working. It was obvious Les was also shouting to somebody twenty yards away.

"Slack out of the starboard fore t'gallant braaaace..."

"Slack out!" echoed Les, still straining, "fore t'galant brace."

"Steady now."

"Aye, steady!" I picked up hint of resentment in Les's voice.

We were just finishing our dinner that evening and the entire family, plus Uncle Dean, Aunt Joan and Les were around the table, which was laden with the remnants of the meal, messy plates and near empty drinking glasses. The Dean and Les scene burst upon us from out of nowhere and caught us completely by surprise. We were in for a treat, a theatrical performance right in our midst, but where would this scene take us?

It was subtle, imperceptible at first. I'm not even sure when it had started. But it was apparent now that the table was moving gently, rocking to and fro, giving the sense that we were seated in a ship's galley, and the ship was pitching and rolling gently in waves. Dean and Les had gotten their feet under the bar that held the table's legs, and were rolling the table gently by the raising and lowering of their toes and forefeet.

"Weather off the port bow, Cap'n, sir! Two points off the port bow at two miles." Les reported this as he capped one hand over his eyes, straining to see, staring off to some imaginary distant clouds.

Dean, the Sea Captain, ignored him. "Damn the weather, Mr. Lee. Steady, Mr. Lee, steady as she goes..."

"Steady, sir."

The pitching of the table became more pronounced now. The waves were stronger and more abrupt, and we could feel the tension growing between the two seafaring men. One plate slid slightly on the table top.

"Weather sir... coming fast..." Les's tone signaled his impatience.

"I said *steady*, Mr. Lee! Now mind your lines and look smart or I'll batten your hatches with the cat o'nine tails, you impertinent cur!"

"Aye, Cap'n, aye..." The poor sailor looked dogged and shamed, yet there was a clear resentment in his demeanor, a not-so-well-masked disgust in his eyes. He muttered under his breath, barely audible "Aye, ya bloody fool..."

"Silence dog!" fired back the captain, hot with a quick rage, his voice thundering across the tipsy table. "I'll not brook your insolence, you mutinous scoundrel – it'll be lashes for you man, or it'll be Davy Jones, by God!"

"Meaning no disrespeck, Cap'n..." cowered Mr. Lee. "But the weather approaches, sir!"

"I've heard ye, man, and I'll decide what and when aboard The Flower!" The fact that this ship, this watery catacomb of roughnecking was so inaptly named caused a few at the table to burst with laugher that just enraged the captain more.

"By damn, you'll pay for this!" screamed the irate captain, pointing directly at us.

"You're an incompetent cap'n and what's been said has been said!" thundered Mr. Lee, bold in his loud defiance.

"Scuppers!"

"Aye, scuppers, then! They's twenty of us and only one of you!" Les met our eyes as he said this, as if to invite us into the coming mutiny.

The captain bellowed at all of us now, "Avast all of ye! I'll have all of ye flogged for this, by thunder!" Just as he said this the ship hit something hard, the rocky shoal beneath her hull, and she lurched in a jarring manner. The table bumped and a glass half filled with water went tumbling, pots rolled and pans slid into one other.

"Now you've run the Flower ashore ya bloody bastard! Scuttled we are!" bellowed Les. Dean barked something back but I couldn't hear what the captain said. I was focused on the sharp carving knife Les had plucked from our serving plate and which he now held by the point of the blade. It was razor sharp and the steel glistened in the light as he waved it wildly. He swooped it over his head and screamed at the captain, "Away with him, mates! Off with his bloody head!" and he sent the knife flying across the table, just over Dean's head. It clattered against the aluminum above our stove just as the ship gave another brutal heave, the table bumped hard, and another drinking glass rocked on edge, silverware clanged loudly on the floor.

The two men sprang up in a flash and went at each other's throats, bellowing oaths and threats as they tussled in our kitchen, knocking chairs over and making a great show if it. It was riveting stuff, impossible for us not be absorbed in.

"Davy Jones it'll be, then!"

"Aye, for *you*!"

Their mock battle carried from the kitchen out to the living room area, and as they tumbled through the passageway and out of our view, we spontaneously erupted into applause and cheers, hooting hoorays for the street actors in our midst. At last we could catch our collective breath. There was nothing quite like dinner and a show aboard The Flower.

And More

1962: Dean flipped a fake detective's badge to a traffic cop outside of Yale Bowl in New Haven and told him to send all the post-game traffic at the next intersection to the right. Dean then drove up and turned left, waving approval to the traffic cop. Dean simply wanted to go home without fighting all the traffic.

1975: Dean walked confidently past cadet guards at West Point, directly to the middle of the football field and, in front of thousands of fans, appeared to pull out exotic equipment so he could take "radioactivity" samples from the fifty yard line. He said he was with the CIA, and they believed him.

1980: Dean got on a bus once and held a roll of blankets in his arms; they were to keep warm in the stadium at the end of the ride. He acted like it was baby, a gently swaddled infant. He pretended to be a foreigner, unable to speak any English and he soon had half the bus cooing and ahh-ing for a baby that didn't exist.

1927 – 2009: All who met Dean Preece learned that any situation has the potential for levity, that audacity can be a powerful thing, and that life is far too short.

Dean entertaining family and friends
with his Hitler imitation at West Point, 1977

Chapter 11

"Vly Summit Winter Olympics" of 1968

(My age: 12)

As kids we rode our bikes and fished in tiny streams. We played in abandoned one-room schoolhouses, some of which still stand today. We built forts and tunnels with bales of hay and dug snow caves in winter. My brother Casey and I tore the bottom out of an old galvanized metal pail and nailed it to the wall in the Dodge barn, then rolled socks and bound them with rubber bands, made a crude ball of the thing, and played "basketball" for countless hours. To us it was Madison Square Garden. We made up names and took on personas and lived out nail-biting, buzzer-beating shots. We ran pass patterns, and threw footballs, after faking handoffs to phantom friends we pretended were there with us. On Saturdays in the fall, local farm boys gathered at one of our family farms, played football and poured our hearts out in sport amongst cow patties and places where granite skimmed the surface – Sherman Townsend and Phil Bell and the Guidons and Walshes and Preeces. We played like Lombardi and Bear Bryant were watching. With our endless supply of green apples in the fall, we played a sort of high stakes dodge ball, and tossed hours of apple-batting practice, using sticks as bats. Snowballs served us for "winter ball," like we were the offseason Mets in Sarasota. We invented games with brothers and cousins that we played long into the night - like "Dungeon," where one team of kids sprinted across our lawn in milky moonlight, while the other team tried to trip them with burlap bags full of soft hay. This was deliciously serious stuff to us kids. It was stuff we dreamed of and ached for and bragged or sulked about for weeks. It consumed us. The work of the farm, as ubiquitous as it was, merely formed the setting, the backdrop in the theater of our childhood; it was only our background music. Like all other kids, work was what we had to do, but play was what we lived for.

1968 was a tumultuous year, even for a twelve year old rural farm kid. Martin Luther King and Bobby Kennedy had each been brutally gunned down, and I watched it and read about it and heard it discussed over the dinner table until I wanted to throw up. Vietnam kept raging and the names of boys from nearby towns showed up in newspapers and on the local news, too often because their lifeless bodies were returning home for burial. The Tet Offensive was in full swing, and American kids were getting the worst of it. It was the high season for Abbie Hoffman and the Chicago Seven and the Students for a Democratic Society. The Democratic National Convention in Chicago was rocked by rioters and violence, and it seemed the country was coming apart right in front of me. I didn't like the world I was hurtling toward, and no amount of "Laugh In" or The Doors singing "Hello, I Love You" or Otis Redding doing "The Dock of the Bay" could distract me sufficiently. Like McCart, our head-turning cow, I wanted to look the other way, wanted to pretend I didn't notice what a mess was out there.

I found distraction in our play, our games. I immersed myself in sports. For me, the Olympics were the thing that year. The 1968 Winter Olympics in Grenoble had Jean Claude Killy and Peggy Fleming, and the Summer Olympics in Mexico City featured Bob Beaman's startling, record shattering broad jump and high jumper Bob Fosbury's remarkable "flop." And late in December of 1968, we manufactured our own "Vly Summit Winter Olympics." I made it consume me.

My father's piercing whistle, coming sharp through the winter night, told Casey and me that he needed us in the main barn immediately. Following our unspoken sibling protocol for such final moments in our games, Casey took the sock-ball and started his final possession from the workbench at the far end of our small Dodge barn. He drove hard to his left, moving toward our dented aluminum bucket-basket nailed to the near wall. I took one step into the lane to block him, and he immediately broke right, powered straight past me to the pail-basket and made it rattle loudly with the sound of a sock-ball score. He was up one.

I was Kelly Greene, a made up person with a made up name on a made up team. Kelly was a small, undersized guard on the "Toledo Flyers" team, complete with the purple gym shorts that I wore over my work pants. Greene was tough as nails, scrappy, and a deadly long distance shooter. He was the only white kid on the otherwise all-black team, having earned respect from the tough kids that played basketball in city streets and on concrete courts with chain-netted hoops. He'd been in these situations before and was unflappable under pressure. Kelly Greene was known for floating monstrous shots high over the barn's internal beams and rafters and watching confidently as the sock ball, unfazed by the closing buzzer, found the bucket and won the game.

I, that is Kelly Greene, took my final imaginary inbound pass and turned to face the defense that was my brother. I paused, took a deep breath and firmed my determination. Then two fast steps forward and a pump fake from my favorite spot, right behind a low rafter beam. Casey left his feet in an all out attempt to block the shot – bingo! Greene pulled the ball back down and glided left into the open space, set up a sweet, soft buzzer-beater from ten feet that would seal it. I released the sock-ball at the apex of my jump, flicked my wrist as if in slow motion and let my index finger fall lazily toward the back of the basket. Glory would be mine… But the shot hit the front of the rim and rattled the bucket, made all the right sounds but for the worst of reasons. Kelly Greene had missed, the game was lost, and I was deflated.

"One more chance!" I blurted out, still in disbelief. But Dad's second whistle, this time angry and irritated – you could tell that about his whistles – ended the game officially. We sprinted toward the barn and our awaiting chores.

When I got to the barn I was surprised to find both my Uncle Dean Preece and my cousin Jim Shanley there. Their two families had arrived minutes ago at our farm. They pulled in at almost the same time, despite three hour-long trips from their different Connecticut starting points. Casey and I were so wrapped up in our game that we never heard them arrive. Of course I was thrilled to see them, and we said our happy hello's before feeding the cows, washing milking machines and closing up the barn for the night.

It dropped to five below zero that night. The next morning was sunny but still brutally cold, and by late afternoon the snow began to fall. Ernie Tetrault's Channel 6 Capitol Region weather forecast reported that we were in for more of the same for the next few days. My father was disappointed because he had been hoping for milder weather that would have allowed us to mix and pour concrete. The extra help from visitors would have made a big difference in pouring a new concrete floor for part of the heifer barn, and Dad was confident and eager to get at it. A few days earlier, he had called Dan McPeek and talked through a construction plan and had all the project management pieces clearly organized in his mind. Jim Duffy was part of the visiting crew, and he endorsed the construction plan which gave Dad further confidence. Like Dan, Jim had a talent for directing projects and orchestrating efforts like this. But it was just too cold to pour concrete; the project was put off until things warmed up.

There were a lot of people at the farm, nineteen of us altogether. We felt housebound and restless, sequestered in too small a space. And this chafed against my father's dogma and doctrine, against his religion, against his deeply held belief that inaction was bad – especially for boys. Dean perceived my father's concern, recognized the check in Dad's deepest constitution and invented a solution that shaped the next few days and touched our hearts forever.

"You fellas ready?" asked Dean, speaking to all of us kids, now gathered in the living room.

"Ready for what?" my brother asked.

"Ready for what?" Dean shot back in a mocking, mimicking, condescending tone. "Why, the Vly Summit Olympic Games, of course. Game one is tomorrow at 10:00 in the morning – touch football. Old folks and little ones versus teeny weenies, and we're gonna whup your asses. Shelton style, old school! Americans versus teeny bobs. Better get ready, ladies."

"All rrright!" we shot back as one. "You old geezers are on!"

We spent the next several minutes buzzing in our kitchen, finalizing who would be on what team, clarifying who was playing and not playing, and generally talking trash in our delighted anticipation.

"I better go with the teenagers" offered twenty-two year old Pat, a college football veteran who was dating my cousin and was making his first trip to the farm. "Not sure what might happen if you older guys run out of Geritol," he said dryly. We erupted with hoots and instantly loved Pat for the well placed cut, especially since he had been so reserved up to this point, and we were trying to get a read on him. He was "in" and we accepted him as one of us, loved him from that moment forward.

"Maybe you'd be more at home painting graffiti on a college classroom building" Dad snickered back at us, part a playful jab and part a reflection of his disgust with a generation that rampaged on colleges all over the country.

"Only writing we'll be doing is tattooing the score on your keesters!" my brother Rick entered the good-natured fray, taunting the adults. It went on like this for some time.

We finally wound things down and headed off to bed. My cousin Jim stayed in our room, and we chatted over the sounds that drifted from his transistor radio. The Montreal Canadiens were hosting the Boston Bruins in Montreal's famous Forum. The broadcast of the hockey game was in French, and I didn't understand a single word of it. Yet it was the perfect way to slip into sleep, consumed with sport. Just as with my father's whistle, the announcer's voice, rather than his words which were so unintelligible to my ears, told me all I needed to know. His matter of fact tone told me the game was being prosecuted, his quickened pace said that the home team had the puck in the offensive zone, and his frantic urgency announced that there were shots on goal. Conversely, I could sense his anxiety when the visitors from Boston were threatening to score. Hockey sounds, not hockey words, gave me refuge and sent me off to a deep sleep that night.

The next morning we milked the cows and had breakfast, then gathered on the road in front of our house, the only flat, snowplowed place suitable for a football game. Our rural dirt road would see only a few cars all day, and even less when the weather was so cold. The youngest kids were sided with the adults, and we teens would stand alone against them. The little kids and old folks called themselves "The Americans," as a way for the littlest ones to know they were on the side of good vs. evil; good being "Americans" and evil being "Teeny-Bobs," as they called us.

The Americans kicked off and the game was under way, but the kick was exceedingly short and recovered by them. "Onsides kick!" shouted my youngest brother Joe, one of the Americans and somebody who took the game seriously. He bounced up off the ball, having recovered it from the snowy patch beneath him.

"Okay, okay!" said my cousin Jimmy Shanley on our side. "No problem, guys. They can have the darned ball, and we'll just shut them down."

We lined up for the snap. When the ball was hiked, the old guys bumped into each other in the backfield which we found hilarious and a bit pathetic. But they quickly recovered and my Uncle Jim Shanley (Jimmy's dad) had faded back as quarterback and was obviously bootlegging left, hiding the ball on his hip. Several of us saw the deception and rushed him, two-hand touched him while still in the backfield, and shouted "way to go!" at each other. Uncle Jim just chuckled at us.

Dean had the ball tucked inside his coat and was standing alone in the end zone. We had been bamboozled.

They kicked off again, and this time it was for real. We returned the ball and promptly threw an interception, as our receiver bobbled the pass right into their arms.

Two plays later they razzle-dazzled us, lateralling the ball to one another and weaving like the Harlem Globetrotters down the field. One of us would make the two-hand touch only to discover the ball had already been passed away. They went on like this for much of the game.

It was rough, but we loved it. The O'Connors, good family friends, had stopped by to say hello, and their kids had entered the fray. Tony O'Connor was three years older than me and tough; he would later go on to play football in college. On one particular play, he rushed the quarterback but was blocked by my father, always the football guard. Dad had hit him hard and had driven him to the ground. Tony thought Dad overdid it a bit and decided to come back just as hard on the next play. He did. He leaped to block a pass and in the process elbowed Dad in the face. Dad's tooth popped out and some blood stained the snow around them. Tony felt terrible, but Dad didn't. He found the tooth and pocketed it, assured Tony that "this is football," and these things are part of the game. He continued to play, didn't slow things down a bit. "That's when I knew I was in a football game, boys," Tony would tell us years later, smiling big as he marveled at the intensity we all brought to those games.

The old folks continued playing football with their style of misdirection and deception. They were neither faster nor stronger. But they were slicker. They cheated of course, throwing forward passes after they crossed the line of scrimmage, claiming catches even after the ball was clearly on the ground, and sometimes carried ball-cradling little ones high over their heads where we couldn't possibly achieve a two-handed touch. But the truth is that they beat us. We figured that even with their cheating, we should have pounded them. We were younger and stronger and quicker. But it didn't matter. Not on that day.

Still, the "Americans," especially the old guys - who called themselves the "Century Club" - paid the price with swollen bruises, twisted ankles, and throbbing knees. Their wounds hampered them for future events, the remaining contests that became part of the Vly Summit Winter Olympics of 1968.

Dean (left, next to another Connecticut visitor), nursing a swollen ankle, holding the day's score totals: "Century Club 56, Teeny Bobs 7"

****

We spent much of that afternoon gloating and complaining, jawing and prodding each other, and at the same time trying to decide what contests would come next. Late in the day Dad came from our attic holding our box of mismatched ice skates and a few cheap hockey sticks he had secretly bought from Mammoth Mart, a general merchandise retail store in Bennington.

"Yeah, hockey tomorrow!" I declared, excited we'd have another chance to win, to make up for our recent loss. Jimmy Shanley had his own gear and played organized hockey, and I knew we'd win because of him. I couldn't wait for tomorrow.

Dad set things in motion. "Oh, and you teen guys need to clear the ice. Can't play in the snow, you know."

We were thrilled and headed toward our frozen pond immediately, bundled in winter clothing, shovels in hand. The work was harder than I expected, as the snow was heavy and the pond seemed bigger than I remembered it being. Ponds shrink in size when you dive and swim in them, when you launch off the diving board and go for maximum height and splash with a cannonball. And they swell larger when you have to walk each icy square foot of the thing, when you have to carry wet snow off every inch of it. But we endured, got it done.

After accomplishing our Zamboni-like ice clearing duties we returned to the farmhouse and burst into the kitchen.

"Ice is ready!" my cousin Kathy Duffy announced. "The whole thing is cleared and we nailed boards together to use as goals. No goalies, we decided – and we also decided you can either play in shoes or in skates."

"Okay, good," said Dad, pleased that the kids were getting into this and becoming consumed with things. Keeping us kids busy was the key to our happiness, and to his. "Did you tape up the hockey sticks? There is black electrical friction tape in the Dodge barn."

"Already got that done," said Casey. "Teeny Bobs are ready for the Americans! Want to start at 10:00 tomorrow morning?" He was anxious to play and hopeful that 10:00 wasn't too early for the adults, who were still nursing bruises and soreness from the football game.

"Tomorrow?" asked my Uncle Jim. "This is a night sport, fellas. You'd better get your team ready – NOW!"

We were thrilled and energized. We milked and did the chores, ate an early dinner and hustled through the knee-deep snow to our pond. Uncle Dean and Uncle Jim were already there and had built what was now a roaring fire, right in the middle of the ice, and there were two smaller fires going, one behind each goal at the farthest edges of the pond. It was a spectacular sight: a giant, grizzly bear of a fire between two gentler, playful cub fires, all glowing in the cold, pitch black emptiness of the winter night.

"Won't that melt the ice?" I was concerned, wondered if these guys know what they were doing. I looked around and saw no ropes or rescue ladders to pull me from the ice that might melt and soften and break beneath me.

"That ice is three feet thick," my father answered, and I was sure he was right. It had been well below freezing for weeks.

Several of us sat on the snow banks that bounded our rink and slipped on skates from our hodgepodge collection, trying to find the ones that fit best. There were ancient, floppy-leathered hockey skates, small sized skates with dual blades, timeworn speed skates with enormously long blades and figure skates for men and for women. Nothing fit well. Some of us decided to forego the authenticity of skating and opted to play in work boots, preferring some stability over the perils of entering the skating novitiate.

Jim Duffy was near the center fire, puck in hand. "Captains!"

Jimmy Shanley skated confidently to him and Dean shuffled in that direction in his boots, went a few feet and took an awkward fall, shot his feet out in front of himself and landed on his back, hockey stick rattling on the ice. "Just testing for ice firmness!" he shot out almost before he landed, and we all burst out in laughter.

The puck was dropped; the game had begun. It was outrageous fun as we hurtled around the slippery surface, tripping and sliding and stumbling over ourselves and each other. Jimmy and my

Dad were the only ones even remotely capable of skating proficiently and the rest of us were absolute wrecks, overdressed and overanxious, like a colony of drunken penguins with hockey sticks. My two uncle Jims, Jim Duffy and Jim Shanley, became some of the best players out there because they simply stayed put and waited for the puck to come to them, a concept lost on the rest of us who were furious in our gang-gaggled pursuit of the elusive puck. We crashed into snow banks pursuing the thing and poked it free from the fire on occasion, erupted when rare goals were scored and screamed protests when the other team scored after holding a competitor.

The farmhouse crew, those not playing, eventually came down to witness the spectacle. They brought a thermos full of hot chocolate for us kids and thermos full of something more for the adults. We went at it again and continued our icy and delightful debacle. It was hard to stop laughing, yet we had to focus so as not to hurt ourselves in a head-whacking fall. We played until we were exhausted.

Teeny Bobs 9. Americans 7. We had won and regained respect after losing the football game. The overall score of Vly Summit Winter Olympics was tied.

****

At breakfast the next morning the teens joined the adults in nursing bruises and complaining of sore muscles. We told and retold stories from the day before, about how this one had caught the long pass or how that one had fallen on top of the puck and almost slid into the center-ice fire. This was our visitors' last full day at the farm, and given the extent of our physical soreness, we assumed that the day would be one of rest and relaxation. We began to talk of playing cards and watching TV.

As breakfast finished, Dean told us all the story of the "Battle of King's Chair." He was a wonderful storyteller, and we loved this particular story, which we had heard several times before. He told us of his childhood friends, of his sixth grade "Southside Gang" that roamed the streets in Shelton, Connecticut. They were good kids but mischievous and full of themselves. They had marvelous names, like Figgie Swanick and Ears Marsden and Thomas Jefferson. He described their tree fort and their stash of girlie pictures. We heard it as every sixth grade boy's Fort Knox and Playboy Mansion. He told us how, purely by chance, on that particular day they bumped into their rivals, the "Northside Guys," at a roadside intersection that had been carved out of the side of a modest hill. The slope of the cut in the hill went up, then back, then up, like a giant chair. "King's Chair" was how they always referred to that spot. The Northside Guys had come to use a nearby ballfield at Ferry School, a ball field the Southside Gang considered exclusively "theirs" during summer months.

Words were exchanged about somebody's sister and poor baseball skills, and early hormones had the sides quickly squaring off. A punch was thrown, though it's still debated today as to who started it – like the shots fired at Lexington Green. Ears Marsden's slingshot went into action, and the fight was on, full force. The Southside Gang, by all reports – fog of war and all, it's so hard to know what truly happened – was getting the worst of it. The hated Northside Guys, led by the muscular Kelpie Goyle, was gaining control. Just then, Southside's Tom Jefferson scrambled to the high ground midway up King's Chair, turned his BB gun on his rivals from this vantage point, and turned the tide of the Battle of King's Chair, once and for all.

Just then, and by mere coincidence, Police Chief Donovan happened upon the scene in his cruiser. Before any of the combatants could figure out what had happened, Chief Donovan had startled them with his police whistle and froze them with the threat of his billy club. He lined them all up and walloped Jeff's (Thomas Jefferson's) BB gun against a telephone pole, bending the barrel of the thing like it was a pretzel. The armistice was thrust upon them, signed. The Battle of

King's Chair was over. The Southside Gang had defended its turf, though punishments were still being handed out.

Chief Donovan was a family friend and drove the Preece boys, Don and Dean, to their Shelton home. He knocked on the door and told Ralph, Don and Dean's father, about what had gone down. Ralph told his friend that he'd handle things with the kids. Gertie (Ralph's wife, Don and Dean's mother, my grandmother) arrived home a few minutes later. Ralph, angry with the boys and ready to deal out some punishment, shared the story with Gertie. She was always a staunch defender of her kids, so much so that she sometimes was blinded to the ruffian side that all boys have, and she denied what was right in front of her. When Ralph had finished giving his report, Gertie responded as she did when she heard her sons had stolen dinghies and cut them afloat in the Milford harbor.

"...Not *my* boys," she said in complete denial. "No... not *my* boys."

We roared at this punch line that we knew was coming, and basked in the warm glow of this favorite among our family's stories.

"That story reminds me," started Jim Duffy. And he told us another delightful tale of how he used to play catcher for the baseball team at St. Bonaventure and consequently had developed a good throwing arm. He told of how the seminarians were "regular guys" too and how they'd occasionally smuggle beer into the place. Jim's job was to throw the bottles away, to fire them out a window and over a high fence where seminarians could secretly retrieve them the next day and properly dispose of the things, thus removing the evidence. The only way to throw anything out of that low window was to throw from a squatting position, like baseball catchers do, like Jim did for years. He chuckled as he told his story, and I saw that sparkle in his eye again; I knew he loved telling that story.

What I didn't know is that the story had a purpose, that he told it as a parable and a lead-in to our next Olympic event. The moment we had our laugh after he finished the story, he announced the next contest. It startled us in its suddenness, as none of us saw it coming; we thought the day would be a lazy one. Not so.

"Okay!" Jim Duffy's tone had suddenly changed. "Each team has two hours to build its forts. We'll do it in the field behind the old milkhouse. Then we'll come back here for lunch. After lunch it's a snowball war – all throws have to be from a squatting position." We all understood in an instant that this was an ingenious way of protecting the little ones. We bigger kids couldn't throw with much power when throwing from our knees or from a squat. It took us a few seconds longer to realize that this rule also gave a big advantage to... Jim Duffy. "Clock starts NOW!"

"Wait," Dad had intervened. "After lunch we need a crew to go the field barn and get a load of hay; the rest of us here will put up a small grist. Five bags of corn. Agway will be here around 4:00 this afternoon."

"Field barn!" I called my spot, anxious to avoid the rasped knuckles that came with putting up a grist, with filling burlap sacks with shovels full of hard ears of corn.

"Grist!" yelled Sue Duffy, who wanted nothing to do with the remote field barn.

And so it went, everybody declaring their preference.

My father nodded to Jim Duffy and Jim spoke again. "Like I said – clock starts NOW!"

We never noticed that the weather was still miserably cold and wet. We were so consumed with building snow forts and preparing for battle, developing attack and defense strategies, and waging our playful war that nothing else mattered: not getting loads of hay or putting up grists nor dealing with fiercely cold weather. We engineered walls and constructed tunnels. We built remote outposts that would allow us to attack from different angles. We manufactured mounds of snowball inventories and positioned them where we thought they'd give us the most advantage. And we waged a fantastic, delightful, exhausting battle that lasted for hours.

I don't know how you keep score in a snowball battle like that, but apparently the adults did. It was declared: Americans 54, Teeny Bobs 19. They were back in the lead, and we assumed the Olympics were over. It was late afternoon. We were cold and tired. And our visitors would be going back to their Connecticut homes tomorrow.

While we were consumed in our snowball war, Uncle Jim Shanley, a self-selected non-snowballer, had amassed all the snow-sliding gear he could find and now had them lined up in our front lawn. There were classic American Flyer sleds made of wood slats with metal rails, metal flying saucer dishes, skis, a toboggan, molded plastic sleds, and even Danny Thomas's kid's bobsled – complete with Danny who had just arrived from the farm next door. Dan had seen our pond fire the night before and wanted in on whatever was going on. Apparently, there was a plan for more contests, and though we were exhausted, our tiredness was overwhelmed by our delight. But it was already late afternoon; time was running out.

Then Uncle Jim explained the plan. "The 1968 Vly Summit Winter Olympics will soon culminate with our final event. The Americans lead right now, by an overall team score of 631 points to 418 points…"

"Boo-hiss," many of us teens shot back – where did *that* score come from?"

Jim continued. "This evening, on the slopes of Preece Mountain, broadcast from the Henry Thomas Memorial Broadcast Booth, we will feature the final event…starting at 8:00 p.m… the main event, illuminated for our cameras by torchlight… the DOWNHILL CLASSIC!"

And so the venue was set. Again, we were giddy with the joy of an unexpected treat. We couldn't get enough of cousins and visitors, so milking every last bit of time together was far more important than resting tired limbs and recuperating from earlier bruises. And we had never been on sleds at night, so the newness of it was that much more thrilling. Our night hockey experience was so fun and so unique we knew that the "downhill classic" would live up to its name.

After dinner and milking, we each packed up rolls of toilet paper and old rags, and some carried poles or sticks that would hold our handmade torches, and we made our way up our hill. Dad and my uncles punched torch poles into the snow every twenty yards or so along a route that covered some of the steeper parts of our hill, and thus marked out a route for us to follow. A can of diesel fuel was brought along, and rags and toilet rolls were soaked in diesel before being lit. Once again, it made for a spectacular sight. We soared along in the nighttime air, slid over the snow that had now crusted over and formed a sort of contoured ice. This sent us flying at high speed, but made it tough to turn or otherwise control our crafts. We were careful to avoid the torches, but Rick couldn't stop his sled and went barreling into a barbed wire fence at the bottom of our run – luckily without serious consequences.

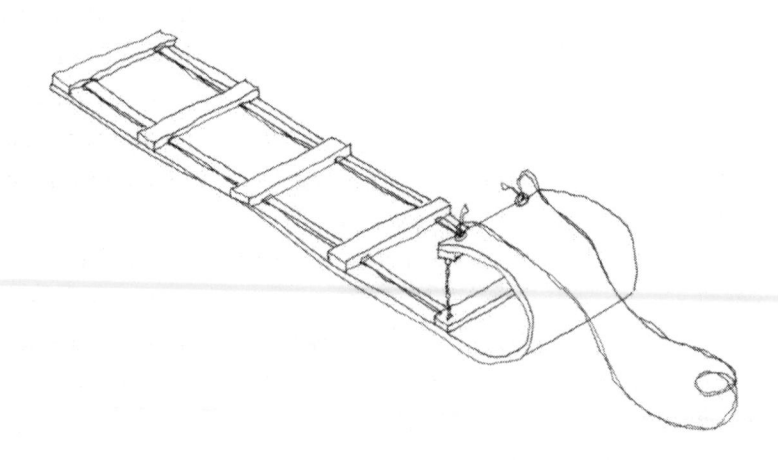

My Uncle Jim Shanley didn't fare so well. On one toboggan run, Uncle Jim, sitting in the back behind a row of kids, attempted to plant his left foot in the snow, to create drag and turn the toboggan away from a torch. But his foot broke through the crusty surface and punched deep into the soft snow below. This exposed his upper leg, his inner thigh, to the edge of the icy crust on the surface. It snapped him off the toboggan and tore through his trousers and gouged his skin, bruising it badly. There was a little blood but not much. It was more the violent force of the thing that spun the large man like a top, purpled his thigh and caused him to limp for the next several days. This mishap signaled to all of us that it was time to bring our night of torch-lit sledding to a close. But of course, only after each kid had "one last run" down the hill.

* * * * * * *

The next morning was sunny and still cold. Our visitors had begun packing their cars and were getting prepared for the trip back to their respective Connecticut homes. Dad had hitched the snowplow to the back of the tractor and was plowing snow out of the barnyard, so we could get back to the business of cleaning barns and operating like a real farm again. Dad's barnyard snowplowing had a rhythmic sound to it, a sort of urr-ump-ahhh-woosh of the tractor going forward and back, the blade scraping and the mounds of snow packing into more mounds of snow.

My brother Joe, who inexplicably didn't get enough the night before, was sledding along the side of the house, along the foot of our hill, along the snow-packed cowpath that ran down across the road and eventually into the barnyard. He would sled a short way and skid to a safe stop and do it again. He noticed us watching him and waved toward us, a sort of "watch this" wave that suggested he was about to show off some newfound sledding acrobatics. He went up the hill to start his run, farther up the hill than I thought he should have.

Snowplowing music played in the barnyard background of the scene. Urr-ump-ahhh-woosh. Urr-ump-ahhh-woosh.

I could see it coming after he went only a few yards down the hill on that sled. The movie ran clear in my mind, fast-forwarded beyond my control and froze me solid. Joe was already going too fast. My brain, as if it were on hyper-dive and outrunning all the brains and perceptions of those around me, was ahead of Joe's, was already several seconds into the future. Urr-ump-ahhh-woosh.

I knew Joe didn't see the events that were about to unfold in front of him. I knew he was focused only ten feet in front of himself, focused only on the next clump of snow and next patch of ice. There was no anticipation in him, no foresight. Urr-ump-ahhh-woosh. He blasted through the ice near the side of the house and approached the icy road crossing at a frightening speed. I saw Dub Touhey sled down that snowy road decades ago, hurtling toward my grandfather's brown Dodge... Urr-ump-ahhh-woosh. I watched helplessly as I saw my neighbor, little Johnny Schmitt sprint out of the barn, unaware of the relentless approach of the truck that would tragically take his life. And then I watched helplessly as my youngest brother, unaware, sped toward my father, toward a man consumed with his work, toward a hunk of mobilized metal that had no soul, no heart. I cringed; I physically cramped in my chest and stomach and involuntarily lunged forward, slightly doubled up but still watching. Urr-ump-ahhh-woosh...

I still cannot comprehend how it happened, though I watched every second of it, gawked, glued to it. Joe hurtled across the road and entered the barnyard far too fast, nearly out of control. Dad had just begun backing up the tractor and snowplow for one more surge, one more shoving of snow into snow. He never did see Joe coming. Through some act of cosmic coincidence, Joe's sled adjusted course ever so slightly to the right, yet he made no attempt to slow the thing. Like a mirage, instead of witnessing the horror of my brother's death, instead of seeing his small body and frail sled devoured by the lifeless, chain-wrapped wheels of our tractor, my brother shot cleanly under the rolling death machine. I still couldn't breathe. I was still frozen.

The blur caught Dad's eye as Joe emerged on the other side and flew out the back of the barnyard. He braked hard. Jerking the tractor and snowplow to an immediate stop, he sent it rocking from its momentum. He was dumbfounded, as frozen as I was. I observed my father as he watched Joe finally slow himself to safety. I saw my father look down into his lap, as his mind pieced it all together in a flash. And I watched him as an onslaught of uninvited tears charged him. He fought them off, locked the brake, and shut down the engine. He was off the now-dead tractor in a second and walked fast into the barn, shaking his head in anger and relief. I have no doubt he broke down in there. Broke down in front of Sheila, in front of Five-Twelve and twenty other cows. He broke down there because he couldn't in front of the rest of us, couldn't let us see how much we meant to him and how desperately he loved us, needed us all. Against all explainable reason, his son had random chance and bad luck thrust upon him in the same way Dub Touhey and Johnny Schmidt did. Yet, unlike Dub and Johnny, it was over and he was spared. I have no doubt my father cried in anguish for their souls, and no doubt he collapsed in gratitude for Joe's safe deliverance.

It took a while to regroup. It took a few minutes to collect in the road for good-byes and farewells. We dealt with Joe's mishap for the most part by joking about it and pretending it wasn't as bad as it was. We ignored the gravity of it as much as we could, and did not mention Dad's quick flight onto the barn. It was over, and we had been spared without reason or rationale. We were all coming out of the private places that each of us retreated to in order to process this in our own unique ways.

It had been a whirlwind of a few days, a remarkable distraction from the cold oppression of heavy winter, and for me from the reality of the tumultuous world that awaited my coming of age. It was at once a glorious time and a time of sobering awareness for me. I was surrounded by an extended family that loved and soared high, failed at times and caused unintended pain at others. We were exactly what families are: authentic, wonderfully imperfect, threaded with God's graces and His grants of talent, opinionated wizards on all but ourselves, sometimes brutally unlucky and sometimes spared beyond belief. I knew I had just experienced something significant. I was aware that Joe's fortune was remarkable. I was aware of the gift of relatives and family, aware of the bonding glue that was their histories and our stories. I was aware of the gift that came in the form of a humble, sometimes crude farm in a remote place with harsh winters. Most of all, I was aware that I would never forget the 1968 Vly Summit Winter Olympics, a special time in a special place.

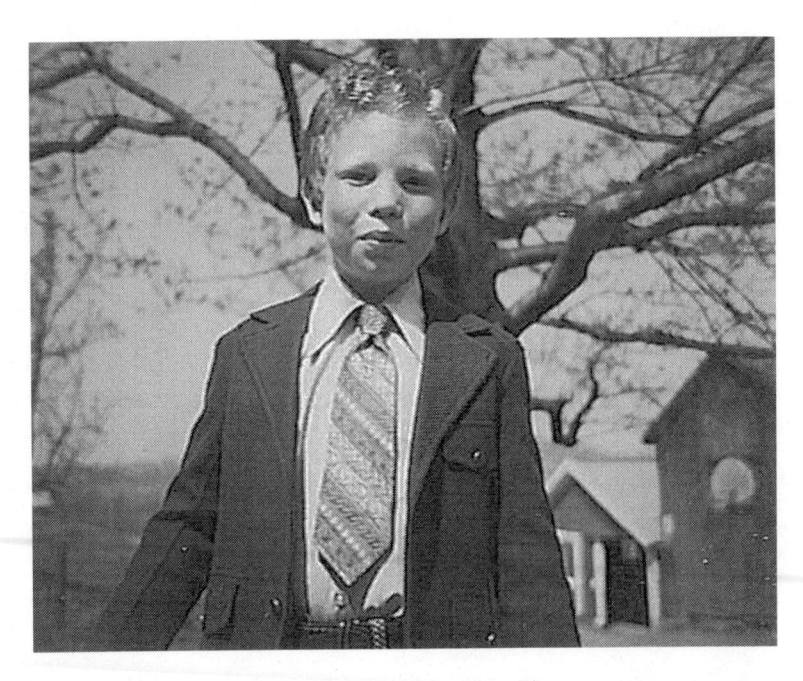

My brother Joe, at about the age of the sled-under-the-tractor incident

Chapter 12

Impetigo Park

(My age: 11)

Haying is the endless summer dance of the dairy farm. It starts with mowing the lush, green fields of June, cutting the alfalfa, clover and timothy, and in the process, releasing their sweet fragrance into the open air. Nothing smells quite as fresh and nature-sweet as just mowed hay. The hay is then immediately conditioned, and when fully dried, it is raked and then baled. Finally, the bales are loaded on wagons and taken to barns where they are packed away for the season, and await their duty as precious feed for snowbound cows. Throughout this haying process tractors hum and machines rumble in their own unique rhythm, filling the countryside with the gentle background music of summer. Like vassals paying tribute to the feudal lord, every hay field makes two annual contributions to the farm, once in early summer and a second time in late summer, the second cutting being milder in volume, but a far greater delicacy on the bovine palette.

Up close, the hands-on work of handling bales is rougher stuff. It scratches and chafes the skin and tears at the fingers of bale handlers. In midsummer, the high sun can bake the hayfield worker as it reflects off the newly barren ground, and off the ever present farm equipment, each metal slab of machine being yet another repository for ever-radiant heat.

But hay dust is the ubiquitous thing. The bone-dry hay, when turned and bent and pounded and crushed into bales, produces a relentless cloud of hay dust that lingers long in the air. Like the mist over Niagara Falls, hay dust is the constant and aromatic proof of the activity beneath it. It is breathed in and slowly saturates the farmer's clothes, becomes embedded in hair and hats, and it permeates nostrils and ears and cakes gently on the tongue's saliva. Sweet, dry hay dust smells pleasant and tastes wholesome enough, albeit foreign and chalky dry. The dust gets everywhere on the perspiring farmer, on arms, faces and sweat-dampened backs, in his eyelashes and in his matted hair. After finishing the job, he wants nothing more than to rinse the stuff off every pore on his body. We had just the thing. It was park and fountain; it was bathtub and glorious wet refreshment. It was free; it was ours; and I thought it was absolutely spectacular: our pond.

The pond was always our after-haying oasis, our Waikiki Water Park. It was the place where we frolicked. It was the place that rewarded our hard work. It was playground and vacation spot and sweet, cool refreshment. It was our long anticipated relief from haying and taxing, physical labor. And it was the place where all that hay dust came off. We absolutely loved it. We'd begin talking about the pond half way through our afternoon haying session, slowly building our anticipation of cool water and buoyant relaxation. It was the prize that drove us to finish our work quickly, to put all equipment away properly, to thoroughly clean up the many loose ends and last details of haying. When we finally got Dad's approval - when he finished inspecting and tallying the haying scorecard in his mind and gave us the okay - it was like we were shot out of a canon. We sprinted toward swim trunks, towels, and pond with newfound energy, raced full out to the water's surface, and plunged into her with the unrestrained ardor of the youthful and innocent.

My cousin Sue, never one for swamps or mud or ponds or any of the dirty stuff of farming, cynically dubbed our pond "Impetigo Park." The name stuck, as things do when they contain an element of truth and are proffered with wit.

> **impetigo** - (im-pi-tahy'-goh) *noun* - *Pathology*
> a contagious skin disease, especially of children, usually caused by streptococcal bacteria, marked by a superficial pustular eruption, particularly on the face.
> *American Heritage Dictionary*

In one sense, Sue was right. The water was never clear, always cloudy with algae and muck from silt on her bottom. Over the years, the pond was populated with muskrats, fish, snakes, turtles and countless bullfrogs. In some years, we pastured cows nearby and they regularly waded in the thing. Being in the farm's lowland, the pond was the ultimate destination of whatever would go downhill. One need only picture a cow and use some imagination to see why Sue would not be caught dead in the waters of Impetigo Park. The rest of us didn't care. We loved it anyway.

Years earlier, Dad had Nelson Petteys dig the deep hole in our low lying field. He hoped that the new pond would drain the surrounding farmland so it could be worked with our tractor, which otherwise was constantly getting stuck in the swampy, mucky, water-saturated earth. The plan didn't work. The place stayed too wet, and unusable farmland remained unusable farmland. But the pond was completed, and Dad decided to turn farming failure into spectacular social success. Indeed he did. He buried a large concrete culvert in one end of the pond and built a dock around it, half on land and half anchored into the pond itself. He built a ladder for swimmers to climb up. He then secured one end of a massive plank to the buried culvert, and extended the other end of the plank far out over the dock; our diving board was magnificent. The pond was forty feet by sixty feet, with a clay bottom near the dock, and it was positioned near our huge, old walnut tree, a regal and picturesque landmark on our farm. Dad planted a willow tree at the west end of the pond, where it would provide him with afternoon shade. He would swim with us briefly and then sit beneath the tree with ice water and a newspaper, while we swam as long as we could.

* * * * * *

It was June 1967, and I had just turned eleven. The Duffys were visiting, and we had just finished haying the back field, the one where fifteen years earlier Henry Thomas plowed with his horses and watched Joe Scully on his new tractor. It was a sweltering hot day for June, humid and hazy, and I had hay dust everywhere. We all did. The knuckles on my left hand ached a bit. I had whacked them on the harsh, unforgiving metal of our baler earlier that day, when the wrench I was turning slipped on the bolt head that was so awkward to reach. But haying was over now. It was pond time. And neither hay scratches on my arms, nor bruised knuckles could mollify my spirits as I walked easily toward our welcoming pond.

The rest of them were already there, having bolted headlong toward the place the moment Dad and Uncle Jim released us from haying duties. But I was determined to take my time, to drink in the scene and appreciate the approach to the place as much as the sanctifying swim itself. Plus I was walking barefoot, a rare thing for the farm boy, and my tender soles weren't made of the tough stuff needed for running unprotected in fields. I had my swim trunks on and carried my towel and a clean change of clothes over my shoulder for the trip back to the house. Step after slow, deliberate step I took in every detail of that perfect scene.

The pond's surface took on the hazy blue-gray of the summer sky and presented itself against a backdrop of distant green maples and nut-brown swamp grasses. The gentlest breeze massaged tree leaves and eased the tall grasses ever so slightly. I heard the water splashing and heard the merriment of happy voices, as my brothers and my cousin Kathy bobbed playfully in the water. Dad was just getting out, and I watched him climb the ladder and walk toward the white lawn chair beneath the softly swaying willow. I tasted powdery alfalfa as I licked my dried lips and smelled the hay dust in my nostrils. As I grew closer to that grand walnut tree and to our glorious pond, I felt the cool air of that little grotto waft its way toward me, inviting me in and promising wet rejuvenation. Though the soles of my feet were tender, I was glad to be barefoot, as it was yet another sensual experience of awareness, and it allowed me to appreciate every single step toward my destination.

That's when it happened.

I unwittingly stepped directly on a large snake, apparently as unsuspecting and unaware of me as I was of it. At first I just felt the squish and instantly knew something wasn't right. Time slowed to a crawl as I looked down toward the all-to-quick writhe that was beneath my right foot. In slow motion the length of snake – I had stepped on the exact middle of it – wrapped upward from each side of my foot, its tail coming up and around my foot one way while its head came up and around in the opposite direction. I let out an involuntary yelp that came to my ears all out of time and off tone, like a slowed down recording of a wounded animal's howl. I panicked fully. Adrenaline coursed instantly and everywhere in me, and my body walled itself off from my brain and control center. My body would do whatever it took and it would do it immediately and utterly on its own.

My chest continued its guttural shrieking while my foot, acting completely on its own, kicked fiercely and launched the serpent toward tree branches, spinning head over tail in the whop-whop-whopping fashion of a football tumbling in flight. My eyes zeroed in on the hurtling snake and my body launched into a full-out, straight-ahead sprint. But without the control center of my brain, my body directed its sprinting right into the flight path of the cartwheeling snake. My brain saw it all and did its lightning-fast calculations of geometry and physics and could tell that my sprinting body was on a high speed collision course with a tumbling snake in descent. Yet it was powerless to issue commands. The snake tumbled ever downward. I ran uncontrollably toward it. The timing was disastrously perfect...

I have no idea how it happened or even *what* happened next, as my next moment of conscious awareness was at the edge of the pond, standing snakeless and flustered while my heart pounded like a jackhammer. As best as I could tell, I had miraculously avoided a collision with the snake, had somehow dodged the thing, and had been spared. Exactly what happened remains a mystery to me, even to this day.

It took a while to regain my composure, and I got no support from the floating peanut gallery who saw nothing and heard only some grotesque sounds from me. My explanation and story about what happened was met with nonchalance and disinterest. They were absorbed in their own world of watery delight and easy recreation. While they mostly believed my story, they didn't think it concerned them. "Forget about it. It's over. C'mon in the water!" was their response.

Though I eventually calmed down, I could still feel the adrenaline which had parts of me shaking many minutes later. I figured a good, physical burst was what I needed and at last I ran toward the diving board and launched into a fantastic cannonball, achieving more height and distance than I ever had before. I was not a big person, so my splashdown was nothing as spectacular as my soaring through the air was. But I was, at long last, in the water. It was everything I had hoped it would be.

Just then we caught sight of Danny Thomas, half a mile distant and tearing in our direction, riding his bicycle at top speed, kicking up a small cloud of dirt road dust behind him. He had haying duties that day as well and noticed our pond party at just the right time. He was always welcome, and we loved to see him coming. A minute later Danny skidded his bike to a stop at the edge of the dirt road, flew down the sloped field to the pond and immediately dove in, perfectly threading the needle by diving through the inner tube we tossed out in front of him. We took turns diving through the floating inner tube and leaping off the diving board for rubber balls thrown out so far, that we were forced to give each effort our absolute, edge-of-control best.

We were so consumed with our diving and ball tossing, that at first we didn't notice Jim Duffy driving the tractor and wagon. He came right to the pond's edge and backed the wagon so that its wheels were almost in water. It served as another launching pad, a second diving platform, set at right angles to the original. We couldn't get enough of it. We ran and jumped and dove, strained for soaring passes and stretched to hit elusive targets in the air and on the pond's surface. It was a wonderful, exhausting, consuming hour of pure childhood joy. Kathy Duffy was athletic and a hard worker, and she caught the most airborne passes that day, made the best dives and won nearly every competition we could dream up.

It sent chills through me when, after surfacing from one dive, Kathy screamed that she had been bitten by a snake. She came flying out of the water and looked under her arm, looked in her left armpit and sure enough, there were the telltale signs of snakebite: two small holes about a half an inch apart, already turning a faint purple. But she didn't panic as I did with my snake encounter. She went to my father who gave it a casual look and told her, "It's a long way from your heart; you'll be okay." But I was unnerved and Uncle Jim thought it best to call it a day, and so we all came out of the water. It was not unusual to see a snake in that pond, but this was the first time anything like this happened, and we practiced more caution in all our future swims.

After deciding that Kathy's bite did not qualify as a full blown emergency, we took turns changing out of our wet swimsuits and into dry clothes in the "Impetigo Park Dressing Facilities." These were more recent additions to the "park," little buildings we relocated from near the farmhouse to the pond earlier that year. We gave the things new moorings and new missions. One was an old smokehouse, about four feet wide and four feet deep, with a full sized door and plenty of room inside for one person to change clothes. Henry Thomas had dried and smoked meats in there, and the wood still held the smoky scent of its heritage. The second was of similar size but of quite different origins. It was an old outhouse. We dragged it off its original foundation and filled in the newly exposed hole in the ground (It was an unpleasant job). We nailed new boards over the seat to form a decent bench, and to build a barrier between us and the history of the thing. Both "private changing rooms" were actually quite decent when washed and scrubbed down, and served their new purpose nicely. But we constantly battled wasps and hornets for ultimate possession of the things, and on more than one occasion had to retreat and yield to the buzzing squatters.

The old outhouse (immediately to the right of the barn) and the smokehouse (standing alone, to the right). "Twinkleberry's apple tree" is the large tree on the right.

The next day we returned to the pond, not with swimming trunks and towels, for we were too snake-rattled for that, but with fishing poles and a can of freshly-unearthed worms from behind the barn. After a fishing trip the previous year, Dan McPeek stocked our pond with a few Battenkill natives. The pond fishing that day was amazing, though everything we caught was small. Most of the fish were bluegills, but we also caught a few bass before returning each one to their pond home. We spotted a turtle at the far end but saw no snakes on that day. Kathy's armpit looked normal, but the two little marks were still plainly visible. "Harmless," Dad said. Kathy wasn't so sure. Neither was I.

Impetigo Park. It was as dirty and nasty and even dangerous at times. It was in some ways just what Sue accused it of being when she named it. It was just what you'd think a pond on a dairy farm would be. But it was also so much more than that. It was our private summer swimming hole, and a place of occasional family picnics and fantastic boyhood fun. It was an after-haying celebration place and a rare treat that could consume the farm boy and make him forget where he was. My cousin Sue wanted no part of Impetigo Park. But the rest of us were dauntless devotees, lovers of our little lake, and unstoppable swimmers in the waters that enlivened us and baptized us into union with that magical place.

* * * * * *

Kathy Duffy returned again in late August and she was again with us at the pond, at Impetigo Park. But this time it was for a different reason. It wasn't for hay dust removal or for a diving contest, not for snake wrangling or fish catching. This time we were there with a few of our cows. This time we were there to bathe them in the pond, to wash them and scrub them clean, to rinse them and wipe them down so that they would be ready for the great event that filled every late August of my childhood, the capstone adventure to every single summer at the farm: the Washington County Fair.

Me (L) and Rick (R) with an Ayrshire cow

Chapter 13

A Day at the Washington County Fair

(My age: 13)

Farming in the summer could be a lonely business. Although summer was the high season for visitors, summer farm work meant long, solitary hours on tractors, mowing, conditioning, raking and baling hay in rural, isolated fields. All this made the farm boy yearn for the company of peers, even to the point of pining for the start of school in September. But the thing we really looked forward to, the magnificent event that brought us both friends and freedom, was the Washington County Fair.

Our 4H club was called Crystal Clovers, and was made up of rural kids from our local quadrant of Cambridge farmlands. We entered vegetables into contests and showed our cows in competitions for highly coveted cloth ribbons. We scrubbed our section of the fair barn clean and strove for "area inspection" scores better than all others. We marveled at horse pulling contests and were delighted with tractor pulls, watching beasts and machines give everything they had. We crawled over new farm equipment on display and coveted the pristine, brightly painted things that promised to make farm tasks easier. These machines were completely beyond our farm's meager financial reach, but like desert mirages, they held the power to enliven our imaginations and make us lust for the unattainable. We scraped and saved all year in order to have a little "walking around money," stuff that gave us access to the rarified air of Ferris wheels, dive bombers, candied treats, and delicious, un-chaperoned autonomy.

As 4H kids attendant to our cows, we stayed at the fair for the whole week. We ate, slept, and lived amidst our cows and amongst friends, and it was always a wonderfully glorious time. Each August we bathed ourselves in around the clock companionship, and stretched our adolescent legs with nascent independence We grew a bit taller and sipped a bit of those magnificent waters from the wellspring of maturity. And each year, as a single unit connected through common experience, we took another collective step toward our future selves.

I remember the fair during that magical summer when I turned thirteen…

Cow Barn Bedroom, Breakfasts and Girls

The tender, lacy light of morning seeped in when the guard quietly opened the barn's large, sliding door. I stayed in my warm sleeping bag, still soggy headed from sleep, and watched the yearling cow in front of me turn her head in recognition of day. She was a reddish brown Ayrshire heifer, solid in color except for the white patch in the shape of Ohio that decorated her forehead. I named her Noel because of her December 25th birthday. She was my ticket to this place, to a week free from haying, barn cleaning, and fetching cows from the pasture. I reached an arm out of my cocoon, stretched my hand toward her and she acknowledged her bunkmate's fingers with a sniff. The bale of straw that was my mattress had yielded through the night, and by morning had adopted every one of my contours. It fit me perfectly, and I did not want to move. Thirteen year old boys cherish their sleep.

The stirrings of the barn began to gently unfold as one farm boy after another crawled from his slumber, sat upright and bleary eyed, finally making his way into Tuesday, the 26th of August, 1969. Some spoke softly, and a few poked slumbering brothers or friends. Somebody at the far end of the huge pole barn bellowed a mournful

"But I'm stiiillll tired!" which provoked some cackles of laughter and retorts from various quarters, as it was designed to do. There was an undeniable fraternity in the place, a connection that registered with a nod of the head later in the day between unnamed strangers who would pass elsewhere at the Washington County Fair, recognizing and silently acknowledging each other as "another boy who sleeps in the 4H cow barn."

My older brother Rick was stirring on the canvas cot next to me, turning in his sleeping bag and preparing to get vertical. Danny Thomas was already up and was making his bed, the only bed in the building. It was a simple, homemade thing. A small iron frame with one stretched-wire spring platform and a three inch mattress over it. One sheet and one heavy blanket. It could not have been much more comfortable than a bale of straw, but we so envied him for that bed. We imagined it made him more rested, smarter, stronger and more full of life. We coveted it as a thing of rare luxury in the midst of our primitive furnishings. The nature of farming was such that farmers had to be resourceful and ingenious, had to constantly make something out of nothing, and had to be creative and find ways to make do. Dan had rescued discarded pieces of the rusted bed frame, substituted remnant limbs from here and there, and welded new life into it. That bed, crafted by the clever and put into service at the fair by the resourceful, testified to all that Dan Thomas was the best farmer in the building.

Serious and conscientious farm boys tended to their cows, brushed them, took them out for water and walked mature cows to the milking parlor. I was neither serious nor conscientious, and so I headed straight for the 4H food booth, a one room wooden building across the lane that served as a functional though inelegant dining hall for herdsmen of all ages. It had picnic tables and simple benches that lined its counters. The benches were merely large planks, wrapped in floral patterned contact paper, resting on stacked cinder blocks. The all you can eat breakfast cost only thirty-five cents, and it was a spectacular part of my day, as all meals are for teenage boys who value food strictly on a cost per quantity basis, and consume it in the open air of summer. When I left the confines of the barn and stepped into open air, the damp cold of the place hit me hard and sent me back for a sweatshirt. It was the grey kind that we all wore back then, before branding of anything and everything appeared on every casual torso-billboarded garment, before cotton capitulated to polyesters, back when grey cotton sweatshirts were simply grey cotton sweatshirts. I grieve their loss.

  Breakfast aromas wafted my way as I advanced a second time, now comfortably sweatshirted, on the 4H booth. Coffee's magnificent, mellow roasted char, full and heavy and wonderfully promising, came at me first. My wakening senses next detected smoky-sweet bacon and then the vanilla-hinted richness of fresh pancakes and maple syrup. I felt like some cartoon character, lifted and led by my nose, floating dreamlike on ambrosial waves of flavor toward the warmth of that life-filled little food booth. It would be pancakes and bacon today, I decided, still only half way to the place. I absentmindedly dragged my fingertips on the first picnic table, feeling the heavy, watery blanket of cool dew that settled on everything open to the early morning sky. There was so much condensation that when my hand left the picnic table it sent a splattering to the ground, enough to both hear and see. I decided I'd sit at the counter, as the benches there would be dry. My eyes were seductively drawn to the grill inside the booth, the hot surface in the middle of the place that was birthplace to those wonderful smells. Bacon sizzled easily while pancakes gently browned, and eggs occasionally hissed as they hit the hot surface. The place was full of welcome and warmth, and the patient buzzings of morning hummed softly around me.

  I nearly choked when she asked me what I wanted. I didn't expect her. The slender brunette girl with the bright smile and endless energy had no idea I was taken with her; she was just going about her business of taking orders and being her normal, infectiously cheerful self. "Uh, pancakes, bacon and orange juice, please," were the only words that finally came tumbling out of me, the first syllable being embarrassingly high pitched. It was my first utterance of the day, and I was still belatedly fighting the final vestiges of puberty. Sandra Thomas, the farm girl who lived less than a mile from me, and to whom I had spoken a sum total of ten words in my entire lifetime, smiled at my order, as if to say I had made an excellent choice. She brightly chirped, "Pancakes and bacon, coming right up!" to both me and the adult working the grill. She carried herself like an experienced maitre d' at some vogue Manhattan eatery: confident, upbeat and stylish, proud of her association with the fine restaurant.

I cringed in private humiliation. *Why didn't I even say hello? I so rarely get to see her – she goes to a different school and so she knows nothing about me – this was the perfect opportunity to say something, anything, except the ridiculous "Pancakes, bacon and orange juice, please." What a fool I am! And what was that "uhhh" at the beginning with the high pitch? Why does that always happen? I am such a blunderer with girls – being on a farm with three brothers all summer doesn't give me any chance to practice chatting with girls, and now I'm completely off kilter. I haven't even brushed my teeth yet. Do I stink? I clearly blew it, but she'll have to come back to deliver the order and I can try to recover then. What should I say? Should I ask her something or tell her something? Better ask something. Is that too forward, too obvious? Would she think I'm an idiot? What is it I should ask?*

"Hi, Gerry." Patti Herrington stood in front of me now, smiling. "How are you? You must have a cow here, huh?" I just stared at her. Unlike Sandra, Patti indeed went to my school and indeed I knew her. Well, at least I knew a little bit about her, and I had at least a few conversations with her, awkward, clumsy things though I made them. I was as taken with Patti as I was with Sandra, as Patti too was sweet and very cute. But Patti was also leggy and tall, and I was so painfully short, and so somewhere in my eighth grade brain I had concluded that I could never have a relationship with Long Tall Patti. The idea of literal friendship never crossed my pubescent mind. The idea of conversation for the sake of conversation, companionship with

235

a girl for its own sake, friendship just for the natural joy of it was simply inconceivable to me. Beyond that, the far-reaching, ethereal concept that dating a taller person is within the realm of possibility was a mind-blowing, unimaginable notion, a transcendental abstraction far beyond my adolescent and insecure reality. Patti Herrington, as cute as she was, and as much as I liked her, was set off limits to me by the unkind God of the Universe, who seemed to me to have dispensed the gifts of height with either an ungodly carelessness or outright cruelty.

"Oh! Hi, Patti!" I blurted out with too much energy, sounding synthetic, which it was, and insincere, which it was not. "Surprised to see you here. Yeah, I've got a heifer here. Do you have a cow?" *Why did I ask that? Of course she has a cow here – I saw it yesterday right next to Danny's cow, and it had Patti's name hanging over it. What a fool! How to recover? Should I ask her how her summer went? Should I ask her if she planned on cheerleading next year? That sounds so lame. She's smiling at my question, so maybe that means she likes me. Or does it mean she thinks I'm a clown?*

"Yep. Just one. Dad said I could only take one, but I was hoping to have two here. Oh well… They make us girls sleep in the bunkhouse, you know. We're all jealous of you guys in the barn. But several of us girls sang songs and told stories until really late; it was fun. How'd ya sleep?" She fingered her brown bobbed hair behind her ear as she talked and it distracted me, made me focus on her dark eyes and I thought about how pretty and friendly she was and – wait, did she ask me a question?!

"Huh?" I blurted back at her, like I didn't hear the person standing three feet in front of me, my vocal chords again betraying me. Damn those things!

"Did you sleep okay?"

But just then I caught Sandra's eye as she waited on the other side of the grill, watching me and Patti talk. Well, it's more accurate to say she watched Patti talk and watched me act like a buffoon. Sandra smiled when our eyes met, and I was again transported somewhere else.

What was that smile? A signal? Is she interested? Or just friendly? What if she thinks Patti and I are dating? Should I do something to make it clear that much as I like Patti, there can never be anything between us because of our incongruent heights, make it clear to Sandra that I'm "available?" Sandra is so bubbly. But she smiles at everybody and would probably smile at the wall if she was alone. Should I smile back?

Patti looked at me as if to say "what's *wrong* with you?"

"Oh!" I again blurted out – my best line of the day. "Yeah, my cow is just a yearling. She's the red one near Danny's. Actually, I forgot, I did see your cow right next to his. Just slipped my mind, I guess." I was dying. Half way through my rambling reply, I remembered her real question about my sleeping, but felt it would be too awkward to go back to it now; it would be like admitting that my mind was wandering.

Patti Herrington, amused by my pathetic befuddlement, giggled the most delightful girl-giggle, shook her head and rolled her comely eyes at me. "Well I guess you probably didn't sleep so well after all!" And she bubbled forth in genuine laughter at my idiotic reply. The laugh just made her cuter, and it was so unrestrained that it turned heads our way, including Sandra's, who now had my breakfast plate and was heading in our direction, smiling big, as always. What was I going to do now? How should I respond to Patti? Should I respond at all? What do I say to Sandra?

"Here ya go! Pancakes, bacon and OJ. That's thirty-five, please," she said with a beaming grin directed toward both me and Patti. "Thanks," I fired back, too abruptly and again too loudly. I fished out the change and handed it to her, speechless, frozen in dumbness. I had no idea what to say.

I want to tell them both that they are adorable and darling and that they make me horribly uncomfortable though it is purely my fault because neither of them did anything in particular to bring this about in me and that I

237

am really not this much of a goof and that I really am a decent person when you got to know me - or that is when I get comfortable enough to show my real self - and I really like Patti though she is so tall as to be out of the question, and if Sandra would just be patient enough with me...

Both girls erupted in irrepressible laughter. The two cutest girls at the Washington County Fair, both my age, both simply trying to treat me like a peer and fellow fair-goer, found my incoherent behavior just too much to bear. Though they attributed it to bad sleep, they nevertheless found me laughably ridiculous, a likeable sot, drunk with weariness from sleeping too close to cows. I joined them in laughter, as I could not do otherwise, and found it to be of great relief. Sandra Thomas and Patti Herrington then both responded to newly arrived customers and I sat alone, wolfing a delicious breakfast, thinking of lines I wished I had thought of earlier. "Hey, how are you, Sandra? What's new on the other side of the Stump Church?" "Hiya, Patti – tell me about your summer!" And other, brilliantly crafted and eloquent conversation starters that so eluded me earlier.

I stood up to leave and both girls waved to me. "See ya, Gerry," said Patti. "Take care, Gerry," from Sandra. "Bye, ladies," I said in return. Ladies? *Ladies?* Seriously, Gerry... I turned and cut my losses, headed toward the 4H barn and cow duties, and felt the awkward delight of a boy who has encountered girls, regardless of how ineptly. "Bacon, eggs and coffee, coming right up!" Sandra's confident, clear voice carried across the distance to my ears, and I thought of the two delightful girls who would unknowingly brighten each day of the fair for me.

When I returned to the barn, I saw something that nearly made me faint. My older brother Rick sat on a bale of hay and on his lap, draping her arm around him, was some high school girl whom I had never seen. I was taken aback, shocked and deeply troubled. Though there was nothing untoward, it felt as if I had walked in on my parents in some compromising situation. At some level, I knew these kinds of things happened, but I never wanted to see it in person. I never wanted to see my parents being anything but Victorian and proper, and I felt the same about my older brother. I was as rattled as I was at breakfast, though for a completely different reason, and merely stood there, dumbfounded. I was introduced to this stranger-teenager, a plain looking, round-faced girl, with dull eyes and coarse blonde hair, cut in straight bangs, smiling at Rick like she had just won a carnival prize. Dumbstruck, I could reply with nothing but a nod. She fawned on him like some familiar old lover, and I could see he found it all deliciously fun. I wanted to flee and see a priest, ask him to exorcise the two of them.

Such was the flailing incongruity of a thirteen year old farm boy encountering girls.

Mauls & Maulings

Maul *[mawl]*
  noun: a heavy, long-handled hammer used especially to drive stakes
  verb: to use roughly
      American Heritage Dictionary

It was a warm, lazy afternoon, and I watched over cows and kept order in the space that was Crystal Clovers Land, while my mates meandered through the fairgrounds, slurped snow cones and played an occasional game of chance. Back in the barn, I casually surveyed the cows and quarters, and finding everything in good order, made myself a seat of hay bales and drifted into late afternoon bliss.

  I nodded into and out of sleep, gone for only a few minutes at a time and only with one foot in slumber's door. As I daydreamed, my eyes fixed on a single wooden post, the corner post of the cow stalls, the post from which all distances were measured and all other stall posts were planted in the ground. Seeing that post reminded me of an old memory and a story that Dad repeated often, always with a grin and always in wondrous disbelief. My mind drifted back nearly a decade to a cool summer evening at the very spot of that corner post. It was 1961 and I was five. The pole barn had just been built and the asphalt alleys did not yet exist. Farmers had rallied here one evening to build the cow stalls that would hold their new residents, bovine guests that would come to this barn for the first time. Until that year, the fair had been held in Cambridge. Now the fair and the cows would come here, to the new fairgrounds in Greenwich.

As my memory drifted back, I saw my father as I saw him then, holding that very post steady for the teenage boys who would hammer it into the ground. A modest hole had been dug to mark the spot, and the brand new fence post rested in it, awaiting permanence. Malcolm Hamilton's strapping teenage sons, John and Carl, stood on the tailgate of a pickup truck that had been backed into position near the post hole. They talked without ceasing, absorbed in brotherly banter and oblivious to those around them. Carl and John teased and jabbered and challenged, and were drowned out only by Malcolm's obstreperous taunts and lampooning encouragements, common only amongst men with deep familiarity and mutual respect. Dad held the fence post firmly and leaned away from the coming hammer blows to protect himself, facing squarely at me. The two maul-wielding young men would do their work from the perch of the tailgate.

"Awwlright c'mon now!" Malcolm shouted to his boys, "he's gonna get bored there waitin' for ya," nodding toward Dad. "You swing them things from the wooden handle end, if that's what's keepin' ya!" With that the two young men each hefted their maul sledgehammers and simultaneously prattle-jabbered a sort of 'who's going first' that quickly set them into reciprocal motion. They alternated swings, first John whomping the post then Carl and back and forth in perfect rhythm, all the while chattering good natured, nonstop taunts at one another. Their blows rapidly grew in fraternal competition, and each thudding, pounding slam was ferocious and stunning to me. I sensed others around us had stopped their own work to watch this scene unfold. I looked to my father's eyes, expecting to see fear. If John or Carl missed the mark with one of those wide arced powerful, high velocity swings, my Dad's arms would be removed and sent half way to China. I had never seen such ferocious power, the stuff that only young men and full grown testosterone-charged teenagers can unleash. The scene held us onlookers spellbound and the Hamilton boys' raw power awed me.

To my pleasant surprise, my father was grinning from ear to ear, swallowing back laughter, and I could tell he too was flabbergasted at their remarkable strength and was equally entertained by their endless banter. These were young men unaware of their own fearsome brawn, blind to their own frightful might. Dad was shaking with joyful amazement and struggling to keep his hands on the post as it vibrated in shuddering pain with each stupendous blow. Each pounding shook the ground and sent splinters and wood dust flying from the pores of the post. Each wallop sent the vanquished post markedly farther into the stubborn ground. Each thundering whack turned another head and held the audience speechless. Each swing sent the post quivering anew. John and Carl Hamilton chatted throughout this spectacle like they were blabbering over a cup of early morning coffee, garrulous but without any sign of struggle or strain of exertion, without so much as a gasp for breath as they brutalized the post and drove it ruthlessly deeper. "Close the damn barn door!" shouted Malcolm, always the entertainer. "It's causing a breeze that's throwing the boys' swings off; gonna hit Donnie!" Dad beamed in glorious entertainment and finally released the post as it had long since gone beyond the point of needing to be held. "Now *hit* the sonnabitch!" teased Malcolm, and to my amazement the two hammerers indeed found another gear. We all watched in wordless amazement as Carl and John savaged it home and finished the job. You could hear a pin drop when they finished; all eyes were on them.

"Jey-hay-sus, let's go fellas! We got stalls to build." And Malcolm Hamilton moved the group of volunteer farmers forward.

"Hey!" I popped upright and shook off the daydream, reluctantly returning to the present. It was my cousin Jim and my brother, who had come to relieve me from barn duty. In the unceremonious changing of the guard, I simply rolled off the hay bale as my brother rolled onto the same comfortable spot. His own daydreams would be coming soon.

Jim and I were flush with four dollars in folding bills which were to last us two days. At twenty-five cents per ride or game, that was enough to make us feel more than comfortably moneyed. We strolled the midway, as if we were investment bankers assessing the landscape and trolling for treasures to be found in the thrill of the perfect ride, or in the conquering of some carnival game and the capturing of a cheap trinket-prize.

We stumbled across our Crystal Clovers 4H Club gang at the bell and hammer game, in which a contestant takes three swings with a large fencepost maul hammer and slams the lever, shooting a metal puck up the tower toward the distant bell. Apparently Danny Thomas had made the outrageous claim that he could ring the bell, a feat of strength we all knew to be far beyond the capability of his thin, angular frame. This was tough stuff, feat of strength stuff reserved for musclebound men in sleeveless, tank top t-shirts with buxom, fawning girlfriends. It was not the stuff of a lanky Crystal Clovers 4H kid, not for the boyfriend of Olive Herrington, a wholesome, sweetheart of a girl. We liked Danny, but he was no Carl or John Hamilton, not yet he wasn't. Danny was waiting his turn, and I could see that the others couldn't wait for him to fail. They were intent on meting out the sort of peer justice that humbles and puts one back in his place when he tries in some way to leave the pack. It is a form of justice we reserve for those we love and consider to be "one of us." The truth is that we just don't want to lose them and can't bear to see them leave the nest. We find it too painful to wish them well and encourage them as they become something larger than anything we had ever seen them being.

Danny Thomas took the wood handled maul, spat on his hands – actually spat on his hands – and rubbed them together in theatrical farm boy determination. He focused, took a deep breath, and walked to the mark, as the modest crowd hushed in anticipation. He wound up in a very deliberate fashion, and gave a mighty, arcing swing that attacked the lever, making the ground beneath us shudder. Ding! It wasn't a faint ring; it was solid, bold and unequivocal. The Crystal Clovers gang gasped in muted disbelief, and a few random onlookers responded with respectful cheers, though all of us were skeptics a mere moment earlier and secretly remained so in our hearts. "Again!" we 4H-ers shouted, wondering if we just witnessed a fluke and hoping, somewhere down deep in our shameful places, that we had. An ugly and selfish part of us did not want him to succeed, as that would somehow send him forth without us, a dreary proposition to us all.

Danny swung again, this time seemingly intent on his aim, and his ranging swing appeared to almost be in slow motion. A second time the heavy metal puck reached the bell, though much less convincingly this time, its ring a lazy afterthought. Despite its understated modesty, that second ring of the bell nevertheless profoundly changed our hearts. That clear and pure sound, gentle though it was, triggered something in each of us and announced our entrance into yet another chapter in our early lives. Our collective skepticism broke with that sound; it broke as with the clear, soft tinkling of elegant crystal shattered. With Danny's second ringing of that bell, we found ourselves casting aside our ugly skepticism, throwing our hearts toward our friend and peer, and hoping with all our might that he would manage it one more time. No longer willful skeptics, we suddenly became the newly hopeful, irresistibly impassioned supporters who wished mightily that he would ring that bell again, and in so doing, would bring a piece of us with him to that glorious new place in adulthood that he was discovering. The crowd's tone changed perceptibly. "Again!" we thundered in unison, now clearly supportive and irrepressibly enthusiastic. Casual bypassers took note and came closer, adding to our numbers and to the general buzzing of interest. "Make it three!" And Danny Thomas lifted that huge maul straight over his head and momentarily paused. Then he put his back fully into the thing, swung it forward and chopped straight down with a frightful, ear-rattling ferocity. I thought he would knock the bell loose and launch it skyward. DING!

Dan, all business-faced and matter-of-fact somber, took his stuffed animal trophy and immediately handed it to Olive. Then he eyed us and finally cracked a smile. The Crystal Clovers members erupted in applause and escorted him off like a champion, like a newly anointed mascot. We took small glories in the fact that Bell-Ringing-Dan was one of us. There was no justice-meting left in us, as it had been shattered by his hammer and wiped clean by the clarion bell of victory. I am sure there were small jealousies, as there could be no other way among teenage boys. But mostly we were thrilled for him, and basked in the idea that perhaps some of that abundant glory rested on us. Dan Thomas, our resourceful metal bed owner, had further established himself as an emerging farmer king, a maul-hammer-wielding champion whose shoulders now seemed larger, and who stood now even a bit taller.

(The next day, away from the eyes of friends, I would take a whack at that game. I failed miserably. I was glad I did not humiliate myself by doing that in front of the 4H-ers or in front of Lida Whitney.)

Carnival Rides and My Miraculous Hand Holding Debut

Late the next afternoon, I set out for a lime flavored snow cone, as the relentless sun had lingered too long, and the air had finally defeated me with its unbroken heat. I sought the incomparable childhood pleasure of cooling down with a frozen, sugar-blasted treat with a shockingly unnatural and brilliant color. A familiar face approached the short line for the snow cones just as I did, and it took me a moment to register Lida Whitney, a Cambridge classmate whom I had not seen all summer. She seemed out of place to me, being so near the stuff of farms and so far from what I perceived as the gentrification of village living. Lida gave me a big smile and a bright hello and said she wanted to see my cow. She was with friends who were altogether disinterested in anything bovine, and so they scattered in different directions. Lida and I naturally teamed up, and after introducing her to the basics of cow husbandry, some of which I made up in order to fill in my knowledge gaps and appear competent, we decided to stroll the midway with our snow cones. I liked Lida as she was always so positive, wore stylish outfits, and loved to laugh. But I didn't know her well, as she was from the other half of the species, interesting to me and appealing, but nevertheless completely alien.

We wandered through the midway, that enchanting place of rides and games and lights. It drew us in with spectacle, with colorful tents and game booths, with chimes and enthusiastic buzzers that announced lucky winners, and with the hawking taunts of relentless carnies intent on prying free our scarce quarters and precious dollar bills. Cotton candy machines whirled for boisterous children, and brilliant candied apples adorned the hands of delighted revelers. The flavor of fresh popcorn scented the air and made it feel like a country kitchen of a place, inviting and familiar. The slow grilling of sweet Italian sausages excited our noses, as did the tangy sweetness of gently grilled onions and the richly charred aroma of roasted green peppers. And everywhere there were strings of lights, fun, gaudy things that floated close in the sky, far beneath the starry, celestial works of art that were beginning to make themselves known in the early evening heavens. "Hey step right up!" the man said. "Win your lovely lady a beautiful teddy bear!" Lida glanced at me and we both giggled in delight, noticing that insistent carnies took for granted that we were a couple.

As we continued our midway stroll, Lida and I discussed what happened during our summers. She did almost all the talking, thank goodness. All I could manage was to toss the conversation back into her court from time to time. We considered this ride then that one, and finally ventured a ride on the Ferris wheel as it promised panoramic views. There is something grand about the Ferris wheel, as it strikes the precarious balance between the raw excitement of pure height and the gentility of easy and predictable motion. It is just the right ride, I concluded as we perused the fairgrounds from above, for a first ride with a girl.

After coming off the Ferris wheel, Lida took me by the hand and raced with me toward the gates for the Octopus, a more intense ride with no waiting line. The man in charge was about to close the gate and start the ride. We made it just in time. The ride lifted forcefully and dropped us without warning, whirled us hard and shoved us into the backs of our seats and pressed our sides together, and all the while carnival tunes floated in the air around us. But I hardly felt or heard any of those things, as I was so consumed with her hand, her fingers entwined with mine. I was actually holding a girl's hand for the first time ever, or perhaps she was holding mine - this was so amazing! Should I pat her hand with my free one? Should I put an arm around her when we ambled along? Should I just "play it cool" instead? What did that actually mean? When do I let go? Did this make us boyfriend and girlfriend or was something more required to achieve that status? Did I want that? After all, I liked Lida, but hardly knew her. What would Sandra think? Did I have a prayer with Sandra anyway? What if she sees me here with Lida? OH MY GOD, I AM HOLDING A GIRL'S HAND!

Lida's hair was golden brown, and she had a small blonde streak in her bangs that was natural and distinctive. I thought she was as pretty as Patti, as sweet as Sandra, and though she arrived into my life that day from out of nowhere, I thought in that moment that she was made for me. Under the soft August moon, amid carnival lights and bells, and the playful, pleasant chimes of midway games, the thirteen year old me swooned for the girl's hand in mine, for her delightful smile and eyes that met mine with innocence, for Lida Whitney, the friendly and fun girl with the adorable blonde streak.

It finally came time for her to leave with her friends, and so I said goodbye, released her hand as she released mine, our hand holding witnessed by all and therefore somehow more meaningful and legitimatized in my mind. I did not try to kiss her. I did not offer a hug. I did not promise to call. I did not state that I had a delightful time and that I hoped to see her soon. In my awkwardness and uncertainty, I just said goodbye.

I would never hold Lida's hand again. I would spend the next four high school years around her, smiling at her and being friendly enough. But I never rekindled that marvelous evening, never found the courage to step forward and take her hand in mine, to stroll along with her as two kids blissfully adrift in the halcyon days of summer, charging toward the next ride at the Washington County Fair.

Chapter 14

Farewell from the Top of the Hill

(My age: 55)

It is August 2011, and I am fifty-five years old. I have climbed to the top of the hill one more time and I stand here now, my foot on the survey marker that pinpoints the peak. Sue takes a photo of me and captures the moment. I am glad she is here, so I can share the experience and thereby delight in it even more. It is utterly calm and silent, and a coming storm has pushed heavy, wet air into the area and has made the horizons hazy and vague. The distant hills merge into the sky in the blurry and indistinct way of their timeless alliance. I am glad I have come. Standing at the hill's summit is the last act of my weeklong visit to this place, a pilgrimage to reacquaint myself with cherished old friends and precious neighbors. To witness what is left of the old farms and to relive a day at the Washington County Fair. To again take in the Battenkill, and the profound silence and haunting darkness of empty rural nights. To study the high school football team, which is now coached by an old teammate of mine. To walk a few local cemeteries and nod at names and salute them in my heart. To visit the Saratoga Battlefield, and to cruise through little towns where Frost, Rockwell, Moses and Anthony lived. I have come to the reconnect with the people and the land. They are one here and so am I, sublimely united with this place and these people in our inseparable song of life.

The barns on our old farm, at the foot of the hill, are nearly all down now, victims of heavy slate roofs and broad, wooden expanses that caught the winter wind like huge sails, unanchored by any weight

Me near the top of the hill, 2011

of farmer's hay since the Preece's departure. The few barns that haven't yet collapsed wilt stubbornly, but time is the most stubborn thing of all, and it will eventually overcome them. The hillside that recedes below me and above what used to be our farm, is overgrown with thickets and groves of trees that signal nature's relentless motion. There are no cows at pasture here now, no beasts to graze the grasses and keep nature in check. Like Henry Thomas's horses, the cows are gone forever. The pond far below, our old Impetigo Park, the place where my brothers and Dan Thomas and I all learned to swim, has been changed dramatically It is greatly expanded and has a pretty gravel border that appears to be a walking path. The magnificent old walnut tree is still there, though it is in decline and will capitulate soon. I wonder if the snakes and turtles are still there. Like the farm itself, the pond I knew is gone.

I wanted to ascend the hill like I used to, back when the farm below was the place I called home and my hill-climbing legs were the effortless spry limbs of an invincible teenager. But because the hill is now mostly woods and scrub brush, the challenging climb would be even more demanding than it used to be. More importantly, the now-treed hillside can no longer offer the beautiful vistas of my childhood. So on this day I chose an easier way. I drove around to the back side of the hill and reached my hilltop objective with relative ease, having secured neighborly permission to hike through the open fields that mark that gentler side of the hill. Just as my mortician ancestors became farmers and thus came to work the soil from the other side, today I approached my childhood place, the top of the hill, from the other side, from the entirely different perspective of decades and direction.

I meant to park the car near the old O'Donnell place, where the two old men farmed with horses while I was growing up. I used to sit on this hilltop and watch them work the adjacent field. I envision it in my mind now, as if I was watching Henry Thomas and his Percherons from across a stone wall of six decades. I intended to knock on the weathered door of their old place and discover who lived there now, and to ask if the current residents had any knowledge of what became of the O'Donnell's. Instead I mistakenly parked at the farmhouse adjacent to the old O'Donnell place, owing only to my own error of memory. The pleasant woman at the farmhouse nevertheless welcomed me warmly and graciously, reported that hers was not the O'Donnell place, stated that it was just beyond the stone wall beside us. Upon hearing my name, her face lit with recognition and she generously granted permission to hike on her property, and we talked of neighbors and local history. She warned me that the trees and shrubs have crowded in everywhere near the top of the hill, and so the views would be greatly diminished versus what I remembered them to be. I was undeterred. My quest this day is not so much about the views but about the visceral mandate in my heart, an insistent siren and calling that demands a voyage to the place that was the lighthouse of my younger years.

It is too hazy today to make out the Bennington Battle Monument in the distance, but I know it is there. The trees obscure Danny Thomas' old farm, Joe Scully's and Robin Thomas', but I know right where they are. Scrub brush blocks my view of the charming little Stump Church and the distant, regal Adirondacks. I look down at young wooded lots that used to be fields, and toward Saratoga, too masked by the filmy obscurity of humidity and harsh afternoon sun to make out any landmarks. But they are there; they will always be there. My internal compass knows this with absolute certainty, and something deep inside me finally rests now that I have returned here. I have my binoculars with me and a notebook in which I can record my thoughts, my captain's log that chronicles reflections on my life's voyage. Years ago this hill gave me perspective on what was out there in the distance and helped me to see beyond my lower horizons. Today this same hilltop, this same crow's nest pushes my lens inward and helps me see different landmarks. Today I will not use my binoculars so much. The notebook is my lens today.

From here I always see more clearly.

From here I see that writing these stories has forced me to resolve ambiguities and logic gaps and historical errors. I see that for me, writing clarifies. It has become foil to my foggy thinking and fence against my faulty logic. Whether my murk is personal, historical or spiritual, writing makes me clarify. The unrelenting stubbornness of written words holds me accountable in ways that my spoken words do not. Like mere ideas, my spoken words come easily and pass lightly, bending to my frivolous will and dissolving the moment they are born. But my written words sit there and stare at me and repeat their consistency and refuse equivocation. My written words talk back at me and they demand clarity from me. They are tough on me; I am grateful for them.

From here I see that "the farm" has never been mine, nor my immediate family's, though I have long thought it was. It is something that belongs to many. The farm was so much more than acreage and cows, barns and brawn, machinery and milking. The farm was and is as much a part of the lives of relatives and visitors as it is part of me. At family gatherings and when talking with old friends and neighbors, I hear the earnestness in their voices that tells me that the farm, that place in time, is no small part of them too. For most, their days at the farm numbered fewer than mine, but they carry the farm in them every bit as much as I do. The farm was adventure, challenge, burden, freedom, and the brutal, inhospitable winds of winter and the warm, gentle breezes of summer evenings on our porch. It was hard work and leathered calluses and long trips. It was safe harbor in the tumultuous 1960's, and it spilled into the decades before and after that. For many, it was a place to go to several times a year and get away. It was a place that at once both drained people and refreshed them. The exhausting work pulled petty concerns from selfish spots, and it pried superficiality from its darkest corners. It refilled the gaps with the simple but enormous power of perspective, and the humbling truth that life is never as complicated as we make it. The farm was so much to so many. It is not mine alone. It belongs to cousins and visitors and the animals of the place, to neighbors and friends as much as to me. "The farm" is theirs too.

From here I see that we were blessed with remarkable good fortune. I think of our many near misses and our charmed good luck, and I see it all now through the sobering perspective of time and maturity. I think of my brothers and how Joe sledded under the moving tractor, how Casey tried to hit me with a flying pitchfork and how I did the same to Rick. I think of Rick's going through a glass farmhouse window and having a shard of glass stuck near his spine and parents rushing him to the hospital; about his bicycle accident and his broken teeth; about the knife cut that sent me toward my own hospital run; about Casey's leap from the top of a fully loaded hay wagon as he hoped to land directly on me and forever destroy my brutal teasing; about cousin Leslee burning the soles of her feet on our scalding hot furnace grate; about how Rick barely dodged the knife I threw at him in anger as he ran up the stairs; about the dangerous and snake-filled slate quarry holes, filled with water of unknown depths at the top of our remote and isolated hill; about how five year old Casey survived seventeen bumble bee stings after he accidentally disturbed a nest; about the out of control fire in our grassy hillside field and how the fire department struggled to get it under control; about how I stood helpless while my father cried and whistled fiercely and came undone as he watched his oldest son drive up the hill on our tractor, fearing he would tip the thing over and be crushed by it; about our electrically-shorted two-way intercom between the barn and the house and how it shocked you every time you touched the thing; about the countless pinched fingers and bruises that came with farm life. I am reminded that we were the fortunate ones. Lou Sardi fell from his barn's rafters, broke his back and died; little Johnny Schmitt was killed at age ten; George Pfeifer was kicked by a cow and was hospitalized with broken bones; a tractor rolled on one of our neighbors and crushed his pelvis; Judy Thomas died at nineteen from a crippling disease; a man at English's farm suffered an electrical shock that nearly killed him; Malcolm Hamilton lost his finger and other farmers lost limbs to dangerous machines; neighbors had barns catch fire from the heat of hay bales that held too much organic moisture; Jimmy Frazier and others died at too young an age in tragic car crashes. We Preeces were the lucky ones. My eyes water in quiet lamentation for those that weren't so lucky. We no more earned our luck than they earned their misfortunes.

From here I see that the people of this place have a tremendous work ethic and remarkable character. Perhaps it is normal small town stuff, common to all small towns and rural communities, but my instincts tell me otherwise. Old friends and acquaintances have become teachers, doctors, nutrition experts, farmers, mayors, pilots, nurses, priests, business owners, parents, government officials, coaches, and more. I wish every one of them lived next door to me, not because of their accomplishments, which are notable, but because of their character. These are up-at-dawn, stamina-filled people, full of industry and joyful perseverance. Theirs is a contagious and enterprising ethos, and it makes me deeply proud to claim roots here, to consider myself one of them, no matter how many decades and miles I have ventured.

From here I see that some goodbyes can never end. My visit here is part of my own thirty year long farewell to this place, and my goodbye will not be final when I leave. It will never be final. That, I realize now, is because the place is in me, and it goes where I go. I will come back from time to time and will again stand on this hilltop spot. It is not about the views, though they are still quietly spectacular. I must come back.

Last, I am thankful for the gifts of place and time, and for family and family lore itself. I am thankful there were many more good times than bad, and that we can celebrate our collective histories together. I have shared only the better parts of our history here; there are worse parts, unpleasant and even shameful ones. But I leave them for now and celebrate only the fonder, happier memories. I am grateful for them.

My mind drifts, and for no apparent reason I reminisce about cookouts at "Duffy Gove," the spot in the farmhouse's yard where we had a little outdoor fireplace and a homemade picnic table. It was a great place in summer, especially when we could pick fresh sweet corn and eat it just a few minutes later. Jim Duffy helped build the brick fireplace, and earned the lighthearted namesake. I remember summer meals coming to us kids through an open window on our front porch, cousins sitting at a card table in the magical outdoors where we were free from the supervisory eyes of adults.

As my eyes take in a distant field I recall my father's self-appointed nickname, "One-Day-Donnie," and I chuckle at how he rarely took himself too seriously. He coined this somewhat self-mocking moniker after achieving a farmer's version of a hole-in-one, mowing a hayfield in the morning and clearing all the bales of hay off it later that same day. It is an exceedingly rare thing, as it requires fantastic weather and exceptionally low humidity, the cooperation of temperamental machines otherwise prone to breakdowns, and a family work schedule that allows for all hands on deck. It happened only one day in twenty-two years for him. He was thrilled beyond imagination, dubbed himself a miracle-farmer named One-Day-Donnie, and feigned that he achieved it by some skill of farming savvy. This was all put on, of course, as he was keenly aware that it happened because of luck and luck alone.

One-Day-Donnie. I will visit his resting place after this trip to Cambridge. In a few weeks I'll make my way to Atlanta, where some of my family lives today and where Dad's remains are buried.

* * * * * *

September, 2011, Atlanta

I am doing it once again, walking alone in a cemetery. The place is a peaceful respite surrounded by urgent drivers and the steady drone of commerce. I stop near Civil War markers for Union soldiers. The Confederate markers are not far away. It is a fitting place for my father, I think. He is amongst war veterans here, people from all over, now interred near others with differing views and near people who, despite their disagreements, gave themselves to the ideal of living the way they wanted, gave their lives to principles in which they believed. I envision him befriending soul after soul, asking each a thousand questions, genuine in his hunger to know them. I step along lightly, respecting the rights of the dead, and I imagine my father's conversation with a Yankee soldier who has heard of Cambridge, of Vly Summit, New York. Though I cannot hear them, I know they talk of that property up there, the hill and the views and the horses that worked the fields, of men who would probably have known Henry Thomas as a young boy, or perhaps they only knew his father. Dad is grinning from ear to ear and nodding his head affirmatively, chuckling in delight as the conversation proceeds. I shall not interrupt him on this visit, as he seems so content, and I do not wish to disrupt his joy. I will ask the angels and the Good Lord for favor upon his soul, and I will share some of these farm stories with him later.

I turn and nod to my Dad's memory; I bid him yet another adieu and continue toward my car, toward my life, toward my future. I am reminded of Frost's poem, the word-artist from beyond the farm's hill, who wrote of his "promises to keep," and his "miles to go before I sleep." I have much ahead of me in this life and I am anxious to get to it.

I reach my car and turn the thing toward the nursing home, where I will pay a visit to Mom. The tires hum softly beneath me as my mind drifts back to an earlier Clare Preece on the farm. I imagine my mother hanging laundry on the clothesline, working in the garden, and chatting with visitors around the farmhouse kitchen table. Fifteen minutes later, I park in the lot in front of the sprawling, sterile building and go in. I am nameless here, another visitor on my way to a standard room with a number on the door. There are hundreds of them here, hundreds of identical rooms and identical doors. It is enough to make one think that the elderly residents of these bedrooms are themselves identical, but I know they are anything but that. Mom is up and is in her wheelchair when I arrive. She smiles when she sees me, and I can tell it takes her a few moments to recall who I am. Her mind is nearly gone and there is nothing she can do about it. I give her a long hug and kiss and give her the time she needs to try to collect herself; she is embarrassed by her rapidly slipping cognitions.

  After only a few sentences we begin repeating what we have just discussed, and I take that as my cue to share with her the photo book I have put together for her. It is a series of photos from her past, from our days at the farm, and she seems to like that. It is easier for her to relate to those times, as they seem to stick in her mind in a way that newer experiences are no longer welcomed to do. It is good to see her laugh and hear her tell her stories, even though the stories have lost important pieces and no longer make sense except to those of us who already know them. I smile anyway and act as if she told it splendidly. She will be gone soon, I know. Her stories will go with her.

  At last I say goodbye and it hits her unexpectedly, as in her crumbling mind she took for granted that the visit would be permanent. She puts on a brave face and pretends to accept that I must go. By the time I reach the front door of the building, she will have completely forgotten that I was there, and at dinner tonight, will tell my brother Casey that she never hears from me. It is not her fault.

  I realize that I have been saying goodbye to her for some time now, as the mother I once knew is already gone. Yet I will continue my ongoing goodbyes as a remnant of her is still here. And there are some parts of her I will carry within me for as long as I am alive, just as there are parts of my father inside me. And parts of the farm and that hill and that time and place too. It is *in* me, always.

I will sit tonight with my brothers in Casey's kitchen and we'll compare notes on Mom's condition. We'll talk about our jobs and about sports and current events, and after a while we'll inch our way toward vulnerability and will share the latest developments in each of our lives. Eventually we will return to some farm story freshly captured in these pages, and one of us will re-tell the tale, and we'll all have a laugh and feel just a bit more connected.

The farm: glue and mooring lines, still uniting us.

The farm

Endnotes

For the interested reader, I offer these endnotes in explanation of particular words, phrases and situations presented in each chapter. My hope is that these comments will illuminate the obscure and enrich your experience.

Chapter 1 - My Past Place

In the opening paragraph, I intentionally use the metaphor of "hang-gliders, soaring forward from the hilltops of our lives." While this is admittedly highfaluting and pretentious language, I nevertheless use it because hang-glider enthusiasts indeed used to visit the farm and would ask to use our treeless hill as a place to take flight. I often climbed the hill with them and once even got to try strapping myself in and launching into the air. I crashed ten feet later, violently. I watched those more skilled than me soar from our hilltop, but I could not yet do it myself. Regardless, these friendly, nameless visitors chatted with me and shared their stories and in so doing, expanded my view of the world.

I could not actually see the Saratoga obelisk from our hill, but the site of the actual battle, near Bemis Heights and along the banks of the Hudson, was visible.

From Van Morrison's *Tupelo Honey* I borrow the phrase "men in granite," which for me takes on a triple meaning when describing my situation at West Point: stoic, unemotional cadets and officers; larger than life heroes captured in the place's many statues; and the living soul of the Corps of Cadets inside the academy's numerous granite buildings. Indeed in October of 1974 I found myself full of self-doubt, overwhelmed and defeated, a blubbering teary mess alone in a stairwell. Ten minutes later my roommate, John Armstrong, talked me out of resigning and that act of friendship changed my life. I am still angry with him…

Chapter 2 - Working the Soil from the Other Side

This is a true story. My father often told of this night and how the experience of waiting for a welder to cut free the dead bodies sickened him. It is the singular event that sent him looking in earnest for a different career. I have invented many of the particulars in order to create what I hope is an engaging story. It is true that Dad loved the Dodgers and followed them closely, that he worked for Sorrell's Funeral Home in Norwalk, that my grandfather worked at Baker Funeral Home on Stratford Avenue in Bridgeport. The family is scant on the details of his accident with the young boy, but I believe it to be true, having heard similar accounts from multiple family members. The incident with the overzealous grieving widow is also true.

The details of the game between the Dodgers and the Phillies is taken from the actual box score and game records for that day's game, but I have invented Red Barber's play-by-play lines. I am certain I have not done him justice.

I close the chapter by stating that my family bought the farm from Henry Thomas, something I believed for fifty years to be true. It is only after writing these chapters that I discovered that Henry had already passed away by that time. The fact is that they bought the farm from Henry's remaining family. My notes on Chapter 3 describe this situation further.

Chapter 3 - From Horses to Horsepower

I set the historical record straight at the beginning of this chapter, on page 21. I have used the real names of Henry's work horses, Betty and Ned. Henry's granddaughter, Beverly relayed to me that her brother Gerald made several failed attempts to ride Ned, a large work horse that apparently was not fond of taking riders. Oh, how I would like to have witnessed those scenes...

Local records do indicate that Floyd Hill lived near Vly Summit as a boarder and hired hand on a local farm, but there is no evidence that he ever worked on Henry Thomas' farm. His role in my story as Henry's hired hand is imaginary.

The O'Donnell brothers, farmers from the other side of our hill, did farm with horses throughout my time there, and even came occasionally to help work our fields with their horses. Joe Scully, Henry's neighbor and later ours, indeed farmed with a Farmall 300, which was considered quite a modern tractor at the time.

Chapter 4 - A Time Between

The descriptions in this chapter are unvarnished truth. I use the phrase "when the sky is blue and the trees are black" because my son, Brian, at about the age of four, coined this phrase as his way of describing the earliest moments of morning. I think he nailed it. As Brian matured, he showed himself to be a highly visual person, and now has his masters in architecture, a field in which the eyes see things people like me see only when told to look.

There are a few farms today that still sprinkle the area, but they are completely different enterprises than anything from my era. They are huge businesses. The leap from Henry's horses to the tractor-powered Preece farm was perhaps less than the leap from the Preece farm to the area's farms of today. Cows are rarely pastured; hay is green chopped or wound into enormous round bales; the farms are highly mechanized and expansive affairs on a scale we never imagined. I admire those farmers who remain viable, as they have had to wholly transform themselves into something that was inconceivable in my day. They are a determined and courageous bunch.

Chapter 5 - Thomases

While what is here is all true, this only scratches the surface of an extended family with deep roots in the area. We quite literally arrived in their midst. Indeed, there were and are many other similar, deep-rooted families there, and I believe that as much as any other factor, these multigenerational families of that area define the uniqueness of the place.

I intentionally use the term "best version of himself" when describing Danny Thomas piloting his go cart in order to honor Matthew Kelly, the author and inventor of this powerful phrase. I had the honor of working for Matthew, and I believe strongly in his message, which is that our purpose in life is to become the best version of ourselves.

I have quoted directly from the Register-Star on page 41, which in its original form, incorrectly reports Dan was driving a John Deere that day. He was actually driving an International. In defense of the Register-Star, Dan made his mark in tractor pulling with a John Deere, and he has farmed with John Deere tractors for decades.

In 2011 I revisited the place and learned that Thomases, Hamiltons, Englishes and more are still there in numbers and are still engaged in farming, though it has changed dramatically. At the 2011 Washington County Fair, I was lucky enough to again watch farmer-tractor-pullers from each of these clans, and in the case of the English family, it marked four generations I have seen compete in this way.

Chapter 6 - Ben English

Again, these are all real events and true stories. Like the Thomases, the English family tree was a spider-like web of nearby farms and local history. I drove by Ben's old farm in 2011 and noted the name on the mailbox still says "English" and the place looks much the same.

In the Runaway Rig section, I purposefully use "it was as if we were watching an enormous, empty, unpiloted airplane plummet toward the earth, a few hundred yards in front of us." Indeed, a U.S. Air Force jet, on a mission out of Westover AFB, Massachusetts, crashed on Ben's farm in 1962. The plane was an F-102A, one of the early supersonic jets, the kind we would have often heard on the farm breaking the sound barrier, and its purpose was to intercept Soviet Bombers. The pilot was killed in the crash and there is a humble roadside marker that attests to the basic facts. Cambridge area citizens erected the monument in memory of the pilot who valiantly stayed with his plane in order to prevent a crash into their hamlet. Though perhaps in a way he didn't expect, he nevertheless gave his life protecting them. The Cold War was on, and it was real. Within a few short hours of the disastrous crash, government agents and military men arrived at Ben's and cordoned the area off, loaded every single piece of debris and evidence on a flatbed truck, covered it with canvas, and left quickly and quietly.

Chapter 7 - Animal Farm

All true. Yielding to softer sensibilities, I declined to be explicit in this chapter about the fate of the animals. I finish the opening section with these understated words, "But it is a tough business that demands all of their fruits and eventually their very lives. Farmer and animal are in it together, fully committed. It is a way of being for them both." First, I was making the point that the animals were eventually sold at auction or slaughtered, something not lost on most readers. But I was also making the point that the farmer gives his life too, not in the same way as the animal does, but nevertheless to a very large degree.

Farming is no eight to five kind of endeavor, and it demands complete commitment from the farmer.

In the section about our sheep, Edward A. Baah, I wrote that his very first pen "sat where it was warmed by the freezer's condensing coils, the thing that made the freezer frozen, the thing that kept our meats in storage, at first made tiny Edward warm." To remove the veil of subtle language and state the thing bluntly, Eddie ended up in that freezer and eventually on our dinner table.

Chapter 8 - Hard Work

These vignettes are true, though made up of multiple events that happened over years and here are strung together in an effort to make the stories more readable (and I changed some names). I chose not to go into similar detail about haying, milking, construction and maintenance, and the many other endless tasks of farming. My experience and specific memories in these areas do not lend themselves to any interesting stories, though the work was undeniably as demanding and relentless as potatoes, corn or manure.

Chapter 9 - Visitors

All true tales. As much as in any other chapter, I am troubled by my failures in writing about visitors, because I believe I have failed to give the reader a true sense for the complexity of these characters. I have written about so few of our visitors, and I fear I have fallen far short of describing their richness of depth and character, far short of capturing their humanity in deserving ways. Perhaps it is enough to simply say that there is so much more to each of these characters, and there were so many wonderful characters I have not even mentioned.

Dan McPeek, Lord of the Battenkill, reminded me in a recent correspondence that when we'd make our fishing excursions, my father would ask him to hide the fishing poles so they would not stick out of car windows or extend from the trunk of the car. Dad was concerned that neighboring farmers, more serious than Dad about the business of farming, might think less of him for playing hooky while there was hay to be gotten in from the fields.

Chapter 10 - Uncle Dean

These stories are all true, and I echo here my general comments on the previous chapter.

Chapter 11 - "Vly Summit Winter Olympics" of 1968

These stories are true, though I have embellished the snowball fight and have woven together several vignettes from across multiple winters. While there was no great single "winter Olympics," winters were a major part of life on our Upstate New York farm, and we went out of our way to entertain ourselves with things like night pond hockey games and torches for nighttime sled runs. Indeed the unrelenting cold often made the more discretionary farm projects temporarily impractical, resulting in periods of winter boredom until warmer weather came, and with it, the start of all-consuming repairs and improvements.

It is also worth noting that the tough winters created their own unique brand of winter work. Frozen water pipes were relatively commonplace and they created some of the most unpleasant of winter tasks. While it took a special blast of cold to freeze pipes in the house, something that occurred only from time to time, pipes in the barns froze often and sometimes with spectacular results. My father fought winter's relentless desire to freeze pipes with burlap bags, heating coils, steady-drip systems, and midnight visits to the barn. He was valorous if not successful. Water molecules crystallized and expanded and, in their unstoppable adherence to physics, tore through pipes and fittings and sent water in a thousand icy directions. We'd arrive at the barn in the mornings, and Dad would mutter his curses and we'd heat and thaw and tote buckets and scrape ice. Dad would cut pipes, and find fittings and solder what he could, or find welders for the rest. It was all just part of farming up there.

Chapter 12 - Impetigo Park

Several real episodes were condensed into a single summer in 1967. They all happened, though not all at one time. I still fear snakes to this day. Today the pond is several times larger than it was back then, and it is rather manicured for a rural pond.

Chapter 13 - A Day at the Washington County Fair

These stories all happened as they have been told. Sandra Thomas, now married and a mom, is still adorable and is still full of irresistible energy. A very attractive woman at my high school reunion some years ago, leaned over and gave me a beaming hello. She could tell I couldn't place her, and she made me guess who she was. After a few clueless moments and zero guesses, I confided to her that I didn't go to high school with anybody that looked as good as she did. I meant it. Patti Herrington finally told me her name, and I blushed like a kid at the fair.

I revisited the Washington County Fair in 2011 and found it to be an absolute delight. Like Impetigo Park, it is greatly expanded from the fair I attended. It was just as much fun to stroll the midway and attend some of the events. It was great to see Dan Thomas, my old neighbor and friend and past state champion compete in the tractor pull. At the fair I watched him take the lead in the tractor pull with his four hundred thirty six inch, quad turbo, super stock tractor. It was enormous and frightfully powerful. As he made the ear-shattering run of over three hundred feet I imagined the kid on a homemade go cart coming down our dirt road, turning the front wheels with his sneakers. I spoke with Dave English and saw him pull. I saw his son pull. I saw his son's son pull. And years ago I had seen his father, Ben pull. Four generations. The other tractor pull competitors had familiar last names: Hamilton, Herrington, Thomas. The next morning I saw the English boy, the latest in the four-generation line of tractor pullers, quarterback Cambridge's high school football team. Like Cambridge itself, he was quietly spectacular.

It was wonderful to chat with some old farmer neighbors and friends, and to amble through livestock barns and read the familiar family names of the animals' owners. But perhaps my greatest fair delight was eating breakfast at the 4H food booth, served by a young girl that could not have been more than ten years old. She did a great job, and I am sure that in a few years, she will be breaking hearts there.

Chapter 14 - Farewell from the Top of the Hill

Indeed I made the trip to the top of the hill and it truly was the literal culmination of a wonderful visit. It was a schedule-packed week that went by too quickly. I was blessed to visit with old friends and neighbors, to hug them and hear their voices and see eyes I have ached to see for years.

My accounts of going to Dad's gravesite and visiting Mom are true too. A short stroll, about the length of a football field, from my father's gravestone, is a Civil War marker for Robert W. Skellie, Company I, 123rd N.Y. Infantry. New York's 123rd Infantry was from Washington County. Company I was mustered in Cambridge. The Skellies still farm there and there is a road there named after the family. I discovered Robert Skellie's resting place only after writing the imaginary scene in which my father talks with a Civil War era Cambridge local and compares notes on Cambridge, Vly Summit, the hill and the Henry Thomas family. Perhaps in the spirit world that scene actually happened; perhaps there is more to my imagination than I ever suspected.

On the day that the local Cambridge newspaper reported the news of Robert Skellie's death, it also notified readers that William H. Tingue had lost his life in the war as well. The dirt road immediately beyond our hill, the dirt road where O'Donnells lived and where I parked my car and hiked the hill most recently with Sue, is named Tingue Road.

Many of my goodbyes are ongoing and will never end. I will return to Atlanta often because of family. And I will return again to Cambridge, to the farm and the hill and the people of that place because of my heart.

Acknowledgements

This is perhaps the most daunting part of my adventure in writing, as there are so many to whom I am thankful and such great risk of inadvertent omission.

I am especially grateful to Sue for her patience and wisdom and endless support; to Brian, Andy and Beth for being there and providing encouragement when I stalled; to Mary for constantly invigorating me and for her invaluable input; to Connie and Kim for their hard work, candor and thoughtful guidance; to Matthew for his remarkable inspiration and insight; to Rakesh, who told me the truth; to Nick, the great enabler; to Casey, Claire, Joe and Rick for their genuine interest and steady encouragement; to Jim, Joan and Leslee for their contagious enthusiasm; to Lynne for her selfless support and for helping me to see the gifts God has given me; and to Chuck for his many affirmations.

I am indebted to Brian for his talented sketches that add so much to what I have written. I am delighted that they are included here. I so cherish Joan's painting, which hangs in our living room and appears on the front cover of this book; it is wonderful.

I also owe a special thanks to Jack Walsh, who unknowingly became my inspiration to attempt this work. At age seventy-eight, after a lifetime of farming in Cambridge, took up a keyboard for the first time ever and wrote the story of his life, telling the reader the way it was. He has since passed away, but I nevertheless thank him for providing me with the amazing power of example.

Lastly, I am so very grateful for extended family, timeless friends and old neighbors who still remain so precious to me after so many years. I hope I am blessed to see you soon. I am grateful for all of you – and for that wonderful place itself.

(L to R) Me, Casey, Mom, Rick, Joe; Thanksgiving, 2011.

Made in the USA
Lexington, KY
02 August 2014